Foundations

The Thomson Wadsworth College Success Series

Andreatta, *Navigating the Research University: A Guide for First-Year Students*, (2006). ISBN: 0-534-64419-8

Beck and Clason, *Light on the Path: A Christian Perspective on College Success*, (2006). ISBN: 0-534-27244-4

Carney and Wells, *Working Well, Living Well: Discover the Career Within You*, 5th Ed. (1999). ISBN: 0-534-35767-9

Clason and Beck, *On the Edge of Success,* First Ed. (2003). ISBN: 0-534-56973-0

Corey and Corey, *I Never Knew I Had a Choice: Explorations in Personal Growth*, 8th Ed. (2006). ISBN: 0-534-60786-1

Gardner and Jewler, *The Essential College Experience with Readings*, 6th Ed. (2006). ISBN: 0-534-59397-6

Gardner, Jewler, and Barefoot, *Step by Step to College and Career Success*, 2nd Ed. (2008). ISBN: 1-4130-3076-9

Gardner and Jewler, *Your College Experience: Strategies for Success Expanded Reader*, 5th Ed. (2003). ISBN: 0-534-59985-0

Gardner, Jewler, and Barefoot, *Your College Experience: Strategies for Success*, 7th Ed. (2007). ISBN: 1-4130-1856-4

Gardner, Jewler, and Barefoot, *Your College Experience: Strategies for Success*, Concise Edition, 7th Ed. (2008). ISBN: 1-413-03075-0

Gordon and Minnick, *Foundations: A Reader for New College Students*, 4th Ed. (2008). ISBN: 1-4130-3287-7

Hallberg, Hallberg, and Aschieris, *Making the Dean's List: A Workbook to Accompany the College Success Factors Index* (2004). ISBN: 0-534-24862-4

Hettich and Helkowski, *Connect College to Career: A Student's Guide to Work and Life Transitions* (2005). ISBN: 0-534-62582-7

Holkeboer and Walker, *Right from the Start: Taking Charge of Your College Success,* 4th Ed. (2004). ISBN: 0-534-59967-2

Lock, *Taking Charge of Your Career Direction: Career Planning Guide, Book 1,* 5th Ed. (2005). ISBN: 0-534-57426-2

Lock, *Job Search: Career Planning Guide, Book 2,* 5th Ed. (2005). ISBN: 0-534-57421-1

Petrie and Denson, *A Student Athlete's Guide to College Success: Peak Performance in Class and Life*, 2nd Ed. (2003). ISBN: 0-534-56999-4

Riesen, Szarlan, and Singha, *Case Studies for First-Year Experience Students* (2003). ISBN: 0-534-26277-5

Santrock and Halonen, *Connections to College Success*, (2007). ISBN: 1-4130-2265-0

Santrock and Halonen, *Your Guide to College Success: Strategies for Achieving Your Goals*, 5th Ed. (2008). ISBN: 1-4130-3192-7

Santrock and Halonen, *Your Guide to College Success: Strategies for Achieving Your Goals*, Concise Edition, 4th Ed. (2007). ISBN: 1-4130-2073-9

Sharf, *Life's Choices: Problems and Solutions*, (2001). ISBN: 0-534-35933-7

Smith and Walter, *The Adult Learner's Guide to College Success*, 2nd Ed. (1995). ISBN: 0-534-23298-1

Staley, *50 Ways to Leave Your Lectern*, (2003). ISBN: 0-534-53866-5

Steltenpohl, Shipton, and Villines, *Orientation to College: A Reader on Becoming an Educated Person*, 2nd Ed. (2004). ISBN: 0-534-59958-3

Van Blerkom, *Orientation to College Learning*, (2007). ISBN: 1-4130-1852-1

Van Blerkom, *Taking Charge of Your Learning*, (2008). ISBN: 0-534-53949-1

Wahlstrom and Williams, *Learning Success: Being Your Best at College and Life*, Media Edition, 3rd Ed. (2002). ISBN: 0-534-57314-2

Wahlstrom, Williams, and Shea, *The Successful Distance Learning Student*, (2003). ISBN: 0-534-57712-1

Weir, *Transitions: A Guide for the Transfer Student*, (2008). ISBN: 1-4130-2279-0

Study Skills/Critical Thinking

Dillon, *Get Connected: Study Skills* (2008). ISBN: 1-4130-3051-3

Dillon, *Making Connections: Reading, Writing, and Study Skills* (2008). ISBN: 1-4130-1410-0

Jenkins, *Skills for Success: Developing Effective Study Strategies* (2005). ISBN: 0-534-63805-8

Longman and Atkinson, *CLASS: College Learning and Study Skills*, 7th Ed. (2005). ISBN: 0-534-62152-X

McKay, *Reasons, Explanations, and Decisions: Guidelines for Critical Thinking*, (2000). ISBN: 0-534-57411-4

Sotiriou, *Integrating College Study Skills: Reasoning in Reading, Listening, and Writing*, 6th Ed. (2002). ISBN: 0-534-57296-0

Van Blerkom, *College Study Skills: Becoming a Strategic Learner*, 5th Ed. (2006). ISBN: 0-534-64540-2

Van Blerkom and Mulcahy-Ernt, *College Reading and Study Strategies* (2005). ISBN: 0-534-58420-9

Walter, Knudsvig, and Smith, *Critical Thinking: Building the Basics*, 2nd Ed. (2003). ISBN: 0-534-59976-1

Student Assessment Tool

Hallberg, *College Success Factors Index*, http://www.csfi-wadsworth.com

Foundations

A Reader for New College Students

FOURTH EDITION

VIRGINIA N. GORDON
THE OHIO STATE UNIVERSITY

THOMAS L. MINNICK
THE OHIO STATE UNIVERSITY

THOMSON ™

WADSWORTH

Australia • Brazil • Canada • Mexico • Singapore • Spain • United Kingdom • United States

THOMSON

WADSWORTH

Foundations
A Reader for New College Students, Fourth Edition
Gordon/Minnick

Publisher: *Lyn Uhl*
Acquisitions Editor: *Annie Todd*
Editorial Assistant: *Daniel DeBonis*
Executive Marketing Manager: *Stacy Best*
Marketing Communications Manager:
   Darlene Amidon-Brent
Content Project Manager: *Karen Stocz*
Senior Art Director: *Cate Rickard Barr*

Print Buyer: *Betsy Donaghey*
Cover Designer: *Ross Carron Design*
Photo Account Manager: *Sheri Blaney*
Rights Acquisition Account Manager:
   Roberta Broyer
Production Service: *Lachina Publishing Services*
Printer: *West Group*

Cover Photograph: © L. Clarke/CORBIS

Library of Congress Control Number:
2006939304

10-Digit ISBN 1-4130-3287-7
13-Digit ISBN 978-1-4130-3287-1

Thomson Higher Education
25 Thomson Place
Boston, MA 02210-1202
USA

For more information about our products,
contact us at:
Thomson Learning Academic Resource
Center 1-800-423-0563

For permission to use material from this text
or product, submit a request online at
http://www.thomsonrights.com
Any additional questions about permissions
can be submitted by e-mail to
thomsonrights@thomson.com

Credits appear on pages 303–304, which constitute a continuation of the copyright page.

This edition of *Foundations* is dedicated
to the memory of
Marilyn E. Hagans
and in honor of
Albert J. Kuhn,
two extraordinary teachers of English.

Brief Contents

Contents

Unit 4
How Should I Expect to Learn?   99

Unit 5
What About Technology?   133

Unit 6
What Are My Rights and Responsibilities as a Student?   163

Unit 7
What Is Diversity and Why Is It Important?   185

Preface

Students entering college face many important decisions involving academic, career, and personal life choices. The purpose of this anthology is to stimulate the thinking of first-year college students about issues they will likely confront during their college years. We hope that, by reflecting on the ideas and insights provided by the writers included, students will recognize and perhaps be comforted by the universal character of the issues they face and will be better prepared to address and resolve them.

This anthology is designed to serve courses that help orient students to college life. In some colleges this text may also be suitable as a reader in first-year composition, and some high schools might find it useful in courses that introduce college issues to prospective college students. In compiling these essays, we have sought to incorporate topics in higher education about which entering college students should have some knowledge as they begin their journey to graduation. In this Fourth edition we include essays on some new topics that students will find informative. These topics include wellness, the role of faculty, time management, academic advising, on-line or virtual students, the Federal Education Rights and Privacy Act (FERPA), and preparing for life after college.

The reader format provides a diversity of opinions and perspectives on a variety of topics. Consequently, it encourages dialogue among different points of view. Because such dialogue is essential to a learning community, students are encouraged to participate in the exploration of ideas, which is how their journey toward knowledge and self-knowledge can best proceed. Instructors are also encouraged to participate in the dialogue, because students will benefit from their example. Journaling activities encourage students to reflect on what they read and how the topics may be relevant to their college life.

The topics are drawn from the common experiences of entering college students. Unit 1 examines the value of a college education by raising such questions as "What is a truly educated person?" and "Is a college education an investment for the future or an end in itself?" It also offers a brief history of higher education and the contemporary American university as they have evolved through the last century. Unit 2 focuses on what you can reasonably expect of college work and how you are likely to change during your college experience. Among the questions discussed are "How will you change intellectually and personally through the college years?" and "How can you learn to become personally effective in college, work, and life?" Unit 3 takes up very practical topics—such as using the library, selecting your major, attending classes, and turning in assignments on time—that relate to the general question "How can you succeed academically?"

Because the act of learning is such an integral part of student life, the writings in Unit 4 offer a variety of perspectives on this important process. Included are practical matters such as the power of memory, how to understand your own learning style, and how to take an active role in shaping how you learn. Unit 5 complements Unit 4 by raising issues about technology—namely, how it can and will affect how you think, learn, and associate with others. The readings in Unit 5 cover different aspects of technology's influence that now permeate our academic, work, and personal lives. From a historical perspective on how technology has evolved to a futuristic view of tomorrow's workplace, the writers in this unit offer a fascinating picture of where we have been and where we might be headed.

Unit 6 introduces the idea of college as a special kind of community, one defined by the common mission of its members: the search for knowledge and truth. Academic freedom (the freedom to express any point of view so that it can be studied and evaluated) is the essential condition of the college community. Because the search for truth is at the heart of the academic experience, certain kinds of behavior are intolerable within it, including, for example, cheating or plagiarism. Unit 7 discusses the value of diversity in a college setting. The dialogue essential to discovering truth places a high value on diversity because, through their diverse opinions and experiences, the varied members of an academic community enrich that dialogue and make it likelier to uncover many truths. Behavior that limits or undervalues diversity, especially discrimination against individuals based on minority group status, weakens an academic community and its ability to serve its primary mission.

The essays in Unit 8 will help you better understand how your professional life is likely to develop and, therefore, how best to prepare for your chosen career in the changing world of the 21st century. Unit 9 looks forward to life after graduation. We believe that post–high school education needs to prepare students for lifelong learning. The essays in Unit 9 encourage you to think about the future so that, even in your first year of college, you begin to lay the foundation for the days after graduation.

In compiling this anthology we have been helped by many students, colleagues, and friends, and we thank them. Mary Ellen Jenkins, assistant dean of the Colleges of the Arts and Sciences, undertook the essential task of securing permissions for reprinting material under copyright and contributed important biographical information about the authors included here. Michael Gifford cheerfully undertook aspects of the manuscript preparation, working with remarkable speed and accuracy. The following reviewers provided input on improvements for this fourth edition: Michele Campagna, Montclair State University; Mark May, Western Kentucky University; Mary Gene Ryan, Charleston Southern University, and Christel Taylor of the University of Wisconsin, Waukesha. Finally, we want to acknowledge the lessons we have learned from generations of colleagues and students in University College at Ohio State who enrolled in and taught University Survey, a course we were associated with for more than 25 years that, in that time, introduced more than 250,000 first-year students to the values and challenges of living and learning in an academic community.

How to Keep a Journal

After most of the readings in this textbook, you will find "Suggestions for Your Journal." We strongly encourage you to get into the habit of keeping a written journal of your reactions to and reflections on your assigned readings. Such journaling will result in a record of your development as you think through both the essays and your experiences as a new student at your college or university. Because many new college students may not know what a journal at its best can be, or how to keep one, we offer the definition and suggestions that follow.

Why keep a journal? The type of journal we are suggesting that you write is a "response" journal in which you will record your ideas and feelings in response to the readings that you are assigned in each unit. Writing a journal can reveal how your thought processes work and how they develop or change, serve as a memory aid, and provide an informal way of keeping track of your ideas that may be less threatening than more formal writing assignments like essays and research papers. Writing in your journal means working to find the right words to express yourself, and so keeping a journal can help you make your ideas more specific, more concrete.

The purpose of a journal is usually to provide a record, often day by day, of the writer's own internal or spiritual growth. In this regard, both journals and the closely related form, diaries, are similar to a document once needed on every sailing ship, the captain's log. The log was a book in which the chief officer of the ship kept a daily record of the ship's travels. Entries were usually brief, providing the ship's location in longitude and latitude and perhaps a sentence or two about important events of the voyage: "Sighted a large group of whales to the west," for example, or "Finished the last fresh provisions today." The ship's log therefore became the skeleton of a history. For some writers, a diary can be very similar to a log. Depending on how much detail an author chooses to include, a diary can be as lean as a ship's log or substantially more informative. An important difference is that the ship's log was intended to be available to others, such as the ship's owners. A diary is almost always intended to be a private document. A journal, in the sense that we hope you will use the word, is similar to a log or diary in that the entries can be made daily and should be dated. Unlike a personal diary, the best journals are written with the expectation that sometime, someone besides the writer will probably read them. Yet they retain a sense of ease and intimacy as though the prospective readers were the author's good friends.

Keeping a journal can encourage you to think more critically by helping you to make connections between what an author has written and your agreements or disagreements with that author's point of view. For example, a typical journal entry may note:

Date: September 30, 2006 [Most journal entries should be dated!]
Essay: "College Major Doesn't Mean That Much" by William Raspberry

As I read Raspberry's advice to his daughter about not choosing a major right away, I wished that my parents had told me this. I felt really pressured to choose a major during orientation since everyone else seemed to know what they were doing. Now that I have been in college for a few weeks, I'm beginning to have second thoughts about majoring in engineering. The trouble is, I don't know what else to major in or even what I might be good at. I don't have to worry about a "career," as Raspberry puts it, if I stick with engineering. But I am not sure what an engineer does all day. Raspberry says to pick a major "on the pleasure principle" for what I enjoy studying. That sure isn't math and physics. And yet I was good in these subjects in high school, and so far in my college classes I have been doing at least average with everyone else in my classes. I think a good way to proceed is to stay in general with the engineering plan but add some other classes in areas—like Theater!—that I really enjoy. Maybe I can find a way to balance both options.

This entry starts with an idea from an assigned essay and develops it with the student's personal point of view, including her examples, generalizations, and relevant personal experiences. A journal entry is usually this length or longer: One perfect sentence might be adequate and expressive, but usually a reflective response will require some development. A paragraph is a common length for an entry, but some may be as long as several paragraphs—even amounting to an essay.

We recommend that you read every essay with an eye for what you personally can learn or take from that essay. Can you apply some comment or suggestion from that reading to your experience? How? Or why not? Our suggested topics are not meant to limit you but merely to serve as possible starting places. In addition, here are some practical tips for keeping a journal that many writers find helpful:

- In journal writing it is permissible to write as you would talk to a friend or trusted adviser. The content is more important than perfection of style, and you will often find the entries are more informative if you think about what you want to express without worrying too much about the style or form of expression you use.
- Write about the insights, feelings and emotions, or problems that you think about when reading the assigned essay. Don't worry if you may seem more negative than positive: It is entirely all right to disagree with an author.
- Sometimes as you are reading an assignment, it is handy to jot down notes with your reactions in a very brief form (just so you can understand them later!). Your journal entry can then be developed from these notes, as you think about them and put them into your own organization.
- Interact with and expand upon what the author is saying but do so in your own words, adding your own ideas.
- Use any creative format that you think best expresses your responses. You may want to write in the form of a dialogue between you and the author or of a letter to a friend or to your parents.

Your course instructor will tell you how your journal entries will be used in class—that is, how they will fit into the course structure and count in your final grade. Some students find that they enjoy keeping a journal and continue the practice even after they are required to do so by a class. Many successful authors keep journals for decades and take from them their ideas for longer essays or books. And some journals have become important historical documents because, like the captain's log of an important voyage, they help others to navigate along one of the paths that eventually we all must find and follow.

The Value of a College Education: Why Am I in College?

S tudents attend college for many reasons. In a national survey by Alexander Astin of UCLA, who has studied each class of first-year students for many years, the largest number of entering students (73 percent) indicated they were coming to college to prepare for a better job. Other common reasons that students gave were to make more money, find a philosophy of life, become a more cultured person, or satisfy their parents' wishes.

Examining your reasons for enrolling in higher education can help you determine what you can realistically hope to accomplish as a student. Because new students may find it difficult to set tentative educational and occupational goals, they usually find it helpful to understand what the college experience is intended to, and can, provide. Such an understanding establishes a foundation on which to shape your personal expectations.

College will open for you an unbelievable range of opportunities to explore diverse fields of knowledge, along with a variety of activities that

Enter to grow in wisdom. Depart to serve better thy country and mankind.

—INSCRIPTION ON THE 1890 GATE TO HARVARD YARD

will help you grow personally and socially. Although you could educate yourself outside the college environment, it is much more expedient and satisfying to learn with other students and from teachers who are committed to creating an environment that supports learning.

In college you will have the time and freedom to delve into many areas of interest that you may not have explored. You will also be exposed to areas of the human experience that you did not know existed. Imagine! In a four-year (now often longer) span of time, you can acquaint yourself with a wide range of human knowledge and experience. Even in a two-year institution, these same opportunities exist, although they will be more focused.

At no other time in your life will you have such a concentrated opportunity for learning. In high school, most of the courses you took were prescribed for you by others. In college, although some majors are more rigidly structured than others, you have more freedom to pursue your personal interests. You are in control of your own learning.

On the other hand, if one of your reasons for being in college is to obtain a job, consider what college can offer you in preparing for your future career. A U.S. Department of Labor study, done with the American Society for Training and Development, identified the following seven basic skills that workers in the future must possess if they are to be successful: learning to learn, competence, communication, personal management, adaptability, group effectiveness, and influence. Many people feel that you will be able to acquire and perfect these basic skills through your college experience. Consciously working to acquire these skills in the classroom, in campus activities, and in social and other contacts will enhance your effectiveness with them by the time you graduate.

The readings in this unit are intended to stimulate your thinking about why you are in college and what you expect from it. The essays present a broad perspective on higher education and its value to the individual, not only intellectually but also as the beginning of a lifelong pursuit of learning. The essays in this unit by Bennett and Cicarelli attempt to reconcile the notion of learning for its own sake with a practical question about careers that students frequently and justifiably ask: "But what can I do with a major in _____?" Gardner tackles the same question in a different way, by defending the (to him) universal value of liberal learning. Bok briefly summarizes the history of American higher education in an essay included here because, when you want to know where you are, it can be helpful to know where you have been. Rudolph's essay on the early years of college football is included to suggest how much college sports have developed. These readings can help you compare your reasons for enrolling in college with some of the goals and objectives of higher education in general. You might also want to discuss with faculty, administrators, and other students your institution's mission and goals for preparing its students for the future.

The Lure of Learning

William J. Bennett

William J. Bennett is an accomplished scholar, teacher, and academic administrator. He was chair of the National Endowment for the Humanities in the early 1980s, Secretary of Education in the Reagan administration, and the nation's "Drug Czar" in the George H. W. Bush administration. Since leaving government service, Bennett has remained an active commentator on cultural issues, publishing more than a dozen books. He has stated that students should be taught "patriotism, self-discipline, thrift, honesty, and respect for elders." He received a Ph.D. in philosophy from the University of Texas and a law degree from Harvard.

This essay reflects Bennett's strong belief in the value of college teaching and its effect on students' learning. His career as an outstanding professor was obviously influenced by those who taught him and brought life to the subjects.

When I arrived at college as a freshman some time ago, I had definite ideas about how I wanted to use my four years of higher education. I wanted to major in English because I wanted to become *sophisticated.** I wanted to become sophisticated because I wanted to land a good job and make big money.

But because of my college's course requirements, I found myself in an introductory philosophy class, confronted by Plato's *Republic* and a remarkable professor who knew how to make the text come alive. It seemed to me and many of my fellow classmates as if we had come face to face with a reincarnation of Socrates himself. Before we knew it, we were ensnared by the power of a 2,000-year-old dialogue.

In our posture of youthful cynicism and arrogance, we at first resisted the idea that the question of justice should really occupy our time. But something happened to us that semester as we fought our way through the *Republic*, arguing about notions of right and wrong. Along the way, our insides were shaken up a little bit. Without quite knowing it, we had committed ourselves to the serious enterprise of raising and wrestling with questions. And once caught up in that enterprise, there was no turning back. We had met up with a great text and a great teacher; they had taken us, and we were theirs.

Every student is entitled to that kind of experience at college. And if I could make one request of future undergraduates, it would be that they open the door to that possibility. College should shake you up a little, get you breathing, quicken your senses and animate a conscious examination of life's enduring questions. Know thyself, Socrates said. Higher education worthy of the name aspires to nothing less than the wisdom of that *dictum*.

These are lofty ambitions. What do they mean in the context of four years of campus life?

*Vocabulary words are italicized in each essay—ED.

3

A college is many things. It is a collection of dormitories, libraries, social clubs, *incorrigibly* terrible cafeterias. But above all, it is a faculty. It used to be said, when this country was much younger, that a log lying on the side of the road with a student sitting on one end and a professor on the other was a university.

That essence has not changed. It is the relationship between teachers and their students that gives a campus its own special genius. "Like a contagious disease, almost," William James wrote, "spiritual life passes from man to man by contact." Above all, a student should look for—and expect to find—professors who can bring to life the subject at hand.

What else should students find at college? They should discover great works that tell us how men and women of our own and other civilizations have grappled with life's relentless questions. What should be loved? What deserves to be defended? What is noble and what is base? As Montaigne wrote, a student should have the chance to learn "what valor, *temperance,* and justice are, the difference between ambition and greed, loyalty and servitude, liberty and license; and the marks of true and solid contentment."

This means, first of all, that students should find wide exposure to all the major disciplines—history, science, literature, mathematics and foreign language. And it means that they should be introduced to the best that has been thought and written in every discipline.

College is, for many, a once-in-a-lifetime chance to discover our civilization's greatest achievements and lasting visions. There are many great books, discoveries and deeds that record those achievements in unequaled fashion. There are many more that do not. A good college will sort the great texts and important ideas from the run-of-the-mill and offer the best to its students. And that offering will be the institution's vision of a truly educated person.

All students have different notions about where they want a college degree to take them. For some, it is law school or journalism. For others, it's public service. That's fine. College *should* be a road to your ambitions. But every student should take the time to tread the ground outside his or her major and to spend some time in the company of the great travelers who have come before.

Why? Put simply, because they can help you lead a better and perhaps happier life. If we give time to studying how men and women of the past have dealt with life's enduring problems, then we will be better prepared when those same problems come our way. We may be a little less surprised to find treachery at work in the world about us, a little less startled by unselfish devotion, a little readier to believe in the capacity of the human mind.

And what does that do for a future career? As Hamlet said, "Readiness is all." In the end, the problems we face during the course of a career are the same kind that we face in the general course of life. If you want to be a corporate executive, how can you learn about not missing the right opportunities? One way is to read *Hamlet.* Do you want to learn about the dangers of overweening ambition? Read *Macbeth.* Want to know the pitfalls of playing around on the job? Read *Antony and Cleopatra.* The importance of fulfilling the responsibilities entrusted to leadership? Read *King Lear.*

Even in the modern world, it is still that peculiar mix of literature, science, history, math, philosophy and language that can help mature minds come to grips with the age-old issues, the problems that *transverse* every plane of life. Students who bring to college the willingness to seek out those issues, to enliven the spirit and broaden the mind, will be more likely to profit in any endeavor.

Reprinted by permission of the author.

 ## Vocabulary

As you think about this essay, these definitions may be helpful to you:
1. **sophisticated**   worldly, wise, knowing
2. **dictum**   a formal authoritative pronouncement of a principle or opinion
3. **incorrigible**   not capable of being corrected, permanently wrong, stubborn
4. **temperance**   moderation in action, thought, or feeling:
5. **transverse**   set crosswise

 ## Discussion Questions

1. How did Bennett and his fellow students initially react to their philosophy class? How did their reactions change?
2. What does Bennett ask undergraduates to do in order to expose themselves to the same wonders of learning that he enjoyed?
3. According to Bennett, what gives each campus its own "special genius"? Have you found this in your classes? Describe.
4. What should students find at college in addition to good teaching?
5. What does the college experience do for a future career, according to Bennett?

 ## Suggestions for Your Journal

Did you decide to come to college because of the "lure of learning"? If so, how do you think that element arose in you? Have you always planned to attend higher education? Did your expectations for college fit the reality you have already found? Be specific in considering these questions, because the details of your experience may fade as time passes.

Have you begun to discover your institution's "vision of a truly educated person"? Write about that vision and the evidence you have already found for it.

A New Debate Is Joined over an Old Question: Is College an Investment or an End in Itself?

James Cicarelli

James Cicarelli is currently dean of the Walter E. Heller College of Business Administration at Roosevelt University in Chicago, Illinois.

In this essay, Cicarelli discusses the objectives of higher education and how to measure its impact on students. He outlines two philosophies and discusses how each is supported by different types of disciplines and institutions.

The seemingly endless debate about higher education is now focusing on the question of what the purpose of higher education is and how best to determine how well colleges and universities are achieving it. Particularly heated right now is the discussion over the pros and cons of so-called value-added *assessment.*

On one side of the debate are proponents of the relatively new view of college as a place where students go to add to their individual reservoirs of information. This philosophy of education emphasizes quantifiable knowledge that can be measured by student performance on nationally standardized tests. The idea is that by testing students before, during, and at the end of their college careers, an institution can discover its educational strengths and weaknesses through "outcomes evaluation"—measuring exactly how much has been added to each student's store of knowledge by the education he or she has received.

On the other side of the debate are those who hold a more traditional view of college as a place where students go to learn to appreciate their cultural heritage, *hone* their skills in critical thinking and communication, and otherwise transform themselves from self-centered individuals into decent and caring citizens. In this view, the emphasis in college should be more on the development of moral principles than on the accumulation of knowledge, per se. Since that sort of outcome is difficult, if not impossible, to measure, the *traditionalist* institution looks to "input" rather than "output," measuring success in terms of the variety and depth of experience to which its students have been exposed.

Despite obvious differences, the two philosophies are not mutually exclusive. Actually, both can be seen as variants of *"developmentalism,"* an approach to education concerned with both the content and the *cognitive* aspects of learning. What set the two views apart are their conflicting methods of assessment, and the resulting controversy is going to dominate the discussion of evaluation for the foreseeable future.

While each side aims to improve higher education, both systems have disadvantages that would make them less effective than their proponents promise. For example, it is foolhardy to judge the success of a college education in terms of how much information the students have accumulated, because so much of it is already obsolete by the time they graduate. Students need to learn how to learn and how to teach themselves—talents that are nurtured by the ability to think clearly and read and write effectively, rather than by the mastery of information whose half-life is often measured in months.

On the other hand, it is pretentious to suppose that a college can teach values or should even try to do so. While most people can accept the broad principles embodied in the old Superman motto—"Truth, Justice, and the American Way"—it's difficult to translate them into working precepts. *Whose* truth? *What* system of justice? *Which* American way? Only in a dictatorship is one set of values taught to all. Yet simply exposing students to competing value systems, without discrimination, leads to confusion, if not anarchy.

Contributing to the controversy are the differences between professional, career-oriented education and general, liberal arts education. The former readily lends itself to the value-added approach because a profession is based on a body of knowledge that must be mastered before the student becomes a practitioner. Mastery of factual information can be demonstrated by passing a standardized test. Such a test shows how well an institution has prepared its students for entry into a profession. In other words, it measures the effectiveness of the education provided. Thus, prospective students interested in a particular career might consider such test results when deciding which college to attend. Unfortunately, that is not foolproof.

A decade ago, for example, when the boom in the oil industry led many colleges to expand their geology programs and others to begin new ones, a bachelor's in petroleum engineering was the hottest degree an undergraduate could earn. Today, most of those programs are as inactive as the West Texas oil fields where all the new geologists and engineers were supposed to find work. Educating for a job can produce graduates who are fit for that job and little else. A liberal arts education, on the other hand, can provide students with skills that transcend specific jobs and can be usefully applied in virtually any occupation.

The general-vs.-professional issue is part of the larger question of whether college should be seen as an investment or as an end in itself. Advocates of the value-added philosophy tend to consider higher education an investment, an expenditure of time and resources that should yield a payoff large enough to justify the initial cost. In their view, society invests a great deal in education, in part because of the hope that the schools and colleges will produce productive citizens who will then ensure that the next generation has the wherewithal to renew the investment. Traditionalists are more apt to view higher education as something one acquires for its own sake, not because it may lead to a good job or some other material gain. If it does result in enrichment in monetary as well as intellectual terms, fine; but the purpose of a college education is to make one better, not necessarily richer.

Whatever else is involved in the debate, a big part of it, for me, has to do with romanticism versus realism. My romantic side, the one that envisions college as a mind-expanding experience, sees the value-added philosophy as an educational straitjacket that demands curriculum conformity at the expense of individualism and experimentation. Reducing the purpose of college to producing graduates who can demonstrate their proficiency on national examinations risks our turning out intellectual clones whose creativity and imagination are suppressed, if not obliterated. Only the traditional approach promises to develop free-thinking citizens who cherish liberty and, therefore, are willing to question authority rather than just accept it blindly.

My realistic side, however, characterizes this line of reasoning as so much drivel. The colleges and universities in the United States represent the entire spectrum of values, from secular liberalism to religious fundamentalism. Students are free to choose the institution that best fits their individual preferences, and national value-added tests would not restrict their choice one iota. In fact, such a system would take some of the guesswork out of choosing a college, because it would show prospective students just how well an institution has done in delivering what it promises.

At this point, it's hard to tell how, if at all, the debate will be resolved. Institutions with no national reputation and few resources will probably embrace the value-added philosophy, since they have everything to gain by doing so and little to lose. Conversely, the better-known, better-endowed institutions will tend to stick with tradition, because they have little to gain and a lot to lose. If the students from the nation's top colleges do well on national standardized tests, they will simply be performing as expected. Should they do poorly, however, even in relative terms, their performance would be taken as a sign that the college or university was doing a poor job, and its reputation would suffer accordingly.

The unknown quantity so far is which side the institutions in the middle, the ones with "average" students and reputations and resources, will take in the controversy. They constitute the majority, after all, and it is their response that will determine the outcome of the debate. Should they tilt toward the value-added side, then evaluating educational results by numbers will become an integral part of the American college system. If, however, they stay on the side of tradition, then "value-added" will, like "relevance," become an interesting footnote in the history of higher education.

Reprinted by permission of the author.

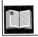

Vocabulary

As you think about this essay, these definitions may be helpful to you:
1. **assessment**   a determination of the importance, size, or value
2. **hone**   to make more acute, intense, or effective
3. **traditionalists**   people who believe an inherited or established pattern of thought

4. **developmentalism**   belief in a process of growth, differentiation, or evaluation by successive changes
5. **cognitive**   capable of being reduced to empirical factual knowledge

 ## Discussion Questions

1. What do advocates of the value-added philosophy consider to be the worth
of a college education?
2. According to Cicarelli, how do traditionalists view higher education?
3. What are the differences between a specific, career-oriented education and a
general, liberal arts education?
4. How does Cicarelli distinguish between romanticism and realism? Which do
you think is the better view? Why?
5. Does Cicarelli think the question of value-added assessment will be resolved?
How?

 ## Suggestions for Your Journal

Write about your current thinking on the major question that Cicarelli
addresses: Do you think of your college education as primarily a way to get a
better job, or do you seek a more general liberal arts education? What factors
might change your thinking on this important question?

You probably have some general education courses to complete as part of
your intended degree program. Do you agree that they will help to make you
knowledgeable about areas of study and thought that you would normally not
be exposed to?

Assume that you have a younger relative or friend who will be entering college next year. Consider writing a journal entry in which you argue for or
against general studies courses using that relative or friend as your primary
audience.

An Uncluttered Perspective: The True, the Beautiful, and the Good

Howard Gardner

Howard Gardner is the John H. and Elizabeth A. Hobbs Professor in Cognition and Education at Harvard. The author of 18 books and several hundred articles, Gardner has argued that there are many kinds of intelligence, not just one, and therefore that there cannot be only one way to measure intelligence. This selection is from his book, *The Disciplined Mind: What All Students Should Understand*. In this essay, he describes three important ideals that should inspire education.

I want everyone to focus on the content of an education—the meat and potatoes: on how that content should be presented, mastered, put to use, and passed along to others. Specifically, I believe that three very important concerns should animate education; these concerns have names and histories that extend far back into the past. There is the realm of truth—and its underside, what is false or indeterminable. There is the realm of beauty—and its absence in experiences or objects that are ugly or *kitschy*. And there is the realm of morality—what we consider to be good, and what we consider to be evil.

To make clearer what I include in these realms, let me mention three topics that I would like individuals to understand in their fullness. My example in the realm of truth is the theory of evolution, as first articulated by Charles Darwin and as elaborated upon by other scientists over the last one hundred and fifty years. This is an important area of science, with particular significance for a developmental psychologist like me. Unless one has some understanding of the key notions of species, variation, natural selection, adaptation, and the like (and how these have been discovered), unless one appreciates the perennial struggle among individuals (and populations) for survival in a particular ecological niche, one cannot understand the living world of which we are a part.

The processes of evolution are fascinating in their own right, as countless budding scientists have discovered. But such understanding has also become necessary if one is to participate meaningfully in contemporary society. Absent a grasp of evolution, we cannot think systematically about a whole range of topics that affect human beings today: the merits and perils of cloning; the advisability of genetic counseling, gene therapy, and various forms of *eugenics;* assertions that "lifelike entities" have been created computationally and that these entities evolve in a manner similar to organic matter; claims that human behavior is best explained by sociobiology or evolutionary psychology.

As my example in the realm of beauty, I select the music of Mozart: to be specific, his opera *The Marriage of Figaro*. This choice begins in the personal. I love classical music, and in particular the works of Mozart; for me, at least, they represent the pinnacle of beauty fashioned by human beings. I believe that everyone ought to gain an understanding of rich works like *Figaro*—their intricate artistic languages, their portrayals of credible characters with deeply felt human emotions, their evocation of the sweep of an era.

Again, such understanding is its own reward; millions of people all over the globe have been enriched by listening to Mozart or immersing themselves in other artistic masterpieces from diverse cultures. Moreover, a sophisticated grasp of Mozart's achievement can be brought to bear on unfamiliar works of art and craft and perhaps also inspire beautiful new creations. And such understanding also proves relevant to the decisions that we make as citizens; which arts, artists, and other creative individuals to support; how to support them; how best to encourage new works; whether there are artistic creations that ought to be censored or regulated, and, if so, by whom; whether the arts should be taught in school, after school, or not at all.

Finally, as my example in the realm of morality, I would like individuals to understand the sequence of events known as the Holocaust: the systematic killing of the Jews and certain other groups by the Nazis and others, before and especially during the Second World War. This event has personal significance, since my family came from Germany and several of its members were victims of the Holocaust. But every human being needs to understand what it is that human beings are capable of doing, sometimes in secret, sometimes with pride. And if the Holocaust is mostly an account of unprecedented human evil, there are scattered incidents of goodness and heroism even in that grim chapter.

Like the study of science and art, accounts of historical events can be intrinsically fascinating. But they have a wider significance. I believe that people are better able to chart their life course and make life decisions when they know how others have dealt with pressures and dilemmas—historically, contemporaneously, and in works of art. And only equipped with such understanding can we participate knowledgeably in contemporary discussions (and decisions) about the culpability of various individuals and countries in the Second World War. Only with such understanding can we ponder the responsibility of human beings everywhere to counter current efforts at genocide in Rwanda and the former Yugoslavia and to bring perpetrators to justice.

The understanding of striking examples of truth, beauty, and goodness is sufficiently meaningful for human beings that it can be justified in its own right. At the same time, however, such an understanding is also necessary for productive citizenship. The ways of thinking—the disciplines—that have developed over the centuries represent our best approach to almost any topic. Without such understanding, people cannot participate fully in the world in which they—*we* live.

One might think that at least some understanding of these well-known topics is widespread. It is therefore sobering to discover that the theory of evolution is considered to be false by one out of every two Americans, and even by 20 percent of science educators. According to the noted scientist Carl Sagan, only 9 percent of Americans accept that humans have evolved slowly from more ancient beings without any divine intervention. As for the Holocaust, about one-third of all Swedish high school students believe that the Holocaust did not take place. Comparable skepticism (if not outright denial) is expressed by various American groups; 20 percent of Americans admit that they do not know what happened in the Holocaust and 70 percent wish that they were better informed about it. Robert Simon, who teaches philosophy at Hamilton College, reports that anywhere from 10 to 20 percent of his American students cannot bring themselves to say that the Nazi attempt at genocide was wrong.

It is not difficult to anticipate a response to this trio of topics: How can one call this an education for all human beings? It is time-bound (the modern era); it is place-bound (Western Europe and places influenced by it); and it is even linked to the author's personal concerns.

"Right and not right," as they say, I would indeed be pleased if all human beings became deeply immersed in the themes of evolution, Mozart, and the Holocaust. There are worse ways to enlarge one's universe. *But—note well—these choices are not privileged, and certainly not uniquely so.* Within the West, there are numerous other scientific theories of importance (Newtonian mechanics and plate tectonics, to name just two examples); other singular artistic achievements (the works of Michelangelo or Rembrandt, Shakespeare or George Eliot); other morally tinged historical events (the French and Soviet revolutions; the American struggle over slavery). And within other cultural traditions, there are abundant examples of the true (these would include folk theories about healing or traditional Chinese medicine); the beautiful (Japanese ink and brush painting; African drum music); and good and evil (the precepts of *Jainism,* the stories of Pol Pot and Mao's Cultural Revolution, the generosity of bodhisattvas).

I am not contending, then, that everyone needs to be able to explain what constitutes a species or to discern the development of melodies and the intermingling romances in a work like *Figaro,* or to analyze the reasons why so many Germans were complicitous in the Holocaust. Rather, what I claim is that "an education for all human beings" needs to explore in some depth a set of key human achievements captured in the venerable phrase "the true, the beautiful, and the good."

Another possible objection. Aren't the categories "true," "beautiful," and "good" themselves time- and culture-bound? Again, this is a valid point, but not a decisive one. The articulated concepts of "truth," "beauty," and "goodness" reflect a philosophically oriented culture; indeed, our first records of explicit discussion of these virtues are the dialogues recorded by Plato in Greece nearly 2500 years ago. Other cultures have developed similar notions, although how they parse the three domains may well differ. However, the beliefs and practices of cultures—the beliefs and practices that they value, transmit, punish, or prohibit—reveal that each culture harbors specific views of how the world is and how it should (and should not) be. And these views embody implicit senses of truth, beauty, and morality.

There is another, more important reason for my endeavor. In the end, education has to do with fashioning certain kinds of individuals—the kinds of persons I (and others) desire the young of the world to become. I crave human beings who understand the world, who gain sustenance from such understanding, and who want—ardently, perennially—to alter it for the better. Such citizens can only come into existence if students learn to understand the world as it has been portrayed by those who have studied it most carefully and lived in it most thoughtfully; if they become familiar with the range—the summits, the valleys, the straight and meandering paths—of what other humans have achieved; and if they learn always to monitor their own lives in terms of human possibilities, including ones that have not been anticipated before. . . .

I've selected my three textbook examples because they are familiar to me, and because they will be familiar to many readers. But I must repeat: there is nothing *sacrosanct* about this trio. Another book, on another day, could focus upon relativity, revolutions, and the *ragas* of southern India. And I would devour such a book. . . .

Reprinted by permission of Simon & Schuster Adult Publishing Group from *The Disciplined Mind*, by Howard Gardner. © 1999 by Howard Gardner.

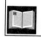 ## Vocabulary

As you think about this essay, these definitions may be helpful to you:
1. **kitschy**   adjective form of *kitsch,* which means sentimentality or tastelessness in decoration or the arts
2. **eugenics**   the science that deals with the improvement of races and breeds through the control of hereditary factors and mating
3. **Jainism**   a Hindu religious sect that teaches reverence for wisdom and respect for animals
4. **sacrosanct**   very holy or sacred
5. **ragas**   musical works that follow a traditional form of the classical music of India

 ## Discussion Questions

1. What is the purpose of education, according to Gardner?
2. What does Gardner mean when he says "the range—the summits, the valleys, the straight and meandering paths—of what other humans have achieved"? Is his metaphor from geography useful?
3. Gardner chooses Charles Darwin's theory of evolution as his example of "the true." Explain why this is a controversial choice.
4. Gardner says that his selection of examples is based in his cultural framework. Using the examples as your clues, characterize Gardner's personal cultural background.

Suggestions for Your Journal

You can apply Gardner's ideas to yourself in several ways. For example, select one new example for each of Gardner's three categories (the true, the good, and the beautiful) but draw them from a very different cultural context than the Western culture that Gardner refers to. Does modifying the cultural context confirm or dispute Gardner's ideas? Gardner's examples for "the true" are based in science. Can you give examples that are not based in modern scientific knowledge?

Assuming that Gardner is right about the purpose, or "end," of education, what steps do you anticipate you will have to take in order to reach that goal for yourself?

The Evolution of Undergraduate Education

Derek Bok

Derek Bok is one of the most respected American academic leaders. He has spent virtually his entire career at Harvard University, where he began teaching law in 1958,
served as dean of the law school from 1968 to 1971, and then accepted the responsibility of university president from 1971 to 1991. In 2006 he agreed to return as interim
president for an appointment expected to last about a year. Bok is the author of many
books, including *Our Underachieving Colleges,* published in 2006, from which the following excerpt is taken.

Until the Civil War, colleges in the United States were linked to religious
bodies and resembled *finishing schools* more closely than institutions of
advanced education. Student behavior was closely regulated both inside and
outside the classroom, and teachers spent much of their time enforcing regulations and punishing transgressors. Rules of behavior were written in exquisite
detail. Columbia's officials took two full pages merely to describe the proper
forms of behavior during compulsory chapel. Yale turned "Sabbath Profanation,
active disbelief in the authenticity of the Bible, and extravagant (personal)
expenditures" into campus crimes.[1]

Most courses were prescribed in a curriculum that usually included mathematics, logic, English, and classics, with a heavy dose of Latin and Greek. In a
typical class, students recited passages from an ancient text under the critical
eye of the instructor. Although many colleges offered courses in the sciences,
such as astronomy or botany, classes were taught more often by invoking *Aristotle* and other authorities than by describing experiments and the scientific
method. By most accounts, the formal education was sterile. Many students felt
that they learned much more outside the classroom in informal clubs and literary societies, where they engaged in debates, read modern literature, and discussed serious subjects.[2]

Despite their quaint ways, colleges before the Civil War were deliberately organized to pursue two important objectives: training the intellect and building character. The most influential defense of the prevailing model appeared in an 1828
report from Yale College, which held that the principal aim of college instruction
was not to supply all the important information that students might some day use
but to instill mental discipline.[3] According to the report's authors, a classical

[1]Laurence Veysey, *The Emergence of the American University* (1965), pp. 33–34.

[2]Frederick Rudolph, *Curriculum:* A History of the American Course of Study since 1636 (1977), p. 95.

[3]"Original Papers in Relation to a Course of Liberal Education," *American Journal of Science and Arts,*
15 (1829).

education was ideally suited to this purpose. Mental discipline was supposed to emerge from hours of demanding work translating ancient languages, disputing *arcane* questions in class, and solving mathematical problems.

Character would be forged by having undergraduates study classical texts, demanding strict compliance with the detailed rules of campus behavior, and requiring daily attendance at chapel. As a culminating experience, most colleges prior to the Civil War offered a mandatory course for seniors on issues of moral philosophy, often taught by the president himself. Ranging over ethical principles, history, politics, and such issues of the day, as immigration, slavery, and freedom of the press, this capstone course served multiple objectives. It set forth precepts of ethical behavior, it prepared students for civic responsibility, and it brought together knowledge from several fields of learning. For many students, it was the high point of an otherwise dull and *stultifying* education.

With the end of the Civil War, higher education began a period of unprecedented reform. Aided by federal land grants and by the philanthropy born of industrial fortunes, college presidents such as Charles W. Eliot, Andre White, William Rainey Harper, and Benjamin Gilman built new institutions and radically transformed old ones. Inspired by the great German universities, these leaders encouraged research, welcomed science, and introduced Ph.D. programs to build new cadres of scholar-teachers.

Undergraduate education soon felt the impact of these changes. The old classical curriculum gave way to offerings of a newer and more practical kind. Instruction in modern languages and literature continued to spread. Courses in physics, biology, and chemistry sprung up everywhere. Private universities introduced new programs in vocational subjects such as commerce and engineering. Public universities carried occupational training even further. According to Laurence Veysey, "such untraditional disciplines as pedagogy, domestic science, and various kinds of engineering were all becoming firmly established at a number of leading universities by the turn of the century."[4]

More radical still were the reforms at some of America's most prominent institutions. At Harvard, for example, President Charles W. Eliot not only rejected the old prescribed classical curriculum, he urged that *all* requirements be abolished, leaving students free to study whatever appealed to their interests. In the end, however, Eliot's vision proved too extreme to survive intact even at Harvard. Although no one wanted to return to the old, classical curriculum, most educators felt that the doctrine of total elective choice went too far in the other direction.

Religious orthodoxy also lost its grip on many colleges. *Nonsectarianism* was increasingly considered conducive to sound university governance. Faith was no longer thought central to the development of moral character. Compulsory

[4]Veysey, p. 113.

chapel began to give way on many campuses, making religious observance little more than another option with a broad array of extracurricular pursuits.

Meanwhile, social clubs and fraternities flourished. Intercollegiate sports took hold, as football games attracted tens of thousands of raucous students and alumni. For many undergraduates, college was not a serious intellectual experience but an excuse for making social contacts and enjoying the good life. As one dean of students, LeBaron Briggs, candidly admitted, "Social ambition is the strongest power in many a student's life."[5] In retrospect, it is likely that the casual attitude toward coursework reflected the spirit of the times more than the nature of the curriculum. Whatever the underlying causes, critics of the elective system seized on such carefree undergraduate behavior as a justification for imposing greater structure on the curriculum. By the early twentieth century both the extreme free-choice model embraced by universities such as Stanford and Cornell and the more rigid, traditional system still in place at Princeton seemed equally out of touch with the times.

By the start of World War II, college curricula were divided between two models. Most public universities offered a wide assortment of vocational majors along with the standard liberal arts concentrations, while achieving breadth through some form of *distribution requirement*. Most leading private universities tended to resist occupational majors (save for engineering and business). Patterns of breadth and depth were nourished by constant growth in the number of courses, made possible by the steady expansion of university faculties. Entirely new disciplines, with courses of their own, gave undergraduates a wider range of options from which to choose electives, fulfill their distribution requirements, or select a major.

In the aftermath of World War II, universities underwent further substantial changes. Encouraged by the GI Bill and later by the demands of an increasingly sophisticated economy, larger and larger numbers of young people crowded into colleges. Existing universities expanded, and new ones were founded. From 1945 to 2000, the number of B.A. degrees awarded annually rose almost eightfold, from 157,349 to approximately 1.2 million.

The rapid growth in the undergraduate population meant that higher education was no longer reserved for the elite but now attracted a majority of American youth. Student bodies became more diverse, as blacks, Hispanics, Asians, and other ethnic minorities entered private and public colleges alike. As applicant pools grew larger, the best-known institutions became highly selective, teachers' colleges evolved into multipurpose universities, and community colleges sprouted like mushrooms.

University faculties responded to these developments in various ways. Although the basic structure of the curriculum remained intact, with its provision for breadth and depth, the steady growth of new knowledge pushed aspects

[5]LeBaron Briggs, *Routine and Ideals* (1904), p. 202.

of science once reserved for graduate students back into intermediate and even introductory college texts. As researchers separated themselves into more and narrower specialties, colleges began developing interdisciplinary programs to focus on large societal issues, such as environmental problems or the impact of science and technology on society. Challenged by a more diverse student population many faculties launched other multidisciplinary ventures in fields such as women's studies, Afro-American studies, and ethnic studies. In response to America's new international prominence, and aided by significant outside support, other faculty members created research centers and interdepartmental programs aimed at understanding more regions of the world such as Western and Eastern Europe, Africa, and East Asia.

As student numbers continued to rise and individual universities grew larger, colleges launched a variety of experiments to provide more individualized instruction, at least for portions of the student bodies. Honors programs were established for qualified students. Research internships offered opportunities for undergraduates to work in laboratories alongside experienced investigators. Freshman *seminars, group tutorials,* and small senior *colloquia* afforded students at least a modicum of personal contact with faculty members.

Meanwhile, advances in technology brought changes in the way professors taught their classes. In the 1950s, the spread of paperback books and photocopiers expanded the depth and variety of course materials far beyond the single hardcover text that had been the staple of most earlier college courses. Several decades later, the Internet brought an even wider array of readings within easy reach of students. Never before had such extensive intellectual resources been so readily available to enhance the undergraduate educational experience.

From *Our Underachieving Colleges* (Princeton, N.J.: Princeton University Press, 2006). ■

 ## Vocabulary

As you think about this essay, these identifications and definitions may be helpful to you:
1. **finishing school**   Until perhaps as late as the 1960s, with the rise of the modern women's movement, a "finishing school" was usually a small, elite private school for girls that emphasized cultural studies and prepared the students especially for social activities. Bok suggests that before the Civil War, the predominantly private, religious schools for men were more intended to polish young gentlemen than to educate young scholars.
2. **Aristotle**   A fourth-century B.C. Greek philosopher whose authority was considered unchallengeable until Galileo and other scientists began to question his writings. In early classrooms, if Aristotle said something was true, it was considered true, even if it contradicted the evidence of the real world.

3. **arcane**   secret, mysterious, or obscure, known only to those approved to learn secret knowledge, with the implication that such knowledge is not useful for daily living in the real world
4. **stultifying**   so boring that it makes the listener become dull headed overall
5. **nonsectarianism**   not affiliated with or restricted to a limited religious perspective
6. **distribution requirement**   Usually a defined part of a structured curriculum. For example, in many colleges, no matter what you choose as a major, you may be required to take some courses in writing, mathematics, science, social science, and so on; that is, the required courses are "distributed" across the curriculum.
7. **seminars, group tutorials, colloquia**   All these terms refer to small classes of specific kinds, with a faculty member as teacher and a limited number of students. A seminar is usually a group of advanced students studying under a professor with each doing original research and all exchanging results through reports and discussions. In a tutorial, a tutor, who is often a junior member of the faculty, coaches a student through a subject, normally without the original research involved in a seminar. A group tutorial is simply a group of students working together with a tutor. (In this usage, the modern notion of a computerized tutorial which takes a user through basic skills is not intended.) A colloquium (plural, colloquia) is not a full-term course but, instead, a single meeting (as short as an hour, as long as several days) at which specialists deliver addresses on a topic or on related topics and then answer questions.

 Discussion Questions

1. Many students today say that they share the sentiment that Derek Bok attributes to early students when he says, "Many students felt that they learned much more outside the classroom in informal clubs and literary societies, where they engaged in debates, read modern literature, and discussed serious subjects." Do you believe that you will learn as much, or even more, outside of classes than in them? What kinds of learning occur outside of class? How is that kind of learning valuable?
2. In talking about the history of why people have attended college in the past, Bok spoke about commerce—today we might say business—courses and engineering courses as "vocational subjects." The term "vocational" nowadays is commonly used to describe classes where students learn to become chefs, or real estate sales personnel, or hair stylists. What are the different uses and implications of this term?
3. Do you agree with former Harvard President Charles W. Eliot who, Bok tells us, not only rejected the old prescribed classical curriculum, but also urged

that *all* requirements be abolished, leaving students free to study whatever appealed to their interests? Would you be happier if you were entirely without requirements? Would you learn as much?

 Suggestions for Your Journal

It is impossible to talk for long about the purposes of education without someone bringing up the idea that a college education should help to develop "character." What do you think is meant by this term? How might a college or university teach "character"? Is that why you enrolled in higher education?

Do some preliminary research into the history of your own college or university. Where in the general picture described by Derek Bok does your current school fit? When was it established? Was it originally a church-affiliated school? If so, is it still, and does that make a difference? How important is research, which Bok says came from a German model?

The Early Years of American College Football

Frederick Rudolph

Frederick Rudolph is Mark Hopkins Professor of History Emeritus at Williams College, where he was chair of the American Studies Program from 1971 to 1980. His book, *The American College and University: A History,* from which this brief excerpt is taken, was first published in 1962 and remains one of the most important and influential modern studies of the history of American higher education.

Football of sorts was played in tenth-century England, where it was largely a matter of kicking a skull or a cow's bladder between towns. The Princeton-Rutgers game of 1869, which inaugurated American football, was in this tradition. During the next decade, initially at Harvard and at Yale, a shift occurred from the soccer or kicking style of play to the Rugby or running style of play. American football, therefore, was a cultural adaptation of the English game of Rugby.[1]

It took a few years for the game to catch on, but its growth was extraordinary. In 1873 football seemed sufficiently ridiculous to prompt a classic remark of President Andrew D. White of Cornell. In response to a challenge from thirty players of the University of Michigan who wanted to arrange a game in Cleveland, President White telegraphed: "I will not permit thirty men to travel four hundred miles merely to agitate a bag of wind."[2] In time Cornell fell fully in line, as indeed did almost everyone else. But no one should have been surprised when within less than twenty years one season's football coach at Syracuse turned out to be next season's captain at Cornell.[3]

Few movements so captured the colleges and universities. In 1881 Michigan—spurned by Cornell less than ten years earlier—went East and played Harvard, Yale, and Princeton in a period of less than a week. A few years later a young bachelor president at Miami University of Ohio all but required his faculty to go out for the team: in those days there were no problems of eligibility. In 1889 the University of the South at Sewanee sent out its team for six successive days of

[1]David Riesman and Reuel Denney, "Football in America: A Study in Cultural Diffusion," *American Quarterly, 3* (1951), pp. 309–205; Thomas Jefferson Wertenbaker, *Princeton 1746–1896* (Princeton: Princeton University Press, 1946), pp. 325–26; William H. S. Demerest, *A History of Rugers College 1766–1924* (New Brunswick, 1924), 428–30; Parke H. Davis, *Football: The American Intercollegiate Game* (New York, 1911), pp. 44–50; Morris Allison Bealle, *The History of Football at Harvard, 1874–1948* (Washington, 1948), pp. 17, 26–28. See also Allison Danzig, *The History of American Football* (Englewood Cliffs, N.J., 1956).

[2]Kent Sagendorph, *Michigan: The Story of the University* (New York, 1948), p. 150.

[3]William Freeman Galpin, *Syracuse University: The Pioneer Days* (Syracuse, 1952), p. 170.

play away from home. At a common-sense hard-headed institution like the Con-necticut Agricultural College at Storrs the official program for physical training had at first assigned the young men to three sessions a week of picking up stones from the college farm; in the 1890's they picked up footballs.[4]

Indeed, the game became so widely adopted that for the first time since the founding of Harvard College in 1636 colleges began to recognize the existence of intercollegiate relations. Institutions that had never found it advisable to con-sult on matters of curriculum now sought means of regulating their athletic relations: from this impulse came the agreement among a number of Midwest-ern colleges in the early 1890s to employ no more than two professionals per game.[5] The need for regulation was generally admitted, for the game intruded a spirit of athletic professionalism into an atmosphere where many believed that it did not belong. One year in the 1890s the University of Oregon football team in three successive contests with three different colleges found themselves play-ing against the same young man.

The game, however, encouraged such a will to win that undergraduate and graduate imagination found its way around any traditional sense of ethics. A senior might invite the fullback on the freshman team to room with him and forget to ask him to share the charges. A student might make a preposterous wager with a star athlete and, of course, lose. Instead, the money might go directly to a father or brother. One college ball player so learned the price of his usefulness that without fear of failure he presented his laundry bill to the team manager with the words "I cannot pay it. You pay it or I do not play." Efforts to regulate the sport had difficulty in keeping up with its growth.[6]

The game prospered. In 1893 New York was thrown into a virtual frenzy by the annual Thanksgiving game between Yale and Princeton. Hotels were jammed. On Fifth Avenue blue and white Yale banners hung from the *Vanderbilt* and *Whitney* mansions. The *Sloanes,* the *Alexanders,* and the *Scribners* displayed the colors of *Old Nassau.* Clergymen cut short their Thanksgiving services in order to get off to the game in time. Clearly, football had arrived.[7]

The movement would continue to accelerate until 1905 when the growing brutality and professionalism of the game created an episode typical of the Pro-gressive period. That year the American public, which was in the process of being aroused by other impurities in the national life, including tainted pork, political machines, and trusts, turned its righteousness on football. Eighteen Americans died playing football in 1905. At Harvard the season provided only two games without concussions. In Philadelphia during the Penn-Swarthmore

---

[4]Amos Alonzo Stagg, *Touchdown!* (New York, 1927), p. 70; Walter Havighurst, *The Miami Years 1809–1859* (New York, 1958), pp. 158–51; Walter Stemmons, *Connecticut Agricultural College-A History* (Storrs, 1931), p. 83.

[5]Allan Nevins, *Illinois* (New York, 1917), p. 2002.

[6]See Galpin, *Syracuse,* p. 169; Charles Henry Rammelkamp, *Illinois College: A Centennial History 1829–1929* (New Haven, 1928), p. 391; Clarence F. Bridseye, *Individual Training in Our Colleges* (New York, 1907), p. 160–62.

[7]Stagg, *Touchdown!,* pp. 150–53; Wertenbaker, *Princeton,* p. 357.

game Bob Maxwell, an outstanding Swarthmore player, was subjected to a beating so systematic and thorough that a photograph, showing him tottering off the field, his face a bloody mess, became a news sensation. That photograph called into action the President of the United States. From the White House Theodore Roosevelt thundered that if the colleges did not clean up football he would abolish it by executive order. And in a bit of moralism which revealed much of the temper of the age, he added: "Brutality and foul play should receive the same summary punishment given to a man who cheats at cards."[8]

On October 9, 1905, coaches and physical directors of Harvard, Yale, and Princeton met with T.R. for lunch at the White House, where he charged them with the responsibility of "getting the game played on a thoroughly clean basis."[9] This was much the same injunction that he, as captain of the *Progressive movement*, was accustomed to delivering to the managers of great American industrial corporations. The football people responded in appropriate fashion. They undertook a campaign of purification and control. In 1906 the forward pass was introduced, taking some of the advantage away from brute weight. Some colleges—notably Columbia, the University of California, and Stanford— gave up football for a decade; others—Northwestern and Union among them— suspended it for a year.[10] But football was not dead.

As the first contact sport to make any headway among young gentlemen in America, it satisfied a whole set of values that under T.R.'s auspices took the name of "the strenuous life." When President Eliot attempted to abolish football at Harvard, Roosevelt erupted with proper vigor: "I think Harvard will be doing the baby act if she takes any such foolish course."[11] And in a 1907 speech before a Harvard audience the same man who had carried the *Big Stick* into the Ivy League just two years before now said: "As I emphatically disbelieve in seeing Harvard, or any college, turn out mollycoddles instead of vigorous men I may add I do not in the least object to a sport because it is rough."[12] Theodore Roosevelt and most of his contemporaries did not object to anything because it was rough. They were not interested in keeping life from being vigorous, even dangerous. They did want it to be fair. And this was all that they demanded of football—a square deal for every player.

[8]Wertenbaker, *Princeton,* pp. 253–54; Riesman and Denney, "Football in America," p. 319; Calvin M. Woodward, *Opinions of Educators on the Value and Total Influence of Inter-Collegiate and Inter-Scholastic American Football as Played in 1903–1909* (St. Louis, 1910), p. 17.

[9]Elting E. Morison, ed., *The Letters of Theodore Roosevelt* (Cambridge, 1952), vol. V, p. 46.

[10]Dwight C. Miner, ed., *A History of Columbia College on Morningside* (New York, 1954), p. 207; Orrin Leslie Elliott, *Stanford University: The First Twenty-Five Years* (Stanford, 1937), pp. 232–33; Dixon Ryan Fox, *Union college: An Unfinished History* (Schenectady, 1945), pp. 35–36; Howard J. Savage et al., *American College Athletics* (New York, 1929), p. 25.

[11]Morison, ed., *The Letters of Theodore Roosevelt,* vol. V, p. 172.

[12]Bealle, *The History of Football at Harvard,* p. 9.

From Frederick Rudolph, *The American College and University: A History* (New York: Vintage Books, 1962), pp. 374–77.

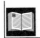 **Vocabulary**

As you think about this essay, these identifications may be helpful to you:
1. **Vanderbilt, Whitney, Sloanes, Alexanders, Scribners**   Wealthy families of New York city who supported different teams in the 1893 game between Yale and Princeton.
2. **Old Nassau**   A nickname for Princeton University. It is also the title of Princeton's anthem since 1859.
3. **Progressive movement**   A political effort to cure many of the ills of American society that had developed during the spurt of industrial growth in the last quarter of the nineteenth century. Theodore Roosevelt was a leading figure in this reform period.
4. **Big Stick**   A term identified with Theodore Roosevelt's foreign policy. When faced with problems, Roosevelt quoted an old African proverb, "Speak softly and carry a big stick, and you will go far."

 Discussion Questions

1. Identify some of the ways in which intercollegiate football is now different from the way it was played at the beginning.
2. It is certainly surprising to learn about intercollegiate football games in which faculty members were part of the team. But what do you think of the idea of a university president requiring faculty to participate as equals with students in designated intramural or intercollegiate activities? What would be some advantages and disadvantages of such activities? How might you go about establishing such a requirement?
3. As Rudolph notes, some schools suspended intercollegiate football when the sport suddenly grew too violent. What might be some reasons to suspend college football today? In discussion, students can be encouraged to take different sides on this issue—as long as the conversation doesn't turn violent.
4. What do you know about the history of your own college's sports program? For example, how long have women been encouraged to participate in intercollegiate competition at your school?

 Suggestions for Your Journal

We tend to think that the world we know today is closely similar to the way it always has been. This essay on the origins of college football shows that things we take for granted today (for example, that members of a college sports team must be enrolled student amateurs at the college) were once very different. Speculate on some of the parts of college life that have probably changed dramatically in the last hundred, or fifty, or twenty years. Where on your campus might you go to do research on the way things used to be at your school?

UNIT SUMMARY

In this unit you have examined many different perspectives about college as an American institution and its meaning and value to you as a student. The following questions can help you think about the viewpoints represented in these readings.

Summary Questions

1. What is a liberal education according to the authors in this unit? How will it prepare you to become a lifelong learner?
2. What are some general goals and objectives of higher education according to these readings? How do they compare with your personal reasons for being in college?
3. Many college students have traversed your campus in the past. What aspects of the history and traditions of your campus are most interesting and important to you?

Suggested Writing Assignments

1. Write an essay about your reasons for being in college. In it describe five goals you wish to accomplish during your first year.
2. How is college different from high school (e.g., teachers, assignments, classroom behavior, course content, learning expectations)? Write about your most difficult academic adjustment.
3. Interview a college teacher in whose class you have learned a great deal. Discuss learning from this teacher's perspective. How does this teacher think learning his or her subject matter can be useful in life?

Suggested Readings

Bloom, Allan. *The Closing of the American Mind*. New York: Simon & Schuster, 1987.

Gardner, Howard. *Multiple Intelligences: The Theory in Practice*. New York: Basic Books, 1993.

Hutchins, Robert M. "The Autobiography of an Uneducated Man." In Robert M. Hutchins, *Education for Freedom*, pp. 1–18. Baton Rouge: Louisiana State University Press, 1943.

Rhodes, Frank H. T. *The Creation of the Future: The Role of the American University*. Ithaca and London: Cornell University Press, 2001.

Rudolph, Frederick. *The American University and College: A History*. New York: Knopf, 1962.

Willie, Charles. *The Ivory and Ebony Towers*. Lexington, MA: Heath, 1981.

What Can I Expect From College and How Will I Change?

What do you expect will happen to you during your college years? The college years are known for the personal and social changes that take place in individuals. New students are likely to notice, first, the academic challenges in the classroom and the social opportunities present at every turn. For many, the increased difficulty of college course work comes as a surprise and the social freedom, which may have been predictable, is more overwhelming than expected.

Furthermore, students usually expect that college will prepare them for a career and will accomplish this in some very specific ways. Students often expect a direct-line or one-to-one relationship between what they study in college and the job that follows graduation. Direct relationships do occur in such fields as engineering and nursing, but more often, college courses teach general skills, not specific job tasks. Students who expect specific training may not see the relevance or importance of this more general instruction.

What we anticipate seldom occurs; what we least expect generally happens.

—BENJAMIN DISRAEL

As time passes, they may become even more confused. For many first-year students, uncertainty about their future career and life is unsettling and worrisome. Their expectations for clear-cut decisions regarding their future may not be fulfilled.

According to many student developmental theorists, these unsettling feelings are common and can be considered normal. Most students need time to master certain developmental tasks that lead to a mature way of thinking and being. For example, as far as personal development is concerned, students need to cope with leaving home, perhaps for the first time. Often both parents and students find this transition difficult.

Some of the best features of college life are the opportunities to make new friends and to meet people who are different from yourself. Some students may find it easy to strike up new friendships, while others struggle with shyness and uncertainty. However, in time these relationships can become one of the most rewarding aspects of college life.

In classes, students are thrust into new experiences with demanding course work. They need to master rapidly moving and complex course content, and some will find they need help with basic learning skills. Academic freedom and the occasional need to drop a course may be new to many students. Some think they can succeed if they work harder, a strategy that doesn't always work. A student's expectations for academic success may take a few detours.

All these developmental concerns are in some sense predictable, as the essays in this section demonstrate. Gordon's essay outlining the theories of Perry and Chickering describes the importance of mastering the various developmental tasks. Family members can be an important support group when students enter college. Bell describes the experiences of both students and their parents during this transition. The essay by Newman and Newman deals with the feelings of loneliness that some students may experience, especially as they begin college. Sears offers suggestions for ways to become personally effective in college, work, and life. Living a process of wellness, according to Travis and Ryan, means you are a changing person who is moving toward a happier life and positive health.

Setting goals, both short-term and long-term, is an important element in the evolution of this highly personal process. Your expectations for what you want to receive and accomplish during the college years will probably change. It will be natural for you to expand and refine your expectations. The essays in this unit may give you some appreciation for the experiences and tasks that others consider important as you progress toward graduation.

The Developing College Student

Virginia N. Gordon

Virginia N. Gordon, who has been a college teacher and administrator, is best known as a researcher, academic advisor, and counselor for undecided students. She received her Ph.D. in counseling from the Ohio State University.

This essay describes two theoretical perspectives on how students change intellectually and personally during the college years. These theories are based on what students have experienced and related to researchers through personal interviews.

By entering college you begin a very exciting and challenging period in your life. Although it may be difficult for you to imagine now, think about yourself on the day you graduate with a college degree. In addition to being a college graduate, what kind of person will you be? How do you expect to change during your college years?

After careful research, many theorists have described how students change and develop throughout the college experience. Social scientists who have studied college students have discovered some patterns and common themes in the way they change. One such theorist, Professor William Perry, of Harvard University, has studied how college students change intellectually and ethically. He developed a scheme to describe the development of the thinking and reasoning processes that takes place naturally as students mature and grow intellectually. Each phase of this development may be likened to a set of filters through which students see the world around them.

Dualistic students see the world in polar terms; that is, they believe that all questions have a right answer and, therefore, that all answers are either right or wrong. Such students are happiest when they find simplistic answers to their questions about the world, and they want to view their teachers and advisers as experts who can give them the right answer. They believe that hard work and obedience pay off. They depend on others to make important decisions for them. Many freshmen begin their college experience seeing through this dualistic lens.

As students develop, however, Perry says they become capable of more complex reasoning and dissatisfied with simplistic answers. They are moving into a *"multiplistic"* view of the world. They begin to see and understand cause and effect relationships. Diversity becomes legitimate because they realize that no one has all the answers. They believe everyone has the right to his or her opinion. They still, however, depend on others to make decisions for them. Some freshmen and sophomores view their experiences through this multiplistic lens.

Perry identifies the next phase, "relativism," as the time when students begin to synthesize diverse and complex elements of reasoning. They are able to view uncertainty as legitimate. They see *themselves* as the principal agent in decision making and acknowledge that they must not only make their own decisions, but also take responsibility for those decisions, regardless of how well or badly those decisions may turn out. Many juniors and seniors fall into this category of "relativistic" thinkers. Because the emphasis in Perry's system is always on how college students tend to think and reason, his theory is called a theory of *cognitive* development.

For Perry, the most advanced phase of cognitive development is one in which students make a commitment to a personal identity and its content and style. Each develops a sense of being "in" one's self, along with an awareness that growth is always transpiring, that change is inevitable and healthy. Students also make a commitment to a defined career area and are able to develop a lifestyle that is appropriate for them. Many students continue in this state of personal growth and development after college.

Through his theory of cognitive development, Perry helps us understand how students view, react to, and assimilate knowledge as they progress through college. It is important to recognize that while college experiences encourage and foster this development, non–college students also mature and develop in much the same way. (It is also important to remember that any theoretical model, no matter how carefully established, is just that: a model. Judgments about how individuals may be measured against a model require great care. And, as you see later, other models are also well established.)

Perry theorizes that growth occurs in surges, with pauses between the surges when some students might need to detach themselves for a while, while others even retreat to the comfort of their past ways of thinking. Ask five seniors to look back on how they have changed intellectually. While they will be able to reflect on their intellectual development in unique and personal terms, the patterns of growth that Perry describes will usually be evident. However, it sometimes takes courage to confront the risks each forward movement requires. Every student has the freedom to choose what kind of person he or she will become, but the forces of growth, according to Perry, will not be denied.

Developmental Tasks

Another theorist, Arthur Chickering, suggests that college students develop in an orderly way on many dimensions: intellectually, physically, psychologically and socially. He describes several developmental tasks, or *"vectors,"* through which students move during their college years. A vector, according to Chickering, is a developmental task that (1) has specific content, (2) shows up at certain times in our lives, and (3) takes two to seven years to resolve. The process is ongoing throughout our lives, and even though we may resolve a task once, it may resurface later. These tasks build on each other; how we resolve one may affect the ones that follow. While these tasks develop in order, they may also be concurrent, so we may be dealing with several at one time. The seven developmental tasks that Chickering has proposed are described next.

1. Achieving Competence

The first task is achieving competence. College students need to achieve competence in several areas: intellectually, physically, and interpersonally. Chickering likens this to a three-tined pitchfork, since all three happen simultaneously.

Intellectual competence involves the skill of using one's mind in "comprehending, analyzing and synthesizing." It means learning how to learn and acquiring knowledge. Most students enroll in college in order to develop intellectual competence. They begin to develop good study habits and the skills of critical thinking and reasoning. They will be able to appreciate and integrate many points of view in their thinking. Ideally, they will enjoy learning for its own sake and feel the excitement of entering new realms of knowledge. Physical competence involves manual skills as well. The recreational value of, and prestige associated with, athletic skills or the creative value of arts and crafts are important to many students. More and more we are concerned that lifelong fitness is important. Recreational skills and interests that one develops in college continue throughout life. Colleges provide many physical facilities for students who seek to develop competency in this area.

Probably the greatest concern of many students is how to develop interpersonal and social competence. They feel a need for communication skills, such as listening and responding appropriately, so they can relate to others individually or in groups. Learning the social graces and how to interact with peers is an important task that most students accomplish early in their college years. Much of this learning happens as a result of observation, feedback from other students, and experience.

When these three competencies are achieved, students feel a *sense* of competence; they sense that they can cope with whatever comes. They are confident of their ability to achieve successfully whatever they set out to do. They respond to new challenges by integrating old learning with new. The task of developing competence is especially important during the freshman year.

2. Managing Emotions

Two major emotional impulses that need to be managed during college are sex and aggression. Maturity implies that legitimate ways have been found to express anger and hate. Sexual impulses are more insistent than ever. Students feel pressured to find answers to questions concerning interpersonal relationships. They move from being controlled by the external rules of their heritage to control by internal norms of self. (Students from rural areas may have different sets of rules, for example, than inner-city students.) Many students are still controlled by the external norms of their peers. Exaggerated displays of emotion are not uncommon: in the past, for example, college students initiated panty raids or held contests for swallowing the greatest number of goldfish.

People often feel boredom, tension and anxiety as normal emotions while their impulsive feelings need to be controlled. Becoming aware of positive emotions such as sympathy, yearning, wonder and awe is also important. Eventually, students learn to be controlled by their own internal set of norms. Achieving competence in the management of emotions means moving from an awareness of the legitimacy of emotions, to acting on them, to controlling them internally.

3. Moving Through Autonomy Toward Interdependence

Another important task for new college students during the first months of college is to achieve independence. A student may be hesitant to try certain new experiences or to approach new people. Such a student is trying to become independent but, as Chickering says, is like a "hog on ice," a little shaky at first. For probably the first time in their experience, many students may be living with no restraints or outside pressures, with no one to tell them when to study or to be home by 11 o'clock. As they act on their own, they may flounder at first. Beginning students may wonder, for example, why they have so much free time. They attend classes for only three or four hours a day and then may squander the rest of the day—until they realize the importance of quality study time.

The student who achieves *emotional* independence has learned to be free of the continual need for reassurance, affection or approval. Such a student has learned to deal with authority figures and feels comfortable with professors or other very important people on campus. There is less reliance on parents and more on friends and nonparental adults. Achieving *instrumental* independence means students can do things for themselves that parents used to do, such as washing the laundry or managing money. They are able to solve problems and use resources on their own.

When the student finally comes to recognize and accept *inter*dependence, the boundaries of personal choice become clearer and the ranges within which one can give and receive become more settled. Autonomous students feel less need for support from their parents and begin to understand that parents need them as much as they need their parents. They begin to see their parents for what they are: middle-aged people with weaknesses just like themselves. Becoming autonomous is a very important task for freshmen to accomplish.

4. Developing Mature Interpersonal Relationships

Developing mature relationships means that students become less anxious and less defensive, more friendly, spontaneous and respectful. They are more willing to trust and are more independent. They develop the capacity for mature intimacy. They can participate in healthy relationships that incorporate honesty and responsiveness. They finally realize that perfect parents don't exist and that Prince or Princess Charming is not coming to sweep them off their feet. They also have an increased tolerance for people culturally different from themselves. They have acquired increased empathy and altruism and enjoy diversity. They are able to develop mature relationships with many types of people.

5. Establishing Identity

The fifth vector, according to Chickering, is establishing identity. This task is really the sum of the first four vectors: developing competence, managing emotions, developing autonomy through interdependence, and developing mature interpersonal relationships. Success at achieving identity will often hinge on how these former tasks have been accomplished. Studies suggest that students generally achieve a coherent, mature sense of identity during their sophomore or junior years.

In addition to these inner changes, students need to clarify their conceptions of physical needs, personal appearance, and sex-appropriate roles and behavior. They identify a personal lifestyle that is theirs. Once such a sense of identity is achieved, other major vectors may be approached. Establishing an identity is the hinge on which future development depends.

6. Developing Purpose

Developing purpose is the vector related to career choice. The questions to be faced for this vector are not only "Who Am I?" but also "Where Am I Going?" Interests tend to stabilize; vocational exploration becomes a serious task. A general orientation toward a career area is achieved first, and then more specific career decisions are made. Students begin to formulate plans and integrate vocational and lifestyle considerations into those plans. An initial commitment to a career goal is made with the move into adulthood.

7. Developing Integrity

Students also need to clarify a personally valid set of beliefs that have some internal consistency. This happens in three stages, according to Chickering. Their values are first (1) humanized, then (2) personalized, and then (3) their beliefs and actions begin to suit each other. During childhood, students assimilate their parents' values. In college, students begin to examine these inherited values to see if they fit them personally. Some values may be rejected while others may be retained. The student's task is to personalize these values by achieving behavior consistent with them and being willing to stand up for what he or she strongly believes. Such a degree of commitment leads to congruence between one's beliefs and values and one's actions. Standards for assessing personal actions are set and are used as guides for all behavior.

Working through these seven developmental tasks is crucial to the college student's successful passage into mature adulthood. How will you be different on graduation day? I hope that you will have no regrets about missed opportunities to become involved in your own development. The college environment offers an almost unbelievable assortment of opportunities in and outside the classroom. There are many resources, including people, who stand ready to challenge and support you. As you move into the world you will be willing to assert the convictions and values you carefully (and sometimes traumatically) learned during your college years. Knowing that everyone moves through these passages of development and that change is inevitable can help you see the more difficult times as periods of growth. In this way you will be able to react positively and productively.

Reprinted by permission of the author.

Vocabulary

As you think about this essay, these definitions may be helpful to you:
1. **dualistic**   consisting of two irreducible elements or modes; a way of thinking that sees issues as black or white, rather than as shades of gray
2. **multiplistic**   numerous or various
3. **cognitive** involving the act of knowing, including both awareness and judgment
4. **vector**   a course or direction
5. **instrumental**   serving as a means, agent, or tool; in this essay, instrumental independence is the ability to live and work on your own

 Discussion Questions

1. What aspect of student development does Perry's scheme address? What is its primary thesis? Do all students fit these patterns?
2. How does a dualistic student view the world?
3. How does Perry describe commitment, which he considers the most advanced phase of cognitive development? How do you reach commitment?
4. What are the seven developmental tasks of college students as proposed by Chickering? Which are most relevant to first-year, traditional-age college students?
5. What, says Chickering, is required to develop an identity? How are the last two tasks of developing purpose and integrity related to identity?

 Suggestions for Your Journal

Sketch your own intellectual development from the time you were a child until now. Where do you think you fit into Perry's scheme? Have you ever consciously experienced a period of intellectual growth? How would you describe it?

Which of Chickering's developmental tasks have you completed? Which will be the most difficult to master?

Trouble with Parents

Inge Bell

Inge Bell was a professor of sociology at Pitzer College. In this essay, she discusses the transition of students as they enter college and the changing roles that develop between them and their parents. The sentences in quotation marks used as examples in this reading are directly from students that Bell talked with in her research.

The last time I went home, I realized that I was visiting my parent's house—not coming home. It was a sad feeling, but also a feeling of independence and maturity. I had to say goodbye to my childhood and the familiarity of my home town, but I realized that I have a whole adult life of my own to look forward to.

Next to grades and love, parents are surely the most frequent cause of *vexation* among students. When I opened up this subject with some classes, the response was immediate. When I asked who was having difficulties with parents, most hands went up.

One young man says, "You come home and they think you are still the same age as when you left. I've been living at school since I was 15 and my parents still treat me like they did when I was 15."

A young woman chimes in, "When I go home, suddenly I'm back with having to be in before midnight or my mother will lie awake and worry until I come home."

Another says, "How do I let them know that I don't need that much parenting anymore? I feel myself falling back into being-your-child-again, and at the same time I witness them go through the transformation into we-are-your-parents. They never see you in any other role—when you return home it's this weird time warp—as if you have never been away."

Another says about going home, "I was a guest but I was also responsible once again for all the old assignments. I had to clean up my room when they wanted me to, not when I wanted to."

Some students found they missed their parents. There is a temptation to slip back into familiar roles. "You kind of want the child role and they want it for you. It is such a contrast to the independence at school."

"I used to just want to get out of the house and be with my friends, now I'm with friends all the time and I like to spend time with my parents. When I go home it's a lot better."

Here somebody asked, "Would anyone want to go back and live at home?" A chorus of resounding "no's."

At the point of leaving home, many students find parents hanging on too hard. "They ask, 'Why don't you come home and visit this Easter, Christmas, or stay all summer?' I want to spend some time with my friends."

My class discussions were with students at small private residential colleges. To balance this bias I got some feedback from a class at a community college where most students live at home. Surprisingly, a slight majority of these students were very well satisfied with their arrangements. In some cases parents seem to have given the child adult status as they entered college:

"My relationship at home with my parents is good. After high school, where my grades were scrutinized by my parents, college has been totally opposite. They leave me alone about my grades. Ironically, I always end up telling them things anyway. I think our 'college' relationship was a positive step in my maturation to adulthood."

". . .They basically stay out of my way. They understand that college, working, and friends is a hard way to live. . . . Their main complaint is that I'm not home enough, I'm never there to talk to, pick up around the house, or watch TV. I have two jobs and school, so it gets hard. All in all, I'm happy with the living arrangements at home. . . ."

In some cases I had the impression that students who live at home are more willing to settle for a lack of *autonomy* because the arrangement is otherwise so useful to them.

"I'm not saying our relationship is perfect, 'cause by far it isn't but I can tell you the more I respect them, the better it gets. So maybe kids should respect their parents more, after all, they do know a lot more than us."

Those who reported not liking life at home had many of the same complaints as those voiced by students living away from home, only in the former case the conflicts have a greater impact on the student's life. "Living with my parents is difficult during college because they tie everything I do to my grades. Their control level is tremendous. Because they are paying for my education, everything in my life must not be private."

"They put a lot of pressure on me by trying to do family functions and continuing family togetherness. They don't understand that as we get older we want to be with friends."

These conflicts are so common, even when relations in the family have been good, that we must look for a *pervasive* cultural pattern. The problem is that for 18 years, your parents protected you, felt a tremendous responsibility for you, tried to ease your path and warn you about the pitfalls of life; and now, suddenly they have to shift gears. They have to trust the wisdom of their own child rearing, and have to trust you to survive your own mistakes. They have to restructure the whole relationship.

At the same time, in our culture, a child is expected to leave home and become a full-fledged adult during the late teens and early twenties. Unlike the situation in many other societies, children are not supposed to remain blindly obedient to their elders. There must be a "breaking free." You all sense this and try to act accordingly. It is, indeed, difficult to go from a highly structured home situation into a very unstructured college situation.

As you meet the cultural requirements of thinking for yourself, you encounter disagreements with your parents. As one student put it, "Can you love your parents and not necessarily agree with them? If you express your disagreement, can they hear where you are coming from such that it doesn't mean you don't love them? If I ever disagreed with my dad, it would be World War III." I asked her if she had actually tried an open disagreement. She said she had not. I urged her to try but be sure that, for her part, the disagreement wasn't part of a desire to reject him in her turn.

Breaking-away is better confronted on concrete issues of parental control: for example, when they demand that you come home by midnight or insist that you have to clean your room on time. Differences of opinion work better if you are just exploring your new ideas with your parents, rather than against them.

Where there has been real love between children and parents, the difficult transition period will pass. It is always surprising to college seniors how much their parents have matured in four years. A few *filial* relationships are so good that the struggle never happens. After listening to the class discussion for some time, one young woman said, "I am really amazed to hear all this because I still live at home with my father, but we don't have any conflict. I think he has always sort of treated me as an equal. I am very comfortable in the situation."

Another said, "Even when you are 30, they'll still have the chicken soup ready. But I think college is the time to branch out. My parents and I are separating, but the relationship exceeds what we had in high school."

In these healthy families, parent and child may enjoy role-reversal, which the child's new adulthood makes possible. An older student said, "My daughter graduated from medical school. We were going to her own home. We were her guests. She was making all the arrangements. What a feeling to have total role-reversal. My daughter worried about my son being late, and I thought, 'Oh, that's what I used to do.'"

Unfortunately, some parent/child relationships are deeply neurotic and tense. Here the struggle to break away can be traumatic for both sides. In dealing with neurotic relationships, the student may be up against raw fear. When we are children parents are all powerful for us. Their nurturance is a matter of life and death. So, it may be necessary to get past this fear.

Sometimes parents pressure students about their choices of major, career, or even extra-curricular activities. "Why don't parents understand that their children have to make their own choices. I think it is because they are distant from their children. They never really see who the child is. My folks used to say, 'Whatever makes you happy.'"

Where you come up against disagreements about college majors and careers, I think you must try to prevail. You cannot let yourself be put into a position of living out your parents' hopes for themselves in your own life. I would advise you to do some thorough research about your desired major, career plan, or summer job prospect. Most college campuses have an office of career planning which gives vocational and aptitude tests. Take these and show the results to your parents. Thus prepared, you will have an easier time staying calm and reasonable—always the position of strength.

Never having been a parent myself, I couldn't tell you how this whole process looks from the parents' viewpoint. So I asked some wise mothers of my acquaintance for some words of wisdom.

"I always looked on college as a maturing experience. Go, have a good time, meet people, broaden your interests. If you also happen to learn something, that's nice. If it contributes to your career, that is remarkable. Actually, my son's extracurricular activity, photography, is now his career."

"I think that college is really the last significant gift you can give your kids. Education in general. One should be generous and gracious about it and grateful that they have come this far."

"This is how we have always felt about children. Parents do not own their children. Children are very special gifts—to be loved, enjoyed, nourished, educated, guided to a recognition of moral values, and to a sense of responsibility and accountability. Then follows the difficult part—a time to trust, to let go, and to hope they've done a good job. Deep inside, mothers and fathers never stop being mothers and fathers, never stop caring, but they can adjust. They can recognize maturity, and value sons and daughters as mature young men and women, capable of making good decisions."

One mother sent along the following poem saying, "For as many years as I can remember I've treasured a very faded clipping that has guided me. It's on my refrigerator right now."

Children Are Like Kites

Children are like kites.
You spend years trying to get them off the ground.
You run with them until
you're both breathless.
They crash . . . they hit
the roof top . . . you
patch, comfort and assure
them that some day they will fly!
They need more string, and you
keep letting it out. They tug.
There is a sadness that goes with
joy. The kite becomes more distant,
and you know it won't be long
before that beautiful creature
will snap the lifeline that binds
you together and will SOAR, as
it was meant to soar—free and
alone! Only then, do you know
that you have done your job.

From Inge Bell, *This Book Not Required* (Fort Bragg, CA: The Small Press, 1991).

Vocabulary

As you think about this essay, these definitions may be helpful to you:
1. **vexation**   something that is troubling, irritating
2. **maturation**   the state of having completed natural growth and development
3. **autonomy**   self-directed personal freedom
4. **pervasive**   diffused throughout every part
5. **filial**   having the relation to a child or an offspring

 Discussion Questions

1. What are some key issues between students and their parents that are discussed in this essay?
2. Why are some students comfortable living at home while attending college, whereas others are not?
3. Our society pressures young people to be independent of their families. How does this differ from other cultures?

 Suggestions for Your Journal

Write about your relationship with your parents when you first left for college and how it was (will be?) different during your home stay over the holiday break.

In what ways would you like your relationship with your parents to change? To stay the same?

Loneliness

Barbara M. Newman and Philip R. Newman

Barbara and Philip Newman are the authors of many books on human development. They are especially well known for *Development through Life: A Psychosocial Approach*, now in its eighth edition. Barbara Newman is professor and chair of the Human Development and Studies Department at the University of Rhode Island. Philip Newman is a lecturer in the same department.

Some students may experience feelings of loneliness as they enter a new and foreign college environment. The authors describe loneliness as a common college experience and suggest that friendships can play a key role in overcoming it.

College brings new opportunities for friendship, but it also brings new experiences of isolation and loneliness. Many college students leave the comfort and familiarity of their support system at home for a new environment. Others break ties with old friends who have gone to work or entered the military right after high school. The early weeks and months of college are likely to bring deep feelings of isolation and loneliness. These feelings are intensified because students usually approach the transition to college with such positive anticipation. They often do not even consider that this change will bring any sense of *uprootedness* or loss.

Loneliness is a common experience of college life. An estimated 25 percent of the college population feel extremely lonely at some time during any given month. These feelings are likely to be most noticeable during the freshman year because of the sharp contrast between the structure of high school life and the independence expected of students in college. However, loneliness can be a theme throughout the college years. The process of becoming an individual brings with it a new appreciation for one's separateness from others. As young people discover their own uniqueness, from time to time they are bound to feel that no one else really understands them.

Your parents may also experience periods of loneliness. They miss the physical presence of a person they love. They miss the daily interactions. Now and again, they may yearn for things to be more like they were and wish to be less separate.

Loneliness can be classified into three categories: *transient*, situational, and chronic.[1] *Transient loneliness* lasts a short time and passes. College students may feel this kind of loneliness when their friends are out on dates and they are alone in the dorm. This type of loneliness may occur when a student is the only one to take a certain position in a discussion; the only black student in a class; or the only one working out in a large, empty gym.

---

[1] These categories are adapted from J. Meer, "Loneliness," *Psychology Today,* July 1985, pp. 28–33.

Situational loneliness accompanies a sudden loss or a move to a new city. Students commonly experience this kind of loneliness when they first come to college, especially if they are away from home. Most of us are *disoriented* when we move to a new town. Going to college is no different. Despite the many new and wonderful facets of college life, most young people experience situational loneliness due to the loss of the supportive, familiar environment of their homes and communities.

Your parents may undergo situational loneliness because of the loss of your presence. Even though they have planned and saved for this opportunity, they may experience intense loneliness following your departure. Rather than trying to create a myth that no one is feeling lonely, parents and college students can help each other through this time by admitting their loneliness and doing their best to reduce it. Frequent telephone calls, letters, and visits home in the first few months can ease the feelings of loss.

Chronic loneliness lasts a long time and cannot be linked to a specific event or situation. Chronically lonely people may have an average number of social contacts, but these contacts are not meaningful in helping the person achieve the desired level of intimacy. Chronically lonely people often seem reluctant to make contact with others. There appears to be a strong relationship between social skills and chronic loneliness. People who have higher levels of social skill, including friendliness, communication skills, appropriate *nonverbal* behavior, and appropriate response to others, have more adequate social support and experience lower levels of loneliness.

You may not recognize that you suffer from chronic loneliness until you are away at college. While children are living at home, parents are usually able to provide the amount of social support their children need. At college, children may find it extremely difficult to replace the level of trust and closeness that were provided by family members and high school friends.

Inadequate friendship relationships may actually interfere with your academic performance as well as your physical and mental health. Substantial research evidence supports the relationship between inadequate social support and *vulnerability* to illness. People who are part of a strong social support system are more likely to resist disease and to recover quickly from illnesses when they occur. Their general outlook on life is more optimistic.

A college student's circle of friends plays a key role in keeping the young person integrated into the social environment. Friends look in on you when you are sick; they make sure you have an assignment if you miss class; they invite you to join them if they are going to a party, a special lecture, or a campus concert. Friends worry about you and remind you to take care of yourself. Friends monitor your moods and prevent you from becoming too preoccupied or too discouraged. Friends value you and support your emerging identity. They understand the importance of the questions you are raising, and they encourage you to say what's on your mind. Building and maintaining satisfying friendships are key ingredients to feeling at home and succeeding in college.

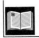 **Vocabulary**

As you think about this essay, these definitions may be helpful to you:
1. **uprootedness**   in psychology, a sense of being displaced
2. **transient**   passing through with only a brief stay or sojourn
3. **disoriented**   having lost a sense of time, place, or identity
4. **nonverbal**   involving minimal or no use of language
5. **vulnerability**   openness to attack or damage

 Discussion Questions

1. What factors may trigger loneliness in a college student?
2. What are the three categories of loneliness described by the authors?
3. How does transient loneliness differ from chronic loneliness?
4. Why are students with little or no social support more vulnerable to illness?
5. What is the hardest part of maintaining a friendship?

 Suggestions for Your Journal

Did you experience situational loneliness when you started college? How did it feel? Do you know students who are lonely? How can building and maintaining friendships be helpful in overcoming loneliness? How can you as a friend help another student through lonely times?

Tips on Becoming Personally Effective

Susan Jones Sears

Well known for her work in counselor education, Susan Jones Sears is a professor emerita in the College of Education at the Ohio State University. In this essay, she offers some practical tips for becoming a competent and successful student.

Whether you are a new college student or a more experienced one, you are probably impressed with the number of talented and highly skilled individuals in your classes—individuals who seem to know more than you do and who are motivated, bright, and dedicated. With increasing competition in the classroom and the workplace, individuals have begun searching for a psychological edge, an advantage to help them excel and be recognized as competent students and workers. Think about the concept of personal effectiveness—personal behaviors and skills that result in enhanced performance in college, at work, and in life. As you begin your college career and prepare for the work world, you can benefit from reflecting upon what it takes to excel.

What are the ingredients of success? During the last two decades, hundreds of books have been written with the intent of helping people improve themselves and increase their chances for success. Techniques for improving your personality, learning to communicate more effectively, and managing stress are all familiar topics to readers who avail themselves of the self-help books in their local bookstores or on the Internet. In the early 1980s, those interested in improving their performance read *Peak Performers* by Charles Garfield; in the latter 1980s and early 1990s, they read *The Seven Habits of Highly Effective People* by Stephen Covey. In the 2000s, Philip C. McGraw is the latest self-help guru.

Today, many books on coaching are generating a lot of attention and discussion. Professional athletes and actors have used the services of coaches for decades, and now ordinary individuals are hiring coaches to give them advice and offer strategies on how to improve their personal and professional lives.

If you study high achievers or personally effective individuals, you begin to see that they function at higher levels not because of a single talent but, rather, because certain factors, taken together, result in greater accomplishment. Individuals who know what they want to do in life, who have a vision, a game plan, or a purpose or goal, are more successful than those who do not. If you have a sense of purpose, you will naturally attract those who are going in the same direction. What is your purpose or goal in life? What are you trying to achieve? Maybe you want to find a major or a career that you will enjoy and [that will] bring you fulfillment, or maybe you want to travel to learn about other cultures. Take a few minutes to think about your goal or purpose for the year.

Replacing Distractions with Energy Boosters

Petty annoyances are often small irritants, but they tend to become real hassles when they are not dealt with. They drain your energy and distract you from your quest for success. Perhaps something around the house or apartment is broken, but you can't seem to get around to repairing it. Or your roommate is a "night owl" and you are not.

Maybe one of your own bad habits is annoying you! Your notes are disorganized and scattered, and when it is time to study for a test, you procrastinate. Or maybe a friend has a habit of making fun of you or putting you down when you make even a small mistake. You have tolerated it but find yourself getting angrier each time it happens. Many of us tolerate petty annoyances and really don't realize how much they are irritating us, wearing us down, and draining our energy. Write down a list of the things you are putting up with or tolerating that are draining your energy. Now set aside a day within the next week to tackle some of these petty annoyances. Try to eliminate everything on your list that you can.

Some annoyances take time to eliminate. If you are having difficulty in a relationship and want to rebuild or repair it, you probably can't do it in a day. But at least you can begin. When you succeed in working through the annoyances that bother you the most, you should reward yourself by indulging in some favorite activity.

Simplifying Your Life

One way to attract something new in your life is to make space—get rid of the clutter, toss out old notes, clothes, and memos, and sell those old books and CDs. Ask yourself: "Have I used this in the past six months?" If your answer is no and it isn't a seasonal item, toss it. If you don't know where to start, take one part of a room at a time. Give your usable items to a local charity. Someone will appreciate what has been cluttering up your space. Getting rid of things you do not need can invigorate you and create the sensation of starting anew.

Once you have rid yourself of the clutter in your life, look at your schedule. If your schedule is packed with stuff to do, people to meet, and places to go, it may be time to simplify. People who are too busy can miss opportunities because they don't notice what is going on around them and don't have time to think. Consolidate your credit cards so you don't spend so much time paying and keeping track of bills. Turn your cell phone off. Before you say yes to a social event, make certain it is really something you want to do.

Managing Your Time Effectively

Do you attend classes, study as hard as you can, and then run to your part-time or full-time job? Do you find yourself complaining that there aren't enough hours in the day? If you feel pressured for time, perhaps you should take a week and track your time in one-hour increments. Keep a notepad in your pocket or bookbag and write down what you are doing each hour from the time you rise until you go to bed. Writing just a few words will allow you to keep track of how you are spending your time. At the end of the week, quickly calculate how much time you spend on major life activities such as attending classes, studying, talking on the phone, sleeping, watching television, listening to CDs, hanging out with your friends, e-mailing or instant messaging. Are you surprised by how you spend your time? In what areas do you think you are wasting your time? How can you reschedule your time so you will use it more effectively?

Learning to Say No

Are you overcommitted with work and social obligations? Do you find yourself participating in activities that don't really interest you? Perhaps you need to learn to say no. Women in particular are brought up in our society to please and to be liked. As a result of this kind of socialization, they find it harder to say no when asked to do favors or take on extra work. Some fear that saying no will turn off their friends, but in reality it doesn't. Often your friends and colleagues respect you more when they learn they cannot take advantage of you. Learning to say no is one way of getting control of your time and your life.

Managing Your Money Well

During the last 20 years, it has become acceptable to have debts. Your parents probably saved money before they purchased a cherished item, whereas you may find it easy to simply charge the cost to your credit card. The costs of immediate gratification (charge it now) can be high. First, the interest rate on debt is high. Second, too much debt can lead to stress that can drain your energy, making it difficult for you to be your best and attract the people and opportunities you want. Instead, if you pay off the balance on your credit cards each month, you will feel lighter, more free, and in control of your life.

Building a Strong Network of Friends

Part of your success in life and work is having some close friends with whom you can laugh, love, and celebrate your and their successes. Be aware of the people around you, and get to know those who are particularly interesting. With our increased mobility, we sometimes have to create our own communities, a circle of friends with whom we feel comfortable and supported. Some create this circle of friends at college or at work, and others find opportunities to create friendships at church or in clubs. Be proactive and create your own network of friends.

Making Time for Yourself

Life can become boring if we do not have something to look forward to. Taking a walk, talking to friends, taking a hot bubble bath, or listening to your favorite music are just a few examples of activities that might be pleasurable and inspiring to you. Taking time for yourself is an important way to keep balanced in today's hectic world. Think about the activities that you really look forward to doing, and then how can you change your schedule to include them in your daily life.

Identifying and Managing Stress

If you are to become truly effective, you must begin to identify the sources of stress in your life and learn to manage stress at work, school, and home. Stress can be either a positive or a negative force. It is negative when it interferes with your ability to function at your optimal level. It is positive when it enhances your performance or your effectiveness. That is the key to stress management.

What does the term *stress* really mean? According to psychologist Donald Meichenbaum, you experience stress when you appraise an event (a demand on you, a constraint, an opportunity, or a challenge) as having the potential to exceed the resources you have available. You may think it's too hard, too frightening, or too challenging. Stressors or events that can create anxiety vary greatly from individual to individual. Three classifications are:

- *external* physical stimuli, such as heat, cold, crowding, loud noises
- *interpersonal* difficulties with others
- *internal* stimuli, such as our own thoughts or feelings

Although stressors are specific to individuals to some extent, universal categories of stressors are environmental stressors, life stress events, and daily hassles.

Environmental stressors include things such as noise, crowding, commuting time, worry about crime, traffic and pollution, economic difficulties, isolation, restricted leisure opportunities, and job insecurity. These often are a function of where you live and sometimes your socioeconomic class.

Life stress events are major occurrences that create stress and require people to change and adapt. Holmes and Rahe identified 43 life events that cause significant stress and assigned each event a weight, using what they called "life change events." Events that call for a greater amount of change and adaptation are assigned a higher number of life change units. For example, the death of a spouse is assigned a very high weight. Holmes and Rahe used their instrument, the Social Readjustment Rating Scale, to measure the amount of life stress a person was experiencing. They found that too many life stress events forced the body to adapt and change so much that those stresses weakened the immune system.

In fact, researchers have made connections between life stress events and both physical and mental illness. Evidence has shown that life stress events contribute to emotional disorders, heart disease, accidents, and other conditions. Whether individuals who experience stressful life events subsequently become ill, however, also depends on their personal vulnerability, as well as the amount of social and emotional support available to them.

Daily hassles (for instance, physical appearance, concerns about weight, too many things to do, and losing or misplacing things) are also stressors. Until the early 1980s, little research had been done on the effect of minor but more common daily hassles. Since then, researchers have paid considerable attention to studying effects of hassles on health. Hassles seem to vary depending on age and, to some extent, the circumstances in which people find themselves. Some common daily hassles for students are:

Taking tests or exams
Worrying about not meeting academic deadlines
Not knowing how to study effectively
Taking hard and demanding classes

Strategies for Managing Stress

Preventive approaches such as relaxation training are important to any stress management program. The term *relaxation training* refers to any technique whose purpose is to decrease the negative symptoms the human body experiences under stress. If individuals can be taught to relax, they should be able to produce voluntarily an alternative physiological response to offset the negative stress symptoms. For example, if a stress reaction results in increases in muscle tension, blood pressure, or heart rate, the voluntarily induced state of relaxation can reverse these increases.

Engaging in a healthy lifestyle goes a long way in managing stress. Individuals who experience the physiological effects of stress are endangering their health. If they also are practicing unhealthy habits that weaken the body's ability to resist stress, their level of stress may increase. Clearly, if you are stressed, you should practice good eating habits, use alcohol only moderately if at all, not smoke, and get regular exercise.

Accepting and Adapting to Change

Change is anything that causes us to shift from old and familiar ways or situations to ones that are new, different, and often challenging. More than a decade ago, Alvin Toffler talked about "waves of change" that are accelerating at a faster and faster pace. The rate of change in today's world is greater than any other time in our history. Global competition, almost unbelievable advances in technology, particularly communication technologies, and a knowledge and information explosion all contribute to this fast-paced change. Learning how to adapt and adjust to change is a critical skill that can be learned.

In times of rapid change, you must be able to adapt quickly. Below are several suggestions on how to adapt to change rather than ignore or resist it:

- Withhold judgment and tolerate ambiguity or uncertainty until you see the results of whatever changes you are experiencing.
- Be flexible and try new approaches.

- Stay current about changes and trends in your field and try to understand their potential impact.
- Anticipate the new skills needed in your field and acquire them.
- View change as part of a natural process of growth.
- Look to the future; don't glorify the past beyond its worth.
- Scan your environment and reassess your goals regularly.

Think about the changes that have occurred in your life in the last 18 months. How did you respond? For example, did you try to avoid change at all costs, complain about the change, reluctantly change, or see change as an opportunity and develop ways to deal with it? At times, change can create situations in which you feel you have little or no control over events going on around you. When that happens, we usually experience anxiety or stress. Although we cannot always control what is happening in life, we can control our reaction it. We can decide how to react to change so it does not overwhelm us.

The personal characteristics and skills outlined above can give you the psychological edge in school, work, and life in general. As you establish your educational and career goals, developing these habits, attitudes and skills can enhance your success in all areas of life.

Works Cited

Covey, Stephen. *The Seven Habits of Highly Effective People.* New York: Simon and Schuster, 1989.
Garfield, Charles. *Peak Performers.* New York: Avon, 1986.
Holmes, T. H., and Rahe, R. H. "The Social Readjustment Rating Scale." *Journal of Psychosomatic Research, 11*(2), 213–218, 1967.
Meichenbaum, Donald. *Stress Inoculation Training.* New York: Pergamon Press, 1985.
Toffler, Alvin. *The Third Wave.* New York: William Morrow, 1980.

From Susan Jones Sears and Virginia N. Gordon, *Building Your Career—A Guide to Your Future,* 3rd edition (Upper Saddle River, NJ: Prentice Hall, 2002). Reprinted with permission of Pearson Education Inc., Upper Saddle River, NJ.

 Discussion Questions

1. What does becoming a "personally effective student" mean to you? Does being a competent college student differ from being a competent high school student? If so, how?
2. Which of the author's suggestions for improving your daily life would be the most difficult for you to accomplish? (For example, do you have trouble saying no when friends ask for a favor?)
3. What are some stressors in your life, and what can you do to alleviate them?

Suggestions for Your Journal

Reflect on your ability to accept and adapt to change. Since you began college, what changes (for example, in your daily routine, in the classroom, in your relationship with your parents) have been the most difficult to deal with? The easiest?

What has surprised you the most about how being a college student has changed your life?

What Is Wellness?

John W. Travis and Regina Sara Ryan

John Travis, M.D., founded the first wellness center in the United States in 1975. He is the author of several books on wellness and cofounder of the Alliance for Transforming the Lives of Children. Regina Ryan is a wellness consultant, editor, graduate advisor in religious studies and human development, and the author of numerous books.

Wellness is the right and privilege of everyone. There is no *prerequisite* for it other than your free choice. The "well" being is not necessarily the strong, the brave, the successful, the young, the whole, or even the illness-free being. A person can be living a process of wellness and yet be physically handicapped; aged; scared in the face of challenge; in pain; imperfect. No matter what your current state of health, you can begin to appreciate yourself as a growing, changing person and allow yourself to move toward a happier life and positive health.

Wellness is never a static state. You don't just get well or stay well. There are many degrees or levels of wellness, just as there are degrees of illness. Nor is wellness simply the absence of disease. While people often lack physical symptoms, they may still be bored, depressed, tense, anxious, or generally unhappy with their lives. These emotional states often set the stage for physical disease through the lowering of the body's resistance. The same feelings can also lead to abuses like smoking, excessive alcohol or drug use, and overeating. But these symptoms and behaviors represent only the tip of the iceberg. They are the surface indication of underlying human needs for such things as recognition from others, a stimulating environment, caring and affection from friends, a sense of purpose, and self-acceptance. Diseases and symptoms are not really the problem. They are actually the body-mind-spirit's attempt to solve a problem—they are a message from the subconscious to the conscious.

Much of contemporary medical practice is involved with chipping away at surface needs. Its orientation is toward treating and eliminating the evidence of disease, and this is important. But it is not enough. It is essential to look below the surface signs to address the real needs. Wellness extends the definition of health to encompass a process of *integration* characterized by awareness, education, and growth.

Wellness, like life, is always a question of balance. It is a dynamic process because there are seeming contradictions to be resolved, apparent oppositions to be integrated, infinite shades of gray from which to choose. In considering the subject of health, for instance, you just don't find absolute answers to questions like: What should I eat? How should I exercise? What form of treatment is best? Rather, you must learn to balance what *you* know with what the "experts" tell you. Even though you are connected with me and everyone else you share this planet with, you are also very much alone, and you must *singularly* make your own life-and-death decisions. (Sounds serious. And it is!) But, if you make your life about self-responsibility and love, then the burden can be transformed into opportunity, and the questions can become the impetus for experimentation, for learning, for trusting, for loving this magnificent and paradoxical creation—yourself.

While some types of illness are genetically determined, and others are the result of environmental or accidental factors that appear to be largely out of our control, a large percentage of the illness we experience is created when we resist the movement and flexibility that characterize life and change. Wellness offers us a bridge to cross over into new territory, to explore different possibilities, to understand the other side of any situation. When we resign ourselves to being helpless victims of disease, when we give up on ourselves, when we hold on to one system and refuse to question it even when it fails to meet our needs, we encourage sickness and death.

To take charge of your own life and health implies taking calculated risks. It means recognizing that you have choices, and it carries with it your willingness to live with the consequences of those choices. For instance, in order to meet a deadline you may place yourself under prolonged stress, neglect your diet, and forget your exercise. These are your choices. If they are short-term, you will probably bounce back easily. But occasionally, they may result in a cold or some other condition that sends you to bed. Are you responsible for the cold? Yes, at some level you are. You may have no conscious awareness of it, but you created the condition that weakened your body and made it ripe for *dis-ease*. If you choose to take responsibility, you may accept the cold as an important message from your body and use it as a chance to rest and rebalance.

Wellness allows us to integrate contradictions like illness and health. It appreciates these as complementary parts of one life process. It is open to new ideas, courageous and noncompulsive behavior. Wellness means we can move freely between seeming opposites, learning from each, growing from both.

Wellness describes the quality of natural health or well-being that is fundamental to human beings. This quality of wellness is *not* dependent on physical well-being for its expression. It is an unconditional state of being that may be *obscured*—but not *destroyed*—by illness. It is therefore possible to discover well-being in the midst of a serious or chronic illness. Although this may seem simple and obvious, it is a major statement that sets the wellness approach apart from the more common treatment approach that measures only our state of physical health.

One aspect of self-love and self-acceptance is allowing disease to be an instructive and positive life force. The lessons that accompany it are essential to the fully functional human being. Since we are all going to die anyway, the test seems to be how we deal with our illnesses rather than how well or how long we can avoid them.

History is filled with example of individuals who experienced personal transformations as a result of serious disease or crippling handicap. For instance, the writings of Helen Keller and the music of Ray Charles have inspired millions of people all over the world. Christopher Reeve's advocacy for the handicapped provides another notable example. Wellness may be encouraged by a physical handicap as much as by a vigorous exercise program or a pure diet. Of themselves, none of these things automatically leads to wellness. When used as tools for self-exploration, for education, for growth, everything leads to wellness.

From *Wellness Workbook—How to Achieve Enduring Health and Vitality,* 3rd edition. (Berkeley, CA: Celestial Arts: 2004).

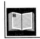 ## Vocabulary

As you think about this essay, these definitions may be helpful to you:
1. **prerequisite**   something that is necessary to carry out a function
2. **integration**   the act of forming, coordinating or blending, into a functioning or unified whole
3. **singularly**   individually

 ## Discussion Questions

1. How do you define "wellness"? Is it similar to or different from the authors' definition? If different, in what way?
2. Discuss the authors' claim that modern medical practice's orientation is "toward treating and eliminating the evidence of disease."
3. What do the authors mean when they say you "need to take charge of your own life and health"? How can you do that?
4. What do self-love and self-acceptance have to do with wellness?
5. Some people are likely to disagree with Travis and Ryan. What do you think are the *least* persuasive ideas that they assert?

 ## Suggestions for Your Journal

How would you describe your current state of wellness? What has been your experience with the mind-body relationship when you've been ill? List the ways you try to stay healthy and if they have been successful. What other healthy habits would you like to incorporate in your daily life and how can you include them? How does being a student help or hinder your staying healthy?

UNIT SUMMARY

The readings in this unit discussed many aspects of college life and its effect on students. Although adjusting to college may take some time, the challenge and excitement of being a student makes this experience unique and memorable.

Summary Questions

1. How do the expectations about college expressed by the readings in this unit differ from your own? How are they similar?
2. How can the college experience help you in your intellectual, personal, and career development?
3. If you were not attending college, how would your life be different? Evaluate the differences.

Suggested Writing Assignments

1. Write a brief essay on how you have changed since your first day in college. How do you expect to change by the time you earn a degree?
2. Describe one experience that you have had with taking control of your situation in life. How did you manage the change?
3. Describe one of your own college experiences that was also described by an author in this unit. Some examples are loneliness, stress, relationships with parents, and classroom experience. Compare your experience with that author's account.

Suggested Readings

Chickering, Arthur W., and Linda Reisser. *Education and Identity*, 2nd ed. San Francisco: Jossey-Bass, 1993.

Gilligan, Carol. *In a Different Voice*. Cambridge, MA: Harvard University Press, 1982.

Nist, Sherrie, and Jodi Holschuh. *College Rules*. Berkeley: Ten Speed Press, 2002.

How Can
I Succeed
Academically?

Academic success can be defined from many perspectives. Some measure it by grade-point average (known commonly as GPA) or by "accume," which is short for cumulative point-hour ratio. A student with a 3.5 GPA, for example, is usually considered more successful academically than a student with a 1.9. Academic success is also defined by one's accumulation of knowledge. Students who, when tested, can successfully throw back to their instructors the facts and concepts they have memorized may be considered academically successful. Still others define success by the salary and prestige of the job they are able to acquire at the end of their senior year. Some students may consider what they have genuinely learned to be the true measure of their academic success. Learning how to learn is a skill that can be used for a lifetime. Successful students will always be intensely involved in their own learning.

Regardless of how a student measures academic success, certain activities in which students engage are

'Tis education forms the common mind.

Just as the twig is bent, the tree's inclined.

—ALEXANDER POPE

essential to the learning process. Among them, reading and writing are two of the most critical. Some first-year students find themselves ill prepared in these basic skills. Most new students who understand the value of these activities work hard to improve their reading and writing skills throughout their college years.

Some other skills closely associated with academic success are:

Communication Skills. These include being able to communicate ideas and concepts effectively in a prepared presentation or in the conversational give-and-take of a committee meeting. Such skills are important in the classroom and marketable in the workplace.

Writing Skills. Students who can express themselves well in writing have a highly marketable skill. The ability to write clear and persuasive reports, proposals, and similar important documents is essential in every work environment.

Organizational Skills. Students need to set goals and priorities and to organize their time and energy accordingly. Self-discipline plays a key role in how students balance their academic life with other personal and social demands.

Analytical Skills. Learning to think critically and logically is important to academic success. Identifying problems and solving them creatively are central to accomplishing many academic tasks.

Research Skills. Students need basic research skills to fulfill many academic assignments. Defining a problem, formulating pertinent questions, using appropriate resources to study the problem, and employing a variety of research methods to solve the problem are all part of the research process that students use constantly.

Computer Skills. These skills include the ability to use a computer and its software to accomplish practical tasks.

The authors in this unit would certainly agree on the importance of the six categories of skill listed above. O'Hanlon outlines the skills necessary for library and Internet research, Gold suggests punctuality, and Brown requires regularity in attendance to class. Burtchaell and Raspberry offer perspectives on selecting a college major that may surprise some readers—especially those who have been conditioned to believe that selecting a college major is roughly equivalent to making a lifelong commitment to a single job. Minnick provides some ways for thinking about elective courses, which are all the classes you take that are not stipulated as some requirement. Schein, Laff, and Allen emphasize the importance of academic advising. Pauk and Owens offer practical ways for managing time, an important skill that students need to succeed. All these readings can have a bearing on your thoughtful approach to course selection.

Major Decisions

James Tunstead Burtchaell

Father James Tunstead Burtchaell, professor emeritus of theology at the University of Notre Dame, served as provost for many years. While holding that title, which in a university is normally the position of chief academic officer and ranks just below the president, Burtchaell lived in student residence halls and saw firsthand the student concerns that he discusses in this reading. Although many colleges strive to get students to decide on a major early, often before being admitted, Notre Dame in Burtchaell's time told students that, as first-year students, they could specify an intent but not declare a major. This essay explains why.

More than two out of every three undergraduates at this university change majors between the time they are accepted and the time they graduate. A good number change two or three times. Any decision that has so many students second-guessing must be tricky, and it is.

The difficulty comes from several directions. First, there are so many options that you had no opportunity to sample in high school. Everyone has some experience studying literature, mathematics, French and physics, but no high school in the country offers electrical engineering. Nor can you get a running start in microbiology or finance or metallurgy or philosophy. More than half of the disciplines we offer are new to you. So how can you have a responsibly cultivated preference early enough to select one as your principal interest here?

Another difficulty is pressure. Some students get pretty clear advice from their parents about what a sensible major would be. Most of that advice tends to have something to do with earning a living after college. And much of it is bad advice.

In the old days there were parents who threatened to cut off tuition money unless their child studied the subject they thought was right. That rarely happens today, but there is another kind of pressure that may be worse. There are few students at Notre Dame whose parents didn't make sacrifices for them to be here. And most students are backed by parents who didn't have, or weren't free to accept, the kind of education they worked hard to provide their children. The result: Most people on this campus walk around with an abiding and compelling sense of gratitude to their parents.

For every student here whose parents have told him what to study, there are a hundred whose parents never breathed a word of instruction on the matter. But most of those hundred, in the privacy of their hearts, want to make a choice that will satisfy their parents. They are drawn to major in subjects their parents can see as oriented toward a useful future. One somehow feels it would be ungrateful to receive a first-rate university education and not put it to maximum use from the start. That is a more *insidious* and damaging form of pressure precisely because there is nothing the parents can do to change it. They had nothing to do with imposing it.

In addition, high school counselors often talk to seniors in a way that is excessively career oriented. They make the student aware, even before she sets foot on a college campus, that she is going to higher studies with an eye toward an eventual profession or job. The message is that it is wasteful to spend four years without any clear idea of where all that expensive study is leading.

Students also have a tendency, especially in their early years at college, to feel crowded by competition. Most freshmen look up and down the corridor the first week they're here and feel intimidated. Everyone they encounter seems to have been a valedictorian, student council president, all-state breast-stroke champion, published poet.

I exaggerate, of course, but most people here *are* used to being at the head of the line. That is how you got here. Now you are at a place with a lot of others who were at the head of *their* lines, and there just isn't room for all of you at the top of this class. So you tend to figure that your choice of study here will have to be canny and careful if it's going to make you competitive with such bright and aggressive classmates.

After a few years you discover everyone else is as normal as you, but by then you've begun to worry that since Notre Dame accepted you it must be a second-rate institution. There are all those other more talented people out there at better places who, when they emerge, are going to have a running start on you. So your choice of what to study is fretful because you have these other, more quick-witted people to compete with.

Those are three difficulties that most of you have to cope with: the subjects are so unknown, the choice is so pressured, and the competition is so strong. Unfortunately these difficulties cause students to stumble into a few classical misunderstandings, which in turn lead them to wrong decisions about their major.

The first misunderstanding is to confuse education with training. An institution that offers you training is trying to provide you with the information and skills you need for a specific career. A law school must acquaint you with how to interview clients, how to plead before a court, and how to draw up proper legal documents. A welding academy will teach you the materials and methods of the trade. Advanced training in computing will prepare you not simply to keypunch or to program, but to create software, to understand the mysteries of central processing, and then to grasp the theoretical underpinnings of applied mathematics.

All of that is training: specific knowledge needed for specific professional or skilled work. It is not education.

Education is the opportunity, through studying a variety of subjects, to gain the information and the dexterity to use your wits and your expression. Education prepares you to *be* someone more than to *do* something. Education is what prepares you to hear more when you listen, to reach deeper when you think, to say more when you speak.

Education is quite different from training, which prepares you in advance to do the tasks that are well known in a given job. Education prepares you in advance to see beneath and beyond what is well known. The principal value that an educated person brings to her career is intelligence. What one wants of an educated person, beyond his skills, is the ability to see into problems that cannot be foreseen. A welder must know in advance all the techniques he has to use, but a banker or a physician or a teacher or a member of the city council is expected to move beyond previous experience and apply his wits to the heart of new problems.

A good university such as this one will give you quite a few skills and a broad grounding of information. But we do not exist to teach skills to undergraduates; we do that in our graduate and professional programs. The result of a college education should be a person whose mind is enlivened and whose imagination is limber. England's Robert Benchley put it in his own peculiar and wise way:

"Gentlemen: You are now about to embark upon a course of studies which will occupy you for several years. Together they form a noble adventure. But I would like to remind you of an important point. Some of you, when you go down from the University, will go into the Church, or to the Bar, or to the House of Commons, or to the Home Civil Service, to the Indian or Colonial Services, or into various professions. Some may go into the Army, some into industry and commerce, some may become country gentlemen. A few—I hope very few—will become teachers or *dons*.

"Let me make this clear to you. Except for the last category, nothing that you will learn in the course of your studies will be of the slightest possible use to you in after life, save only this: That if you work hard and intelligently you should be able to detect when a man is talking rot, and that in my view is the main, if not the sole, purpose of education."

People fortunate and qualified enough to receive a university education will make their living by their wits. You will be served less by what you *have* learned than by what you *can* learn.

The good thing about education is that it matters hardly at all what subjects you choose to study. You can be educated in any discipline, because there is no direct connection between an educational subject and a specific career. So never ask what you can *do* with your major.

This touches on the second classical misunderstanding that has led so many students astray. The choice of a major is not the choice of a career. Undergraduates are not making lifetime decisions. When they imagine they are, it can be paralyzing.

As you know, Notre Dame has delaying tactics to slow you down in the selection of a major. Before coming here most of you speculated about your eventual career, and then about what course of study you would select. You arrived here ready to declare a major, but the Freshman Year of Studies would not allow that. The most you were permitted was to designate an "intent." We wanted you to get the maximum exposure and experience here, and a year or two more of self-knowledge, so that your intellectual curiosity and interests could ripen and the decision would be more sound, more considered.

Let me say a bit about that. Some talents show themselves early in life. If you are an excellent athlete, you already have the coordination and stamina and pleasure from sports in your early teens. Nobody suddenly develops into a star athlete in her 30s.The same is true for mathematical ability. If you are good at quantitative understanding, you are already good at it in junior high school; in fact, you tend toward high achievement in math and other related subjects. You know science is your strong suit, and you come to college aware that you will study science and excel in it. Then things go wrong. Physics will begin to bore some of you. You will conceal from your parents that you signed up for a few extra theology courses, and you'll write poetry by flashlight under the covers at night. You may plug on and earn good grades, but with less and less appetite. It is *disconcerting* to develop a new range of interests when your track record of achievement and satisfaction is so definitely in another direction. But that is what happens when a new range of talent begins to mature and to rival other talents that had declared themselves earlier. No one tells you in advance that philosophical thinking matures later than mathematical thinking. The choice of a major needs to be slowed down to allow you to get confirmation of your emergent strong interests and abilities.

But even then, near the close of your sophomore year, you are only choosing a major, not a career. Still more developments and experiences will come. Fixing on a lifetime career when you are a sophomore in college is like getting engaged at 14.

What you study here may have little necessary connection with what you will do later. We give baccalaureate degrees in about 40 disciplines and in many combinations of subjects. But people graduate in philosophy and end up lawyers. They study mechanical engineering and end up as business executives. They get degrees in English and go to medical school, do art history and run the family business, choose chemistry and go into politics. They major in sociology and become priests. They finish in accountancy with their CPAs and choose to be homemakers and mothers.

Even if they emerge from a program most students would consider a direct pipeline to a specific profession—architecture, for example—they are really much more free than you would suppose. Do you know how many people with degrees in architecture practice architecture? About half. So consider yourself enhanced, rather than caught, by what you choose to study. You are not making a lifetime decision, you are making a decision for the next two or three years . . . or until you change that decision.

This is not to say that there should be no natural growth from study to career. It does imply, however, that educated people have such enormous advantage and versatility that they retain a basic freedom to do whatever they please in life. To have graduated in any discipline that Notre Dame offers in no way forecloses career possibilities. It has become increasingly the case that you will enter a career that requires or provides specific training. About 60 to 70 percent of you will go on to graduate or professional schools; others to corporate training programs. Do not suffer a failure of nerve by imagining that you are more attractive to employers if you have more advanced professional training. For then you will forfeit the unrepeatable and more valuable opportunity to get an education first.

You have talents that will be enormously attractive to employers, talents so superior that you are free to make your living by your wits, your versatility of understanding, your imagination. Don't double-think the future.

The temptation is to figure out your career and then choose the studies that lead up to it. That is exactly the wrong way round. You are not ready to choose a career, except in the most tentative and speculative way. You are barely ready to choose a major. Select what you want to study with the belief that it will lead you to the point of deciding—well, not quite your career, but what you will do after graduation. What educates you best is not what you figure will lead somewhere, but what you now believe will give you most enjoyment. Pick your major on the pleasure principle, for what you most enjoy studying will draw your mind in the liveliest way to being educated.

If you want to study medieval history, don't fret about what you can do with it. You are not at a trade school. If you want to study marketing, do it because you find marketing the most fascinating subject we offer. If you came to Notre Dame determined to become a physician but in your freshman year you couldn't stand math and you failed chemistry and you threw up over your laboratory frog, there's a message there. It's not that you are incapable of becoming a doctor, but that the kind of disciplines that govern a doctor's work do not really appeal to your appetite. If in the meantime drama has caught your eye, then make that your choice and let the future handle itself. Or, more accurately, let it help you to become more qualified to determine the future. If throughout the course of four years you progressively follow your intellectual nose into what fascinates you most, when you emerge you will be in a much wiser position to choose the threshold of the proper career than you were at the start.

In the meantime don't feel pushed to make the decision prematurely. Our curriculum is versatile enough that the decision can be reviewed and postponed and changed. I am not arguing for indecision or instability. I am merely pleading for a sense of freedom, a certain responsible recklessness about study, that too many students feel guilty about having.

Let me put it this way. Imagine you are told now that on graduation day you will die. It will be painless and gentle; you will slowly and beautifully fade, right here on the main quad, with family and roommates gathered round, the Glee Club singing under the trees, and *Father Hesburgh* giving you a potent final blessing. Knowing of your death now—realizing that whatever your major is, it can never lead you into a career but will be only for your pleasure and fascination— would it make any difference what you choose to study in the interim? If it would, then you ought to change. Ironically, what you then choose will lead you, by steady and proper pacing, into the most reliable future.

It is essential to realize that any major can lead to any career, and that the best major is the one you choose with no lookout out of the corner of your eye to where it will lead.

Once that is cleared up, the difficulties are less difficult. Yes, most of the majors possible here are subjects you cannot have studied before. So use the first and especially the second year to explore. Use the freedom the curriculum provides. Far too many men and women graduate from here and come to this regret: If they had it to do over again, or had had the nerve earlier, they would study another subject.

As for the pressure from parents whose approval you seek, remember: If you are mature enough to undertake university studies, you have to be mature enough to choose those studies. You might choose unwisely, but it should be your choice.

Parents who virtually demand what their children will study at college are misguided and, fortunately, rare. I think parents ought to have the freedom to suggest or lobby for a choice of major, but you take away your parents' freedom if you transform their cue into a command. Parents ought to be able to promote an idea without children complaining they are being forced or browbeaten. If your parents do suggest a course of study, give it serious thought, but don't pretend you owe it to them to follow their recommendation.

And don't get up a guilt if you choose another major, because you may in fact be trying to make *them* feel guilty for something they never did.

And if you feel tempted to make a curriculum choice to gain your parents' respect: don't. If you have anything to be grateful for, it is that your parents have wanted you to get the best education within your reach and theirs, precisely so that you could and would make these kinds of decisions responsibly for your own satisfaction. If they didn't want you to develop independent judgment, they would have kept you home.

How can you choose your major to sidestep most of the rush-hour traffic of competition? By ignoring competition. Only about 40 percent of your fellow Americans manage to enroll in college, and only about half of those graduate. Virtually all of you at this University will complete your degree requirements. That puts you among the top fifth of all people your age. And among that 20 percent, only the most highly qualified are competitive for admission to a university like Notre Dame, which means you have educational opportunities that rank you among the top one or two percent in the country.

It makes one feel uneasy to hear such talk of exclusiveness, but these are simple facts. So when you get uneasy because everyone in the corridor seems pretty swift of mind, calm down. You are moving among classmates who have the same advantaged education you have, who have been *sieved* through highly selective admission processes. After a while they may begin to look ordinary enough, but they aren't. And you aren't. The older one gets and the more experience one accumulates, the more clear it becomes that the number of really quick-minded people is small. You wonder how the world gets by with so few. Rather than imagining yourself as part of a large, capable crowd trying to crush through a narrow doorway of opportunity, it is more realistic to understand you are advantaged to an embarrassing degree, and there aren't nearly enough of you to go around.

To select a major program of study wisely you need not figure out what other people want of you. You need to figure out what you want. And that's not easy. It requires much self-knowledge.

But that is both what education gives and what education requires. William Johnson Cory, a Cambridge man, expressed impatience when critics complained that English schools were offering an education that was not useful enough. Education was not supposed to be useful, he retorted.

"You are not engaged so much in acquiring knowledge as in making mental efforts under criticism," he continued. "A certain amount of knowledge you can indeed with average faculties acquire so as to retain; nor need you regret the hours that you spent on much that is forgotten, for the shadow of lost knowledge at least protects you from many illusions.

"But you go to a great school, not for knowledge so much as for arts and habits; for the habit of attention, for the art of expression, for the art of assuming at a moment's notice a new intellectual posture, for the art of entering quickly into another person's thoughts, for the habit of submitting to censure and refutation, for the art of indicating assent or dissent in graduated terms, for the habit of regarding minute points of accuracy, for the habit of working out what is possible in a given time, for taste, for discrimination, for mental courage and mental soberness.

"Above all, you go to a great school for self-knowledge."

There are crucial freedoms that others can neither keep from us nor give to us. We must take possession of them ourselves. The sense of freedom that leads one to follow his or her own sensible instincts into a major course of study, confident that if one does that, then—and only then—will one be ready to make other even more crucial decisions: that is the sense of freedom I urge upon you before it is too late, and even before it is too early. Go ahead.

And after you have made your choice, remember that your major is only a minor portion of your higher education. You are invited—prodded—to surround and enliven your mind with elective courses. Relish them. The instructors in your discipline believe that you can never study enough of it, and some of us would advise you to take every elective our discipline has to offer. That is because we hanker to have our students love what we love, and this tempts us to tempt you to forgo your education and begin training in our field. Instead, browse in the clover.

When I was an undergraduate in philosophy, we were directed to read only primary sources; only the great thinkers, not the secondary folks who wrote textbooks about them. Excellent. But in retrospect, the good times were the hundreds of hours when I got lost in the stacks of the library and read my fascinated way through an education that no one had planned, but was lavishly provided.

Your duty is to enjoy. Nothing you might do could be more useful.

Reprinted by permission of the author.

Vocabulary

As you think about this essay, these definitions—and one identification—may be helpful to you:
1. **insidious**   harmful but enticing or having a gradual but cumulative effect
2. **dons**   the British educational system's equivalent of college teachers
3. **disconcerting**   unsettling or emotionally disturbing
4. **Father Hesburgh**   for more than twenty years, the legendary president of the University of Notre Dame
5. **sieved**   filtered

 Discussion Questions

1. What are the three difficulties that cause undergraduates to make wrong initial decisions about a major?
2. For Burtchaell, what distinguishes training from education? Give some examples of your own for training.
3. According to Burtchaell, what should a "good university" provide its students?
4. Based on your experience and that of your friends, is Burtchaell correct in saying that new students have insufficient information to select a major?
5. Burtchaell's final two sentences may have surprised you. Did you expect a serious teacher to draw this conclusion? How does he justify it?

 Suggestions for Your Journal

Write about how you chose your academic major. If you have not decided on a major yet, discuss why you have not done so.

What is your reaction to Burtchaell's ideas about not putting pressure on students to make a choice too soon in their first year? Do you agree that choosing a major is not necessarily choosing a career? Why?

Do you agree or disagree with Burtchaell that choosing a major should be done on the "pleasure principle"? Why?

College Major Doesn't Mean All That Much

William Raspberry

William Raspberry is a widely syndicated columnist who works with the *Washington Post* Writers Group. In this brief essay, which was first published as one of his regular columns, he stepped away from his usual commentary on the Washington scene and grew more personal as he counseled his daughter about approaching the question of what college major to select.

Soon to every *fledgling* student
Comes the moment to decide.
But since Angela's a freshman,
My advice is: let it ride.

With apologies to James Russell Lowell, that is pretty much my counsel to my daughter, who is about to begin her first year in college. Soon enough, she'll have to face the sophomore necessity of choosing a major—whether or not she's decided on a career. In the meantime, I tell her, don't worry about it.

A part of the reason for my advice is the memory of my own struggle to decide on a major. I eventually had four of them, none of which related to what was to become my career. But the more important reason is my conclusion, regularly reinforced, that majors just don't matter that much. The latest reinforcement is from John Willson, a history professor at Michigan's Hillsdale College, who having heard once too often the question "But what do I do with a history major?" has decided to do what he can to put his students at ease.

"Every sophomore has a majoring frenzy," he wrote in a campus publication. "It is typical for sophomores to say, 'I want to be an anchorman. Therefore, I will major in journalism. Where do I sign up?' They act like they have had a blow to the *solar plexus* when I say, (a) Hillsdale has no major in journalism, and (b) if we did, it would no more make you an anchorman than a major in English makes you an Englishman."

But rather than simply repeating what professionals already know, or urging colleges to dispense with the requirement for declaring a major, Willson has reduced his advice to a set of rules and principles.

The first, which college students often find incredible, is that aside from such vocational courses as engineering or computer science, any relationship between majors and careers is largely incidental. Physics majors are hardly more likely to become physicists than business majors to become *entrepreneurs*. The rule that derives from this principle: If you wanted your major to be practical, you should have gone to the General Motors Institute.

65

The second principle is that students (and colleges) should delay the necessity of choosing for as long as practicable. "Most students (and even more parents) have rather vague notions of what the subject of any given subject is. . . . Talk with your parents, but don't let parents, teachers, media experts, television evangelists or fraternity brothers pressure you into a majoring frenzy before you know what the major is all about." In short: All things being equal, it is best to know what you are talking about, which may even prevent majoring frenzies.

The third is a quote from the Rev. James T. Burtchaell (writing in *Notre Dame* magazine): "Pick your major on the pleasure principle, for what you most enjoy studying will draw your mind in the liveliest way to being educated." It's good advice, and not only for students at small liberal-arts colleges. A few years ago, the University of Virginia published a booklet, "Life after Liberal Arts," based on a survey of 2,000 alumni of its college of arts and sciences. The finding: 91 percent of the respondents not only believe that liberal arts prepared them for fulfilling careers but would also not hesitate to recommend liberal-arts majors to students considering those same careers. The "winning combination" derived from the Virginia survey: a liberal-arts foundation, *complemented* with career-related experience and personal initiative.

Colleges aren't assembly lines that, after four years, automatically deposit students into *lucrative* careers. What is far likelier is a series of false starts followed by the discovery of a satisfying career. In the Virginia survey, for example, only 16 percent reported being happy with their first jobs.

Willson's advice, the results of the Virginia survey, and my advice to Angela come down to the same thing: Major in getting an education.

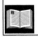 ## Vocabulary

As you think about this essay, these definitions may be helpful to you:
1. **fledgling**   a bird at about the age it learns to fly; here, metaphorically, someone getting ready to start independent living
2. **solar plexus**   a *plexus* is a gathering or network of nerves, and the solar plexus is located in the abdomen; a blow to the solar plexus will cause the victim to double over in pain
3. **entrepreneurs**   people who start and maintain businesses, taking the risk for the sake of possible profit
4. **complemented**   not *complimented* or *flattered* but completed and perfected by something else
5. **lucrative**   profitable

Discussion Questions

1. What reasons does William Raspberry give for his assertion that your choice of a major is not as important as many college students think?
2. How do you react to Raspberry's thesis that any relationship between majors and careers is "largely incidental"? Why is this perceived connection made by so many students?

 Suggestions for Your Journal

Raspberry and Burtchaell clearly agree on some important points about selecting a college major. What argument does Raspberry add to the discussion that Burtchaell does not mention? Which author do you find more persuasive? Why?

Want Good Advising?
Take the Initiative!

Howard K. Schein, Ned S. Laff, and Deborah R. Allen

This essay was written for the *Daily Illini,* the student newspaper at the University of Illinois at Urbana-Champaign. The authors hoped that by introducing basic advising tricks to undergraduates, they would become active members of the campus community and learn how to use the university better. The authors are professional academic advisors in a variety of higher education settings.

What is good academic advising? In its broadest sense, academic advising should involve an assessment of your personal values, a plan for attaining intellectual fulfillment, an investigation of career direction, and a look at the real world from objective and subjective positions. In a large sense, academic advising should lead you to ask: "What does all this mean to me?" Advice givers and their resources should help you learn how to answer this question.

Good academic advising is aimed at giving you the skills to answer the key question: what does this all mean to me? It's like all good educational experiences and all well-taught courses. It's a process that helps you learn to plot your path through college. It should help you orchestrate courses, resources, and other opportunities into an educational experience personally fit for you and one that seduces you into becoming personally involved in and responsible for your own learning.

The only thing you are going to get from your college programs catalog is a bare scheme of curricula, and its presentation will hardly tell you what you need to know. On most large campuses, for instance, you can study literature though several departments, such as English, Chinese, French, Russian and comparative literature. However, do any differences exist between these tracks, and if they do, what are they? Do they offer different opportunities to utilize the resources of the campus, and will your career marketability be affected if you choose one track over another? For that matter, what does a person with a bachelor's degree in literature do after graduation?

Consider another example: Is the best route into medical school through traditional science? What nontraditional programs offer a route that is more attractive and offers better alternatives than the standard pre-med curricula? If such programs exist, how do you find out about them? You won't be able to answer these questions by consulting your college programs catalog. More important, you don't want to wait until your last year of college to begin to search out the answers.

So what do you do?

First, you need to understand the role of advising and advisors in your academic life. You are responsible for the academic choices that affect your education. Don't assume that the advice you receive represents the only, correct, or beneficial alternative for you. All that academic advisors can do, at their best, is advise from the perspective of their personal and professional experiences, but their professional experiences do not necessarily given them a comprehensive view of your institution. For example, departmental advisors know about their own department's requirements, but they aren't paid to know every detail of the campus. Still, many have underground networks of people who can give them information about nondepartment opportunities, and you can access this information, but only if you take the time to sit, talk, and ask. Remember that when you talk with an advisor you are receiving consultation. Advisors are not there to tell you what to do; they are to give you information to help you make a decision. The appropriate synonym for "advise" is "recommend" not "command."

Second, faculty and professional advisors are not the only advisors with valuable recommendations. Take advantage of parents' and friends' knowledge and pay attention to information you read, see, or hear. You cannot make a good decision until you learn how to determine what's going on around you.

Third, large universities can be big, impersonal places, and they will stay that way if you sit back and expect to maneuver through your degree like a customer moving through a buffet line. Smaller schools have their own problems: How do you maximize the relatively few resources available? Think about the difference between getting a degree and getting an education: The two are not necessarily the same, and how you pursue these options will determine whether you become a victim of the system.

If you receive inadequate services and support, you may not have made the effort to discover the offerings at your college. You need to find and create your own community, consisting of deans and faculty members, counselors, residence hall staff, and advisors with whom you can talk on a casual and personal basis and who can give you the inside road map to your campus. This will take time and effort, but the benefits will be worthwhile. With a good set of personal contacts, you will discover that most of your academic goals can be accomplished, and you can open up fields of study for yourself that are hidden beneath the surface of curricular requirements.

Finally, it's up to you to know the rules, requirements, and resources of your campus. If you don't understand the reason for a requirement or a rule, or if you have unanswered questions, you need to ask for assistance, and you need to keep on asking until you get answers that make sense! Each college differs in how it handles rules, exceptions to rules, the substitution of courses to meet requirements, and other such issues. Don't assume that you know everything about any rule, constraint, or restriction until you check the information, and then double-check it. Many times you will find the hidden loopholes that allow department heads and deans to make exceptions to rules, and often you will find someone who will help you accomplish your objective. However, you will never know about these possibilities if you sit passively and make assumptions about the information you think you know. If you are not active, the system, with absence of malice, is going to do a number on you.

From "Giving Advice to Students," National Academic Advising Association (NACADA) Monograph Series, No. 11, pp. 30–31, 2004.

 Discussion Questions

1. What do the authors consider good academic advising?
2. The authors use literature as an example of the wide range of course topics that could be taken within fields of study that are offered on a campus. Name some courses in other academic disciplines that would be interesting to take to broaden a business major. What courses would broaden a psychology major? An education major?
3. What do the authors say is the role of advising and advisors in students' academic life?
4. What are four steps that students can take to ensure they are getting the best possible academic advice?

 Suggestions for Your Journal

What are your expectations from academic advising? What happened the last time you visited your advisor? Did the exchange answer all your questions? Why or why not? What can you do to take better advantage of your advisor's knowledge of the curricula and campus and community resources?

Controlling Your Time

Walter Pauk and Ross J. Q. Owens

Walter Pauk was the director of the Reading Study Center at Cornell University and over the years has published more than 100 books, including eight editions of *How to Study in College,* considered by many to be the gold standard for sound study advice. Ross Owens works with *InfoWorld,* a computer trade newspaper, as executive managing editor. He has written numerous articles on Internet-related topics.

Time is a precious and irreplaceable *commodity.* As she lay on her deathbed, Queen Elizabeth of England (1533–1603) reportedly said, "All my possessions for a moment of time." How you use time can determine your success or failure in college. If you use time wisely, you'll prosper. If you use it poorly, you'll fail the job you came to do. That's why the management of time is the number-one skill to master in college.

Yet students frequently squander time. A survey conducted at Fordham University found that college freshmen spent roughly one-third of their waking hours engaged in social activities or idle leisure during a typical weekday. This "free time" amounted to nearly twice the time they spent studying. And on the weekend the ratio of social and idle leisure time to study time for the same group was almost six to one!

Although the students in the survey seemed to waste time routinely, you needn't put yourself in the same position. You can gain extra time in two ways: (1) by doing a job in less time than usual, and (2) by taking control of your time. The first way requires you to study more efficiently. The second way requires you to save time by reclaiming "hidden" time and improving your time habits and to better manage your time by sticking to a schedule.

All of us have claimed that we don't have enough time to accomplish what we need to do. But the fact is that everyone is allotted the same amount of time: twenty-four hours a day. Many of us allow a lot of this time to go to waste by failing to realize it is available in the first place. In addition, it's often our day-to-day habits and activities we no longer notice, that save time or waste it. You can put your time to better use by pinpointing areas of "hidden" time and cultivating time-saving habits.

Finding "Hidden" Time

There's a lot of valuable time in your day that is being overlooked, simply because you didn't realize it was time you could use. For those who flush tiny slivers of soap down the drain or toss small scraps of cloth into the wastebasket, there are others who combine these slippery bits and pieces into a whole new bar or stitch discarded shreds into a comfortable quilt. Think of all the time you spend standing in line or even waiting for a traffic light to change. If you could find ways to make use of this "hidden" time, you could almost certainly add hours to each week.

Carry Pocket Work

Many situations may leave you with a few moments of unexpected free time—a long line at the bank or supermarket, a delayed bus or train, a wait at the doctor's office, a lunch date who arrives late. If you make a point to bring along a book, a photocopied article, index cards on which you've written key concepts, vocabulary words or formulas, you'll be able to take advantage of otherwise frustrating experiences.

Use Your Mind When It's Free

Some activities may afford an overlooked opportunity for studying if you're prepared. For example, if you're shaving, combing your hair, or washing dishes, there's no reason you can't be studying at the same time. Since many of us tend to "zone out" in such situations, they are excellent opportunities to use time that might otherwise be squandered. Attach small metal or plastic clips near mirrors and on walls at eye level. Place a note card in each clip. Do a problem or two in math or master some new vocabulary words as you eat a sandwich at work.

Record Study Information

Another way of using hidden time is by listening to information you have recorded on audiocassettes or MP3 files or burned onto CDs. Recorded information enables you to keep studying in situations where you're moving about or your eyes are otherwise occupied, such as when you're getting dressed or driving. In addition, recorded information can provide a refreshing change from written material.

Employ Spare-Time Thinking

You can make the most of the moments immediately before or after class by recalling the main points from the last lecture as you are heading to class or by quickly recalling the points of a just-completed lecture as you're leaving class.

Use Your Subconscious

At one point or another, you have awakened during the night with a bright idea or a solution to a problem that you had been thinking about before bedtime. Your subconscious works while your conscious mind is resting. If you want to capture the ideas or solutions produced by your subconscious, write them down as soon as you wake up; otherwise, they'll be lost. Many creative people know this and keep a pad and pencil near their beds. For example, Nobel Prize winner Albert Szent-Gyorgyi said, "I go to sleep thinking about my problems all the time, and my brain must continue to think about them while I sleep because I wake up, sometimes in the middle of the night, with answers to questions that have been eluding me all day."

Changing Your Time Habits

Habits, by their very nature, are things we do routinely without even thinking. Most of us are unaware of our habits unless someone or something draws attention to them. A good way to take inventory of your time habits is by keeping a daily activities log. From the time you wake up to the time you go to sleep, note all your major activities, the time you started and finished each, and the time each activity consumed. With your day itemized on paper, you can gain a clearer picture of where your time is being spent and where it's being wasted. Once you have concrete evidence of a daily activities log before you, you can begin to eliminate your time-wasting habits and develop or reinforce the time-saving ones.

Defy Parkinson's Law

Parkinson's Law says that work expands to fit the time allotted. To avoid running out of time, work Parkinson's Law in reverse: For each task, set a deadline that will be difficult to meet, and strive to meet that deadline. Each time you achieve your goal, reward yourself with some small but pleasant activity. Take a break. Chat with a friend. Stroll around the room. Have a special snack, such as a bag of peanuts (keep it in your desk, to be opened only as a reward). If you fail to meet a deadline, don't punish yourself. Just hold back your reward and set another goal. Positive reinforcement is powerful in effecting a change in behavior.

Obey Your Alarm Clock

How many times do you hit the snooze button on your alarm clock before you finally get out of bed? Even one time is too many. Set your alarm for the time you want to get up, not for time you want to start getting up. If you can't obey your alarm, you'll have a hard time sticking to your time schedule. After all, it doesn't even buzz.

Limit Your E-mail and Internet Time

As marvelous as they both can be, e-mail in particular and the Internet in general can be tremendous "time sinks," swallowing up hours in a typical day. Rather than checking it constantly, designate specific times during the day when you read and send e-mail. It's true that e-mail has sped up communication, but it's a rare message that can't wait a few hours before being read or sent. The same applies to any Web surfing you may do, whether for schoolwork or pleasure. Time has a tendency to fly by as you click from one link to the next. You can help keep things under control by setting a timer when you surf and returning to your studies when the timer goes off.

Take "Time Out"

Reward yourself with regular short breaks as you work. Learning in several small sessions, rather than one continuous stretch, increases comprehension. In one study, students who practiced French vocabulary in three discrete sessions did 35 percent better on an exam than those who tried to learn the words in one sitting. So take a breather for ten minutes every hour, or rest for five minutes every half-hour. Whichever method you choose, keep your breaks consistent. This way, you will study with more energy and look forward to your regular rests. When you return to your desk, you'll find that you feel more refreshed.

Listen to Your Body

All of us are subject to *circadian rhythms.* That is, we have periods when we are most wide awake and alert and other periods when we're sluggish or drowsy. In general, we're sleepiest a few hours before dawn and twelve hours later, in mid-afternoon. In keeping with these natural cycles, we're widest awake about every twelve hours, usually at mid-morning and again in mid-evening. Knowing this can help you plan the day's activities more strategically.

1. *Schedule* cerebral *tasks for mornings and evenings.* Reading, writing, problem solving and other "thinking tasks" should be done when you're likely to be most alert.
2. *Save active behavior for mid-afternoon.* Fieldwork, lab work, exercise, and errand running are best done at this time of day when more sedentary activities may make you feel drowsy. If you're not a heavy coffee drinker, a cup of coffee might get you through the afternoon slump.
3. *Resist the temptation to sleep in on the weekends.* Changing your sleep schedule on the weekends can have a chain reaction effect on the following week. You may find yourself feeling jet-lagged on Monday or Tuesday if you sleep in on Saturday or Sunday.
4. *Read in the morning; review in the afternoon.* Scientists have discovered that short-term memory peaks at about nine o'clock in the morning and that long-term memory is strongest at about three o'clock in the afternoon.

Keep a Notepad Handy

Stray thoughts and worries can really cut into your ability to concentrate. They can also eat up valuable time. The best way to deal with these distractions is to get them out of your head and onto a piece of paper as quickly as possible, then return to your work. Writing these thoughts down can result in an additional time-saving bonus. Getting started is often the hardest part of shifting from one activity to another. Your jottings may provide a needed jump-start to overcome the *inertia* that seems to characterize the outset of a new activity. If so, they may save you some valuable time. Although spontaneous scribblings can sometimes provide guidance as you are moving from one task to the next, a far better strategy is to come up with a schedule and stick to it.

Sticking to a Schedule

A time schedule is a game plan, a written strategy that spells out exactly what you hope to accomplish—during a day, a week, or even the entire term—and how you plan to do it. Committing yourself to planning and keeping to a schedule can seem a bit frightening at first, but following a schedule soon becomes a source of strength and a boon to your life.

Most people understand the supreme importance of time and the value of sticking to a schedule, yet many of us continue to waste time needlessly. Why? Perhaps it is because we are human beings, not machines. Learning to use time wisely after years of wasting it doesn't happen by simply flipping a switch. Controlling your time is ultimately a matter of developing the right mindset. If the dying words of Queen Elizabeth and the compelling evidence in this essay haven't been enough to convince you to change your time-wasting ways, perhaps the following tidbits about time will finally make things click.

Ten Valuable Tidbits about Time

1. One of America's greatest composers, jazz giant Duke Ellington wasn't ashamed to admit that "Without a deadline, I can't finish nothin'."
2. If you've got a long list of things to do but you're spinning your wheels, start with the easier tasks. Getting one done makes the next one easier. Build momentum.
3. Be a *contrarian.* Go to the library when almost nobody is there. Get into the dining-hall line before the crowd. Get the reserved books before the line forms. The time you save will add up quickly.
4. Make decisions wisely by asking, "What are the alternatives?" Make a list of the alternatives and then put pluses and minuses alongside them. Learn this process. It will save lots of time.
5. Don't spread yourself thin by attempting to become an "information junkie." This scattershot approach takes up a great deal of time and can still leave you feeling stressed and dissatisfied. Just make sure that you gain a firm grip on your own field.
6. A lot of time is lost by looking for misplaced notes, books, journals, and reports. Make an unbreakable rule: a place for everything, and everything in its place.
7. "Most people," says motivational speaker Anthony Robbins, "would not see an awful movie a second time, yet they play the same bad memories over and over again in their heads."
8. When you're really through studying, spend an extra fifteen minutes studying just an extra bit more.
9. If the thought of saving time sounds sensible but uninspiring, ask yourself this simple question: What do I want to save time for? Suddenly the efficient use of time may take on a significance that it never had before.
10. A Sanskrit proverb puts everything in proper perspective:

   Today well lived
   Makes every yesterday a dream of happiness
   And every tomorrow a vision of hope.
   Look well therefore to this day.

From *How to Study in College,* 8th edition (Boston: Houghton Mifflin, 2005).

Vocabulary

As you think about this essay, these definitions may be helpful to you:
1. **commodity**   an economic good
2. **circadian rhythms**   rhythms occurring in approximately 24-hour periods or cycles
3. **cerebral**   relating to the brain or intellect
4. **inertia**   indisposition to motion
5. **contrarian**   a person who habitually takes a contrary position or attitude

 Discussion Questions

1. Pauk and Owens list several ways to find "hidden time" in your day or week. Which of these have you tried? How much time did it save? How did you use the time that was saved?
2. What specific suggestions do the authors give for changing your time habits? Which ones seem the easiest to implement? The most difficult?
3. How much time a day do you spend answering and sending e-mail and on the Internet in non-coursework? Which of the authors' suggestions for controlling time spent this way could you use? How?
4. Do you use positive reinforcement during your study time? If so, what kind of positive reinforcement works best for you? If you haven't used it, would you consider trying it? Why or why not?
5. Which of the "Ten Valuable Tidbits about Time" are you already using? Which ones are you interested in implementing? Why?
6. Some people may find that some of the suggestions in this essay are unrealistic. Do you? If so, how might you adapt or replace them for the same objective of making your time work for you?

 Suggestions for Your Journal

Write about your concept of time and how it affects your life as a student. What are your strengths in managing your time? In what areas do you need to improve your time management? Of the many tips in this essay, which ones do you already practice? Which ones, if any, could help you make better use of your time? Will your concept of time change after you graduate? In what way?

The Right Stuff: Research Strategies for the Internet Age

Nancy O'Hanlon

Nancy O'Hanlon is an associate professor of University Libraries at The Ohio State University, where she has taught library research skills and developed online courses in using the Internet and other technological tools for beginning and advanced researchers. In the following reading she explains why students need to develop good research strategies, especially given that information defines the age. Books, she reminds us, will also always be an important tool for any research undertaking.

Tom Wolfe describes the unique qualities that enabled the first U.S. astronauts to meet unknown challenges as "the right stuff." For these explorers, "the right stuff" was not simply courage, but a unique combination of daring, skill, experience and a persistent determination to succeed:

> ... the ability to go up in a hurtling piece of machinery and put his hide on the line and then have the moxie, the reflexes, the experience, the coolness, to pull it back in the last yawning moment—and then to go up again the next day, and the next day, and every next day. ... A career in flying was like climbing one of those ancient Babylonian pyramids made up of a dizzy progression of steps and ledges, a *ziggurat*, a pyramid extraordinarily high and steep; and the idea was to prove at every foot of the way up that pyramid that you were one of the elected and anointed ones who had the right stuff and could move higher and higher. ... (Wolfe 24)

Research today challenges us to navigate effectively through Internet space. At one time, knowledge of the library and skill at using printed resources were sufficient preparation for finding useful information. Today, the Internet, particularly the World Wide Web, is the vehicle for most research. The sheer volume of information available through this medium is staggering, like the Babylonian pyramid in Wolfe's vision. To be a successful researcher also requires "the right stuff"—imagination and flexibility, well-developed searching skills, persistence and the ability to evaluate information coming from diverse sources.

Why is it important to learn research skills? During college, students are expected to find information in order to answer academic research questions, understand important societal issues and analyze complex problems. Information supplied by teachers and textbooks is no longer the sole basis for learning. College students are exposed to a wider range of information and must make judgments about the relevance and credibility of sources. In *The Craft of Research*, Booth, Colomb and Williams state that "Those who can neither do reliable research nor reliably report the research of others will find themselves on the sidelines of a world that increasingly lives on information" (Booth 6). They also contend that "We are *inundated* with information, most of it packaged to suit someone else's commercial or political self-interest. More than ever, society needs people with critical minds, people who can look at research, ask their own questions, and find their own answers" (Booth 3).

Too Much Information?

How much information is available to researchers in the Internet age? Consider the following estimates provided by a study published online by the University of California, Berkeley:

- The world produces between 1 and 2 exabytes of unique information in all formats (print, digital, broadcast) each year. An exabyte is a billion *gigabytes*. If stored on floppy disks, the stack would be 2 million miles high.
- Digital information comprises the largest amount of this total. The Internet is the youngest and fastest growing medium today. In 2000, the World Wide Web consisted of roughly 2.5 billion static, publicly available Web pages and is growing at a rate of 100 percent per year.
- Another group of Web pages is dynamically generated and stored in Web-accessible databases. This "deep Web" is estimated to be 400 to 550 times larger than the static "surface" Web.
- Taking all kinds of Web information into account, there are 550 billion Web-connected documents, and 95 percent of this information is publicly accessible. 7.3 million new pages are added to the Web per day. (Lyman, Executive Summary)

Much of this Web-accessible information is not available in any other format. For example, *NameBase: A Cumulative Index of Books and Clippings*, http://www.namebase.org. is a database containing information about people, groups and corporations who have been influential in politics, the military, intelligence, crime and the media since World War II. These names have been drawn from various books, articles, and government documents recovered using the Freedom of Information Act. Because of the way it is constructed, this database allows users to find other names that appear on the same pages and thus uncover potential relationships or connections between individuals and groups. *NameBase* is a unique part of the "deep Web" that could be useful both to investigative journalists and to students.

How can you locate useful research tools like *NameBase* among billions of Web sites? Some rules of the road for effective searching of the Web information space are described in the next section of this essay.

Smart Search Techniques

In the years since 1994, when the World Wide Web was invented, a number of powerful search tools have become available to help Web users locate information hiding within this mass of billions of documents. These tools fall into two basic categories: Web directories and Web indexes (or search engines). Success hinges on choosing the right tool as well as using it effectively.

Web directories are lists of sites, along with brief descriptions of their content, selected and compiled by knowledgeable editors. Directories can be browsed by topic and are good starting points for most Internet research because they offer quick access to the best known and most useful sites.

For example, the *Internet Movie Database*, http://www.imdb.com. is widely recognized as an excellent site for finding information on film casts, credits, plots, and characters. It is relatively easy to identify using a Web directory like the *Britannica.com Internet Guide*, http://www.britannica.com., which assigns one-to-five-star ratings to sites in each of its topical categories.

If your information need is not met by sources listed in Web directories, you can search one of several large Web indexes to locate relevant documents. Web indexes are created by software programs called "spiders" or "robots" because they work automatically, crawling from one Web page to any others that are linked to it, harvesting information. The spiders collect every word on each Web page and store them in a huge index or list. When you enter a search, this index is what your search words are matched against.

The companies that own these search engines report that most people enter only one or two search words. When you consider the size of these Web indexes (millions of documents, with thousands of words in each document), this search strategy (or lack thereof) seems doomed to failure. You must use more than one or two search terms in Web indexes in order to narrow down search results and make them more relevant to your specific research question.

Search engines are quite literal and don't deal well with words that have multiple meanings. Using a variety of relevant search words can help with this problem as well. For example, a search for the word "spider" might retrieve this essay, since that word is used several times. [But] if you were looking for information about the insect, rather than the Web software program called a spider, you could get better results by including other search words that also describe what you want (such as "insect" or "arachnid").

Three other techniques will help to improve your chance of success when searching in large Web indexes. First, learn to use search qualifiers in order to specify the importance of your search terms and indicate any relationship between them. For example:

- To require that all of your search terms are included in each document found, you may put the plus sign (+) before each term.
  Example: +spider +arachnid +tarantula
- Use the minus sign (–) before each word that should be eliminated from your results.
  Example: +spider – Web – robot
- Use quotation marks to indicate when search words should be treated as a phrase.
  Example: "brown recluse spider"

It is also important to develop intelligent limiting strategies. In many search engines, it is possible to limit or screen search results by different variables, such as type of site (for example, government, military, educational, or commercial). This technique can be especially fruitful when you want to find varying perspectives. For example, you could limit a search for information on campaign finance reform to government Web sites, in order to learn the viewpoints of elected officials on this topic.

Finally, use specialized search tools, ones that focus on a particular topical area, whenever possible. By using specialized resources, like *FindLaw*, http://www.findlaw.com for legal topics or *Achoo*, http://www.achoo.com for health-related research, you are searching only the portion of Web space that is relevant for your research topic and are thus more likely to find good results.

Evaluating Information Quality

When we use the phrase "good results" in this context, we really mean search results that appear to be useful based on a quick look at the Web page. Determining the quality of information found on the Web actually takes more effort and some special techniques.

It is relatively easy and inexpensive to "publish" information on the Internet. On one hand, this open environment often permits you to see more sides of a topic than you might when relying only on printed sources. For example, when doing research on sweatshop labor in developing countries, you may be able to locate first person accounts and discussions of working conditions in overseas factories, reports of watchdog groups and other kinds of information sources that are difficult or impossible to find in print.

At the same time, because there is no real filtering mechanism to check accuracy, one cannot accept at face value the information found on the Web. In *Evaluating Internet Research Sources,* Robert Harris notes that on the Internet, information exists on a continuum of reliability and quality:

> Information is everywhere on the Internet, existing in large quantities and continuously being created and revised. This information exists in a large variety of kinds (facts, opinions, stories, interpretations, statistics) and is created for many purposes (to inform, to persuade, to sell, to present a viewpoint, and to create or change an attitude or belief). For each of these various kinds of purposes, information exists on many levels of quality or reliability. It ranges from very good to very bad and includes every shade in between. (Harris, Introduction)

Harris further notes that when evaluating information sources, there is no single perfect indicator of quality. You must make inferences from a collection of clues. Here are three important variables to consider as you review and evaluate sources:

Purpose: Consider both the purpose of the source as well as the purpose of your research when determining which Web sources to use. Sites published by advocacy groups (such as the Sierra Club or the American Civil Liberties Union) may include fact sheets, position papers and findings from scientific research studies. These groups may present evidence to support their cause but ignore contrary findings. If you are attempting to understand an organization's mission or find evidence that is representative of a particular viewpoint, advocacy organization Web sites can be quite useful. Look elsewhere for a balanced treatment of controversial issues.

Authority: The most credible information is provided by writers who have education, training or life experience in a field relevant to the information. You can read the jacket blurb to find out more about the author and the scope of a printed book. On the Web, look for an "About Us" link to find brief information about site authors and their credentials.

But inquiring minds may want to check credentials or learn more than Web site authors tell us about themselves. If the author is an organization rather than an individual, what is their reputation? You have access to the tools that will help you to locate this kind of information. Search in a Web index to find other documents that the site authors may have published. Use your college library's catalog and online reference databases (of newspaper, magazine and journal articles) to locate works in print written by or about individuals and organizations.

Content: When evaluating the content provided by a Web site, there are a number of questions to consider. These are the same questions that one would ask when evaluating the content of any information source.

- First, does the information appear to be accurate? Factual information may be checked in other sources.
- Is there an attempt by the author to be objective? Opposing viewpoints should be presented in an accurate manner. Harris notes that "there is no such thing as pure objectivity, but a good writer should be able to control his or her biases." Does the author use a calm, reasoned tone or resort to inflammatory language? Does the site author have a vested interest in the topic, one where "the messenger will gain financially if you believe the message . . ."?
- Finally, does the author cite evidence to support claims and then document (provide references to) these sources, so that they are easily available for further research? Harris recommends that you "triangulate" an important information source, finding at least two other sources that support it. References supplied by an author can help in this process, but you should look for other sources as well.

A World Beyond the Web

Does all important information live on the World Wide Web, somewhere among the exabytes? In a word, no. Despite its size and scope, not everything useful for research is on the Web. There are numerous holes in this fabric—many important printed books and articles will never be available online, because their conversion to digital format is not cost-effective.

For example, when studying about focus group interviews for a marketing or sociology class, you should read *The Focused Interview*, the seminal work on this subject written by Robert K. Merton, an eminent sociologist who invented the technique. This book was first published in 1956 and a second edition appeared in 1990. Neither work is Web-accessible.

Although it is important to learn how to search effectively on the Web and to evaluate the information found there, it is equally important to understand that there are projects for which Web research will not be sufficient. The college library will continue to be important to successful research, despite the phenomenal growth of online information. It is the place where students can expect to find the most important or influential works on many subjects as well as personal assistance and advice about research problems from librarians. Having "the right stuff" for research in the Internet age involves the willingness to explore all spaces where information and knowledge abide, not just the most obvious ones. Booth states that by learning and practicing the craft of research, you

> . . . join the oldest and most esteemed of human conversations—the conversation conducted by Aristotle, Marie Curie, Booker T. Washington, Albert Einstein . . . all those who by contributing to human knowledge have freed us from ignorance and misunderstanding. They and countless others once stood where you now stand. Our world today is different because of their research. It is no exaggeration to say that, done well, yours will change the world tomorrow. (Booth 7)

Works Cited

Booth, Wayne C., Gregory C. Colomb and Joseph M. Williams. *The Craft of Research*. Chicago: University of Chicago Press, 1995.

Lyman, Peter and Hal R. Varian. *How Much Information?* University of California, Berkeley: School of Information Management and Systems. 30 October 2000, http://www.sims.berkeley.edu/how-much-info/

Wolfe, Tom. *The Right Stuff*. New York: Farrar, Straus, Giroux, 1979.

Vocabulary

As you think about this essay, these definitions may be helpful to you:
1. **ziggurat** a form of early temple with the general shape of a pyramid but with recessed tiers that appear as huge stairs or ledges around the structure
2. **gigabyte** a unit of computer information. The basic unit is a binomial bit (that is, its value must be either 0 or 1). Eight bits make a byte; 1,048,576 bytes make a megabyte; and 1,024 megabytes make a gigabyte.
3. **inundated** flooded; overwhelmed

 Discussion Questions

1. What is the difference between a Web index and a Web directory?
2. What does O'Hanlon mean when she talks about a "search strategy"?
3. Explain the use of these signs in searching for information on the Web: -, +, and "   ".
4. What kind of questions should you ask when evaluating a Web site? Give some examples that O'Hanlon does *not* provide for evaluating a Web site with respect to its purpose, authority, and content.
5. O'Hanlon says that we still need to consult books for much of our information. Is she right? Explain your answer.

 Suggestions for Your Journal

Sometimes a student's first experience in a college library can be overwhelming. What were your impressions the first time you walked into the main library at your college? Do you feel more comfortable doing research on the Web or with traditional book searches? Why? What library or computer skills are you lacking? Where can you get help to improve these skills?

Fourteen Ways of Looking at Electives[1]

Thomas L. Minnick

Thomas L. Minnick is Special Assistant to the Vice Provost of Minority Affairs and former associate dean of University College at The Ohio State University, where he completed his bachelor's, master's, and doctoral degrees in English. He is a specialist in the
English Bible and the writings of William Blake. In this essay, he encourages you to
think before you schedule your electives so that they can complement your required
course work by helping you to achieve some of your goals for college study.

Electives are what is left over for you to take once you deduct all your
required courses.

Typically, a college degree is made up primarily of several kinds of requirements. These may include courses required of all students, no matter what degree
they may have decided to seek; such university-wide requirements are often called
"core" or "general education" requirements. They are likely to include some basic
mathematics, one or more courses in college-level English composition, and several courses distributed among the social sciences, sciences, and humanities. Does
everyone at your institution need to take some history? Then history is probably a
general education or "core" requirement for your institution, whether you are
working toward a bachelor's degree at a university with an extensive graduate program or toward an associate's degree at a community college.

Additionally, you are likely to have to complete some courses that everyone in
your degree program needs to take. For example, students working toward a
degree in engineering, no matter what area of specialization, all typically need to
have at least a year of college physics, mathematics through differential equa-
tions, some basic course work in engineering graphics, mechanics, and chemistry. Similarly, business students are all required to study economics (both
"micro" and "macro"), accounting, statistics, marketing, finance, and the like.
Requirements shared by everyone aiming toward a specific degree are usually
called "program requirements" or "degree requirements."

A third kind of required course work is that which you complete for your
major. Major requirements might include an introductory survey course (or a
series of them), usually taken by first- or second-year students while they learn
the dimensions and variety of the major field. English majors are likely to be
required to take a survey of American literature and another of British literature, for example. In some colleges they may be required to have a course in
research methods for English majors. And some majors require that everyone in
the program complete a senior year "capstone" course that puts—or attempts to
put—all their previous major work into a *coherent* perspective.

---

[1]With apologies to Wallace Stevens. (Gentle reader, Wallace Stevens wrote a thoughtful poem entitled "Sixteen Ways of Looking at a Blackbird." You might enjoy it.)

Once you add up all these kinds of requirements (general education, college, and major), you are likely to find that there are still some classes you need to take to complete your degree. At the university where I work, which follows the quarter system and sets 196 quarter credit hours as the minimum for an undergraduate degree, the university-wide general education core and the college/program requirements usually total about 100 credits. Major programs vary dramatically but average about 45 credit hours. Deduct 145 from 196 and you get 41 credit hours (or eight to ten classes) that are not specified. For these, which are "electives," our students can take just about anything they like. This essay is about some ways you can use these extra classes to your advantage.

1. To explore possible majors. Many students enter college without knowing what they want to study for a major. An undecided student can use elective hours to explore several possible major programs, usually by taking the appropriate introductory survey classes. Do you think you might like Forestry? Sign up for a basic introduction to the field and find out through that class whether you really have an interest and/or an aptitude for it.

2. To serve as a cushion. This use of electives is closely related to (1) above. Suppose you started college as an engineering major and then discovered that you lack the commitment or the focus to be an engineer, so you change programs to business. You will probably have taken some classes in your first term (engineering graphics, for example) that are not required in your new major. Electives allow you to move from one major to another without losing useful credits: in this example, the engineering graphics class will still count toward graduation, and it served the purpose of helping you make a sound decision on a new major. Electives give you flexibility—within reasoned limits—to change from one program to another without losing credits or unduly prolonging your degree work.

3. To develop a focus or cluster outside your major. Perhaps you don't really want to be limited to a single concentration. If your college does not provide for dual majors or minors, or if you don't want to complete *all* the work for a second major but would like an additional focus to your degree, electives can provide the way. Imagine that you have decided to major in Elementary Education but you also have an interest in the History of Art. Using your electives, you can build your own concentration in art history by taking the courses in that area that attract you. In this way you may be able to select your art history classes more freely than a formal major might allow—limiting yourself to national schools (American painting) or individual styles (contemporary art) that you really like, while official majors may need to follow a strictly prescribed *regimen* of courses.

4. To explore your career options. Nationally, one of the most frequently selected electives is the career exploration course. Such courses usually fall into one of two categories—fairly general in approach and scope, or quite specific. A general approach can help you assess your personal characteristics, such as your interests, abilities, values, and goals. It can also help you explore educational and occupational fields that might match your personal interests and strengths.

Some courses include information about techniques for writing your résumé and for presenting yourself effectively in job interviews. These general career courses can teach you career decision-making strategies that will be useful throughout your life. The other, more specific type of career course is often limited to specific career opportunities in the area (or areas) related to the department teaching the class: "Careers in Agriculture" would be such a course that focuses on, and discusses in very specific detail, the career options available to people with a specific kind of education. Such a course typically provides very helpful information about specific employers who look for and hire graduates with a particular educational and career background. Career information courses—whether general or specific—can help you enhance your understanding of who you are in relation to your academic major and related career opportunities and, in so doing, prepare you for the work world.

5. To enhance your marketability. A popular use many students make of their electives is to build a business focus—even if they are not pursuing a business degree. Suppose you are an English major who likes and knows something about computers. By adding several advanced computer science courses to your English major, you become more competitive for job offers that want a liberally educated student with added skills. Your focus might take the form of several courses from a single department (a number of marketing classes, for example), or several related classes from a variety of departments (a marketing class, a course in beginning accounting, a class in business management, a course in personnel issues). A business major might like to take classes in the language and culture of a specific part of the world in order to be better prepared to do business with that part of the globe.

6. To develop a talent you have neglected. Are you good at singing or playing a musical instrument? Perhaps you don't want to major in that area, but it would be a shame to give up that *expertise* or let it *languish* while you complete your undergraduate studies. Take a class in singing, or join one of your college's choral or instrumental groups. Register for drawing or painting, or making pottery, or creating art on the computer. Sign up for a basic photography class. Electives can allow you to pursue and develop interests and talents that you do not plan to turn into a major, but that you should not neglect. Because the credit you earn with electives counts toward your graduation, you do not need to feel that courses you take just because you want to are wasted.

7. To get, or stay, fit. I am often surprised by the number of college students I talk with who participated strenuously in high school sports. Both men and women find physical exercise and competition to be challenging and exciting. Yet often, when such students get to college, they neglect their interests in being fit, largely, I think, because they equate college courses with "serious" work and sports with play. However, getting fit and staying fit are lifelong activities that help you to work and think better. They also promote a healthful lifestyle because people who have worked to keep fit as a rule avoid destructive activities like drinking alcohol to excess and smoking. If your college has a good physical education facility and offers you courses in activities you have never tried, take a

few elective credits to learn and practice some of these activities—oriental martial arts, for example, or caving, or whitewater rafting, or working out on the
high ropes. And all these physical activities can be great for helping to cope with
the stress of college work.

8. To develop skills in leisure time activities. Once you begin your career,
your work will take up much of your life, but it will always be important for you
to make time for enriching activities—especially when you are away from the
stimulus of a learning environment. Develop the habit of reserving time for
thoughtful entertainment. Electives may provide just the opportunity you need
to learn more about theater, fine art, music, and similar interests. Do you like
jazz? Check your school's course catalogue to see if there are classes in American
music, or nonwestern music, that might help you to better understand the origins and history of jazz. Do you like attending plays? Take an introductory theater course, or take an acting class and try out your talents in a learning setting,
or sign up to help build scenery and earn college credit while learning more
about the technical details of putting on a performance.

9. To learn to help others. Most universities provide courses, often for modest amounts of credit, in such helpful skills as first aid and cardiopulmonary
resuscitation (commonly abbreviated to "CPR").These skills can help you in getting summer work. More important, knowing how to help others in an emergency can actually save a life—maybe even your own. Less dramatic but also very
helpful are opportunities to provide tutoring and similar assistance to others at
your university or in your neighborhood. Interested? Ask your adviser if there is
a program where you can tutor underprivileged kids or read a textbook for a
blind student or help in adaptive physical education for handicapped students.
These experiences can teach you a great deal about yourself and may provide
some of the greatest personal rewards of your college experience.

10. To learn life skills that will be useful later. For example, many business
schools provide a "service course" (so named because they teach it as a service to
students from outside their own college) about basic financial matters, like
establishing credit, managing your income, buying a home, planning for financial independence, selecting basic insurance, and the like. Courses in family
financial planning for nonbusiness majors are likely to accentuate the practical
and introduce theory only when absolutely necessary. Many other departments
offer the chance to learn material that will have lifelong practical value. Basic
courses in public speaking and communicating effectively in small groups apply
to almost every later career; go to the Communications Department to find
them. Most sociology departments offer a class in the varieties of modern marriage, or the sociology of the family—with obvious utility for later experience.

11. To learn to understand and appreciate different cultures. Studying
other cultures can help you prepare for working with people from those cultures
in your life after college. Most of your life will be spent in the 21st century, and
experts predict that there will be *no* majority culture in America in your life.
Many American cities in the south and west—Dallas, Los Angeles, Miami—
already have no dominant majority group, only larger or smaller minorities.

Even if you plan to live in a largely *homogeneous* small town, chances are you will be doing business with, or your children will need to do business with, the larger multicultural world. If you find that a little frightening, take a class in dealing with other cultures and you may find it exciting instead. Check with the appropriate language departments, and you are likely to find some classes taught in English that will help you understand the patterns and values of cultures different from your own.

12. To learn study and time-management skills. Most two- and four-year colleges now provide organized help for students who need better study habits. This need is not restricted to students who did less than well in high school. Often, good students could earn better than average grades in high school with only modest investments of study time—and have consequently developed weak study habits that need to improve in the face of more difficult, more rapid college instruction. Would you like to read with greater comprehension? Could you manage your time better than you do? Check with your advisor for information about classes that teach effective study skills, time management, and related learning skills. Even if these are offered *without* credit, and so are not technically "elective hours," consider them carefully, because they can greatly improve the quality of your work as a student.

13. To develop leadership skills. Usually students turn to their extracurricular experiences (student government, interest clubs, other campus associations) for training in leadership. But there is a significant body of writings about various leadership qualities and styles, and your institution is likely to offer at least one credit-bearing class in leadership. Such courses are often taught as "laboratory courses"—that is, you get practical training in a hands-on way. If you are aiming toward a professional career in a management position, you ought to get some experience in leadership, and such a course may be your best route toward it.

14. To take some courses just because you will enjoy them. In the best of all possible worlds, every class you take would be one that you love to attend, and I hope that many of your required courses—in general education, in classes that relate to your degree program, and certainly in your major—fit this description. But in the real world we are bound to spend our time in, you may find yourself required to take some classes you enroll in only because they are required. If you anticipate that such a course is coming up next term, you may successfully balance it with an elective class that you take just because you want to take it: perhaps you've already had the instructor, and you really enjoyed his or her previous course, or perhaps you've always had a hobby of reading about a specific area, so taking a course in it as an elective would help round out your knowledge of that field.

How can you select classes for Use Number 14? I encourage my advisees to imagine that they have just won the lottery (tonight at $35 million!) and have spent a chunk of it having fun—traveling the world, buying your parents a mansion and each of your friends an expensive car. Eventually, you tire of doing nothing, however nicely you can now afford to do it, and you realize the permanent attraction of learning. In such a case, what courses would you take? Assuming you do not financially *need* a degree, you could just take the classes you want. If you were free in this way, what classes would you sign up for? Make a list of them, then sign up for them as electives!

Reprinted by permission of the author.

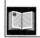 **Vocabulary**

As you think about this essay, these definitions may be helpful to you:
1. **coherent**   consistent
2. **regimen**   a systematic plan
3. **expertise**   the skill of an expert
4. **languish**   to be or become weak or enervated
5. **homogeneous**   of the same or similar kind or nature

 Discussion Questions

1. How are electives defined in this reading? How do they fit into the general structure of degree requirements?
2. What kind of electives can enhance your chances of finding a satisfying career?
3. Through what kind of electives can you acquire skills and knowledge that may be useful for your future leisure-time activities?
4. Although taking extra courses in your major is not listed as a way to use elective hours, would this be a good way to increase your mastery of the subject? Why or why not?
5. How can you expand your understanding and appreciation of other cultures through electives? Why is this a particularly good use of electives today?

 Suggestions for Your Journal

What has been your impression of the function of electives in the curriculum? Which of the 14 reasons for selecting electives appeal to you the most? Why? Look at the list of courses in your college's catalogue. If you could select any courses to take just for fun (and not worry about a grade), which would you choose? Why? What does this tell you about your choice of major?

Please! It's Only Seven Minutes Late, Professor

Joel J. Gold

This essay describes Professor Joel J. Gold's "solution" to overdue student papers. However, after recounting a student's experience with a late paper to his classes, he was the recipient of one class's payback.

Toward the bottom of the large *pseudo*-wooden door of my faculty office is a small hand-lettered sign that reads: PAPER SHREDDER. An arrow points to the space under the door where students are always sliding things, such as late papers and requests for letters of reference. My colleagues see the sign and make little jokes, but most of them don't really know the story behind it.

It began simply enough a few years back, when I was telling a class about the next essay. Allowing myself to be jollied away from the usual deadline of class time on Thursday, I told them the papers could be submitted by 5 P.M. Friday, but no later. At 5 o'clock, I would leave and turn on the paper shredder, so that anything slipped under the door later would be automatically shredded.

Now it should be obvious that in these *straitened* times no garden-variety English professor is going to have a paper shredder at his disposal. They all grinned back at me, and I figured we understood each other.

By 4:50 on Friday, all but three papers had been turned in. In a few minutes I heard someone running down the hall, and a young man thrust his paper at me. "Plenty of time," I said. He looked almost disappointed that he was not the last. At 4:57 the next-to-last paper arrived. "Am I the last one?" the young woman wanted to know. Again disappointment.

Well, now it was 5 o'clock, and one paper was still out. It was possible that it would not arrive, but the student was one of my conscientious overachievers. She was probably triple-checking her footnotes. I decided to wait.

I shut my door. I turned out my light. Then I pulled a chair up behind the closed door, gathered a couple of sheets of old copier paper in my hand, and sat down to wait. At seven minutes past, I heard footsteps hurrying toward my office. Whoever it was stopped right outside. And panted for a few seconds. Then the paper began to come in under the door. There in the dark, I was ready.

With exactly the degree of pull you get when you try to make change for a dollar in one of those airport change machines, I tugged slightly and evenly at the proffered paper. For a moment, the person on the other side gripped the paper more tightly. Then, probably surprised at herself, she let go. Her paper was mine.

I took the copier paper I had been holding all this time and began as noisily as I could to tear it into bits and pieces. There was dead silence on the other side of the door. Then I said aloud. "Chomp, chomp, CHOMP." Audible gasp outside.

"Please!" she said. "It's only seven minutes late." The thought of what it might look like outside that door to a passerby got me giggling. (I know, I know. It was unworthy of me. But I pictured a stricken young woman, talking to the door: "Please, door, it's only seven minutes late.") Perhaps the muffled giggling or the implication of the "Chomp, chomp, CHOMP" had just registered, but I heard the closest thing to a "Humph!" I have heard in real life before she stalked off down the hall. I suppressed my giggling, collected my papers and my *composure,* and went home.

She wasn't in class the next time it met, and I told the story—without names, of course. The class loved it. "Chomp, chomp, CHOMP!" they kept repeating throughout the hour.

I told the story again the following semester and the one after that—you can get a lot of mileage out of a good story. Students began to ask me about the paper shredder, and that's when I decided on the sign for the bottom of the door.

For a couple of semesters it was Our Joke. But you know how it is—sooner or later the old retired gunslinger is going to have to draw one more time. One of my students actually had the nerve to say, "You're always telling us about what you did to other classes, but you don't ever *do* anything about it." Now it was my turn for a "Humph!"

So amid the groaning about the deadlines for papers in my course, "The Comic Spirit," was born the idea for One More Twist. Essays were due Friday by 5 P.M. "And then the paper shredder," they chortled. "And then the paper shredder," I said.

When 5 P.M. came, and six papers were still missing, I gathered up what I had, turned out the lights, and went home. That weekend I spent much of my spare time tearing paper—all kinds of paper—into tiny bits and dropping them into a brown paper sack.

On class day, I secreted my nearly full shopping sack inside a large book bag and went upstairs. I *surreptitiously* pulled it out and hid it in my reading stand, planning to *discourse* on the papers at the end of the period.

It worked out even better. Halfway through the period, as I was shifting from *Northanger Abbey* to *Alice in Wonderland,* one of my anxious worrywarts raised his hand. "When," he wanted to know, "will you be giving back the papers?"

"I'm glad you asked me that," I said, quite sincerely. The students were now all waiting for the answer, not paying much attention to my hands, which were reaching in behind the reading stand to move the sack into position.

"Those of you who turned your essays in by 5 o'clock last Friday will get them back at the end of next week." A slight groan: They had hoped it would be sooner. They always do. For the rest, those who slid them under the door some time after 5 P.M.—and I'm afraid I don't know how many of you there actually were. . . ." By now, they were hanging on every word. The sack was in ready position. "But those of you who turned your paper in late (I had lifted the sack high above the desk) should come up after class (I turned the sack upside-down and thousands—thousands—of little shreds of paper were fluttering down over the reading stand, the desk, the floor) and identify your papers. If you can."

There was an explosion of laughter, stamping feet, pandemonium, as the shower of confetti continued for several seconds. They could not believe that a university professor would do anything so idiotic.

"Now," I said, in my best professional rhythms, "let us consider the scene in which Alice finds the caterpillar sitting on a mushroom."

At the end of the period, while I tried to get as many of the tiny bits of paper into the wastebasket as I could, I saw a few of my students in the doorway, pointing at the debris. They were apparently explaining to friends and passersby what had just happened in the classroom. And I don't think they were discussing the Mad Hatter or the March Hare. At least not directly.

I knew that somewhere down the road the old gunslinger would probably have to draw one last time, but I reckoned I was safe for a couple more semesters.

I didn't have quite that much time.

Given everything else that had gone on in my honors satire class, I might have known they would be the ones. I had, of course, recounted to them the story of the paper shredder.

The day I realized just how closely they had been listening was the day their papers were due. As I unlocked my office door, I saw on the floor a few hundred strips of shredded paper. Without quite understanding what had happened, I gathered up the scraps and carried them to my desk. There, I found that the segments could be fitted together and deciphered. I appeared to be in possession of 10 or 11 (it was a little hard to tell) essays on ". . . andide and Saint Joan," "The Innocents in *Volpone* and *Can . . .* ," and "Satiri . . . *Travels*." Page numbers helped me piece parts of essays together. Then I realized that the scraps were all on copier paper. On a hunch, I went to see the departmental secretaries. Grinning widely, they handed me a large envelope filled with the originals.

Those wags in the honors class had copied their essays, shredded the copies, slid them under my door, and given the originals to the secretaries to whom, obviously, they had explained the whole scam.

And up on Boot Hill, the old gunslinger's tombstone reads: Those Who Live by the Shredder, Die by the Shredder.

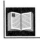 ## Vocabulary

As you think about this essay, these definitions may be helpful to you:
1. **pseudo**   false
2. **straitened**   hard up, short of money
3. **composure**   calmness of mind, bearing, or appearance
4. **surreptitiously**   secretively, as if afraid of being caught
5. **discourse**   verbal exchange of ideas

Discussion Questions

1. What happened to the student who turned in her paper seven minutes late?
2. How did Gold get even with the class that began to doubt his story about the paper shredder? What was their reaction?
3. How did one class "get even" with the author? How did Gold react to their prank?
4. What policies do your professors have about late work? Should there be a campus-wide policy on this issue? Why or why not?

 Suggestions for Your Journal

Have you ever turned in a late assignment? What was the result? What do you think is a fair reaction to students who turn in papers late? How would you react to Gold's policy if you were in his class?

Under what circumstances do you think it is acceptable for you to turn in a paper late? If you turn your assignments in on time and others turn in theirs late without penalty, have you been treated fairly? Why?

Why I Don't Let Students Cut My Classes

William R. Brown

William R. Brown is professor of English at the Philadelphia College of Textiles and Science. In this essay, he presents his opinions on why students cut classes and describes how he arrived at his no-cut policy in his course. The positive results from enforcing his policy are also described.

Last year I announced to my classes my new policy on absences: None would be allowed, except for illness or personal emergency. Even though this violated the statement on cuts in the student handbook, which allows freshmen cuts each term up to twice the number of class meetings per week and imposes no limit for upperclassmen, my students didn't fuss. They didn't fuss even after they discovered, when I telephoned or sent warning notices through the mail to students who had missed classes, that I meant business.

Part of their acceptance of the policy may have resulted from the career orientation of our college, but I don't think that was the main reason. After I explained the policy, most seemed to recognize that it promoted their own academic interests. It was also a requirement that virtually all of them would be obliged to observe—and would expect others to observe—throughout their working lives. It had to be Woody Allen who said that a major part of making it in life is simply showing up.

I told my classes about recent research, by Howard Schuman and others, indicating that academic success is more closely tied to class attendance than to the amount of time spent studying. I shared my sense of disappointment and personal *affront* when I carefully prepare for a class and a substantial number of students do not attend. I think they got the message that the policy is not arbitrary—that I care about their learning and expect them to care about my professional effort.

I don't claim to have controlled all the variables, but after I instituted the no-cut rule, student performance in my classes improved markedly, not so much in the top rank as at the bottom. In fact, the bottom rank almost disappeared, moving up and swelling the middle range to such an extent that I have reassessed my evaluation methods to differentiate among levels of performance in that range. The implications of so dramatic an improvement are surely worth pondering.

Additional benefits of the policy have been those one would expect to result from a full classroom. Student morale is noticeably higher, as is mine. Discussions are livelier, assignments are generally turned in on time, and very few students miss quizzes.

The mechanics of maintaining the policy kept me a little busier than usual, especially at first, but the results would have justified a lot more effort. I called or mailed notes to several students about their cuts, some more than once. I eventually advised a few with *invincibly* poor attendance to drop my course when it seemed that an unhappy outcome was likely. They did.

No doubt this kind of shepherding is easier in a small college. But it can work almost anyplace where a teacher cares enough about the educational stakes to make it work. The crucial element is caring.

At the first faculty meeting of the year, I confessed what I was doing. After all, I was defying college policy. I told my colleagues—at least those not cutting the meeting—that it rankled me when I had carefully prepared a class and a fifth, a quarter, or a third of the students didn't show. I thought my classes were good, and I *knew* Faulkner, Austen, and Tolstoy were good. What had been lacking in my classes, I said, was a significant proportion of the students. I told my colleagues that I believed my problem was not unique but was true of college classes everywhere, and that I was doing something about it.

Although no one seemed to attach much importance to my ignoring college policy, few of my colleagues gave me active support. Some were agreed that a 25 percent absence rate in a college class was not alarming. Others felt that college students must take responsibility for their studies, and that we should not feel liable for their losses from cut classes. One implied that if students could bag a lot of classes and still pass the course, it reflected badly on the teacher.

If professors have enough drawing power, another said, students will attend their classes. (How do you *parry* that?) Still another pointed out that if the professor covers enough material, there will be no time to waste taking the roll. In a large lecture, someone said, who knows who is there and who isn't? After the meeting, one *wag* told me I should consider using the acronym PAP for my "professional attendance policy," but congratulated me on at least evoking an interesting discussion in a faculty meeting, something rare indeed. It was easy to conclude that most of them preferred not to see a problem—at least their problem—in spotty class attendance.

Why do students cut so frequently? I can cite the immediate causes, but I first want to note the enabling circumstance: They cut because they are allowed to. They cut because of the climate of acceptance that comes from our belief that responsibility can be developed only when one is free, free even to act against personal best interests. That this is a misapplied belief in this case can be easily demonstrated. When substantial numbers of students do not attend, classroom learning is depreciated, student and teacher morale suffer, and academic standards are compromised. Students who miss classes unnecessarily are hurting more than themselves. With our *complicity,* they are undermining what colleges and universities are all about.

Students cut for two general reasons. They have things to do that appear more important than the class, or they wish to avoid what they fear will be painful consequences if they attend. In regard to the first, nursing an illness or attending family weddings or funerals are good excuses for missing a class. But other excuses—the demands of outside jobs, social engagements (including recovering from the night before), completing assignments for other courses—are, at best, questionable.

The other general reason is more disturbing and perhaps less well recognized. A few years ago, I asked several classes what they most disliked about the way courses were taught, and the answer was plain—anything that produced sustained tension or anxiety. I believe cutting is often a result of that aversion. The response of students to feelings of personal inadequacy, fear of humiliation, or a threatening professorial personality or teaching style is often simply to avoid class. This response feeds on itself, as frequent absences make attending even more threatening.

But what accounts for frequent cutting where the teacher tries to make the material interesting, knows the students by name, and approaches them with respect, help, and affability? I accept that question as unanswerable. I simply tell my students: Attend my classes regularly or drop the course. That's the rule.

Reprinted by permission of the author.   ■

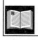 **Vocabulary**

As you think about this essay, these definitions may be helpful to you:
1. **affront**   an insult
2. **invincibly**   incapable of being overcome or subdued
3. **parry**   to evade, to shove aside
4. **wag**   joker, smart-aleck
5. **complicity**   association with or participation in

 Discussion Questions

1. What, according to Brown, does research indicate about academic success as related to class attendance?
2 What happened after the author instituted his no-cut rule?
3. What benefits did he see after enforcing the policy?
4. What reaction did he get from his colleagues?
5. Why, according to Brown, do students cut classes?

 Suggestions for Your Journal

Have you ever cut a class? If so, what were the consequences? If you put yourself in the place of your instructor, how would you be affected by students cutting your class? Do you think students appreciate a teacher who cares enough about them to institute such a policy? For what reasons would you cut a class? Can you answer Professor Brown's "unanswerable" question about why some students cut classes, even when all the positive aspects of the course are in place?

Unit Summary

The writers in this unit offer many perspectives on how to be a successful student. One defining purpose of college is to learn about our intellectual and cultural heritage. To be intensely involved in learning requires great concentration and many skills. The readings in this unit have offered many suggestions for accomplishing this.

Summary Questions

1. How do the readings in this unit suggest you can become a successful student?
2. What tasks or strategies described in the readings could you adopt to improve your own attitudes or behaviors toward your academic work?
3. What skills do you hope to acquire in college to help you in your future work and in living in general?

Suggested Writing Assignments

1. Write a brief essay describing the qualities of a successful student and why you selected those qualities.
2. Select one reading in this unit and write about your personal experience with the academic concern it describes.
3. Several authors in this unit write about various approaches to learning. Describe how your own approach to learning is the same as or different from the ones they describe.

Suggested Readings

Arthur, John. *A Concise Guide to College Success: Carpe Diem*. Upper Saddle River, NJ: Prentice Hall, 2003.

Lawrence, Gordon. *People Types and Tiger Stripes*. Gainesville, FL: Center for the Application of Psychological Types, 1982.

Pauk, W. *How to Study in College,* 4th ed. Boston: Houghton Mifflin, 1989.

Robson, James B. *Beginning College 101: How to Achieve Real Success in College*. South Plainfield, NJ: College and Future Company, 2001.

Uchida, Donna, with Marvin Cetron and Floretta McKenzie. *Preparing Students for the 21st Century*. Arlington, VA: American Association of School Administrators, 1996.

How Should I Expect to Learn?

The act of learning is so ingrained in our everyday life that we usually take it for granted. However, as psychologists who study learning professionally can demonstrate, learning is a complex process that operates differently for many people. Learning can be defined in many ways. It is not only the acquisition of knowledge and skills by instruction or study; it is also an accumulation through experience. Although students enter college after years of "learning," many find that college learning offers new and exciting challenges.

A great deal of research on how people learn has provided important insights and tools to enhance our understanding of the process. David Kolb, a business professor, has suggested that the demands of different academic disciplines require students to use different learning styles or approaches. Howard Gardner takes a multifaceted view when he discusses eight "intelligences," which he describes in terms of a set of abilities, talents, and mental skills (see pp. 101–102). Daniel Goleman writes

I am not young enough to know everything.

—James M. Barrie

about "emotional intelligence," which includes both personal competence and social competence. Goleman suggests that emotional intelligence will be especially important in the future workplace where emotional competencies will be increasingly essential for excellence in every job.

Many researchers believe there is a relationship between the knowledge that exists in the mind and the situations in which it was acquired and used. Successful learning also depends on the individual's past experiences and attitudes toward the learning process. Perhaps the most important factor in successful learning, however, is the motivation or desire to learn.

This unit offers many perspectives about learning. James reviews some newer ideas about intelligence. Siebert and Gilpin provide insights into students' varied approaches to learning. They point out that the learning circumstance or situation for one person may require a different approach than for another. Schein, Laff, and Allen emphasize the importance of using faculty in and out of the classroom. Hellyer, Robinson, and Sherwood offer tips on how to use your memory. Distance education—as described by Michael Dertouzos—is increasingly being viewed by some as the learning mode of the future. To complete this unit, Schank presents some profound ideas about how we will learn 50 years from now.

Understanding Who Is Smart

Jennifer James

Jennifer James is an urban cultural anthropologist and a highly regarded business speaker. A university professor for 14 years, she is the author of six books and has written a weekly newspaper column. In this essay James writes about a new vision of intelligence and how "system thinking" can help us understand change.

The debate over intelligence is a debate over higher standards. Over the past forty years, researchers of all kinds have uncovered the weaknesses of our tests and shown new respect for a broader-based definition of intelligence that reflects more than traditional fact retention and computation skills. Educators, in particular, are looking for a battery of tests that is more predictive of real-world success. The designers of a school testing program in California, for example, put a premium on the skills required for "reasonably deciding what to think and do." Among other things, students had to be able to determine the relevance of information, distinguish between fact and opinion, identify unstated assumptions, detect bias or propaganda, come up with reasonable alternatives or solutions, and predict possible consequences. Intelligence is the ability to make adaptive responses in new as well as old situations.

At Harvard, philosopher Nelson Goodman wanted to understand why some people were "creative" and others were not. In his work, Goodman expanded the concept of intelligence from "How smart is he or she?" to "How is he or she smart?" Motivation and interest in the task at hand—along with traits such as concentration, intention, purpose, drive and tenacity—emerged as important influences.

Howard Gardner, a psychologist who helped to conduct this research, thought of intelligence as the ability to solve problems or create products. He devised the following list of eight primary forms of intelligence (to which I have added one of my own):

1. **Verbal/linguistic intelligence.** This form of intelligence is revealed by a sensitivity to the meaning and order of words and the ability to make varied use of the language. Impromptu speaking, story-telling, humor, and joking are natural abilities associated with verbal/linguistic intelligence. So, too, is persuading someone to follow a course of action, or explaining, or teaching. Will Rogers had this form of intelligence. Good journalists also have it.
2. **Logical/mathematical intelligence.** This form of intelligence is easiest to standardize and measure. We usually refer to it as analytical or scientific thinking, and we see it in scientists, computer programmers, accountants, lawyers, bankers, and, of course, mathematicians, people who are problem solvers and *consummate* game players. They work with abstract symbols and are able to see

connections between pieces of information that others might miss. Einstein is one of the best examples of someone with this form of intelligence.

3. **Visual/*spatial* intelligence.** Persons with this form of intelligence are especially deft at *conjuring* up mental images and creating graphic representations. They are able to think in three-dimensional terms, to re-create the visual world. Picasso, whose paintings challenged our view of reality, was especially gifted at visualizing objects from different perspectives and angles. Besides painters and sculptors, this form of intelligence is found in designers and architects.

4. **Body/kinesthetic intelligence.** This form of intelligence makes possible the connections between mind and body that are necessary to succeed in activities such as dance, mime, sports, martial arts, and drama. Martha Graham and Michael Jordan delighted audiences with their explosive and sensitive uses of the body. Because they know how we move, inventors with this form of intelligence understand how to turn function into form. They intuitively feel what is possible in labor-saving devices and processes.

5. **Musical/rhythmic intelligence.** A person with this form of intelligence hears musical patterns and rhythms naturally and can reproduce them. It is an especially desirable form of intelligence because music has the capacity to alter our consciousness, reduce stress, and enhance brain function. For example, students who had just listened to Mozart scored higher on standard IQ tests than those who had spent the same period of time in meditation or silence. Researchers believe that the patterns in musical themes somehow prime the same neural network that the brain employs for complex visual-spatial tasks.

6. **Interpersonal intelligence.** Managers, counselors, therapists, politicians, mediators, and human relations specialists display this form of intelligence. It is a must for workplace tasks such as negotiation and providing feedback or evaluation. Individuals with this form of intelligence have strong intuitive skills. They are especially able to read the moods, temperaments, motivations, and intentions of others. Abraham Lincoln, Mohandas Gandhi, and Martin Luther King, Jr., used interpersonal intelligence to change the world.

7. **Intrapersonal intelligence.** Sigmund Freud and Carl Jung demonstrated this form of intelligence, the ability to understand and articulate the inner workings of character and personality. The highest order of thinking and reasoning is present in a person who has intrapersonal intelligence. We often call it wisdom. He or she can see the larger picture and is open to the lure of the future. Within an organization, this ability is invaluable.

8. **Spiritual intelligence.** This form of intelligence is tentative; Gardner has yet to decide whether moral or spiritual intelligence qualifies for his list. It can be considered an *amalgam* of interpersonal and intrapersonal awareness with a "value" component added.

9. **Practical intelligence.** Gardner doesn't list this form of intelligence, but I do. It is the skill that enables some people to take a computer or clock apart and put it back together. I also think of practical intelligence as organiza-

tional intelligence or common sense, the ability to solve all sorts of daily problems without quite knowing how the solutions were reached. People with common sense may or may not test well, but they have a clear understanding of cause and effect. They use intelligence in combination with that understanding.

QUALITIES OF MIND

Rate yourself on each of these forms of intelligence. What are your strengths and weaknesses? How are they reflected in the kind of work you do and your relationships with others?

	Low				Moderate					High
	1	2	3	4	5	6	7	8	9	10

1. Verbal/linguistic
2. Logical/mathematical
3. Visual/spatial
4. Body/kinesthetic
5. Musical/rhythmic
6. Interpersonal
7. Intrapersonal
8. Spiritual
9. Practical

Don't let this list intimidate you. There is increasingly strong evidence that intelligence can be taught, despite ongoing arguments about genetic predetermination. Also, the levels of each of these forms of intelligence can vary from one person to the next. Albert Einstein had a high degree of logical and spatial intelligence, but his lack of personal skills was legendary. He left those details to others.

Regardless of the forms of our intelligence, we also need to know how we think. Researcher Gail Browning studies approaches to problem solving. She identifies four "styles" that people use to process information: analytical, conceptual, structural, and social. She concludes that most of us use more than one of them, depending on the problem before us. Her work helps us visualize thought processes, something that makes communication and negotiation easier. When forming a creative and productive team for problem solving or futuring consider combining different thinking styles.

Analytical thinkers are the most logical. They must have facts, figures, directions and reasons to approach problem solving. They want to design a system. They see themselves as straightforward, clear and purposeful. In a team meeting they ask, "Is this feasible?"

Conceptual thinkers accept information in almost any form. They enjoy a challenge and often plunge into the problem-solving process before considering what direction to take. They want to paint a picture. They don't mind mistakes. They usually suggest, "Let's look at this problem in a different way."

Structural thinkers draw comparisons and look for systematic links to determine the source of a problem. They prefer creating flow charts. They organize the components of the problem and the possible solutions and ask, "How does this apply to our situation?"

Social thinkers are the facilitators of group process. They talk to everyone; they weigh all the solutions equally; they may identify the best solution but not know how they reached it. In a team situation they ask, "What do you think of this idea?"

Review these four styles and combine them with the nine forms of intelligence outlined. Try to identify yourself and imagine how different problems or situations engage different aspects of your intelligence or thinking style. Create a perfect team for a problem you are currently trying to solve. What ideal set of minds would potentially be the most intelligent and the best at processing?

British researcher Edward De Bono, in a series of books on intelligence, believes he has the answer. He adds the term lateral thinking to this mix. He sees it as the most productive thinking process because it is easily taught and allows everyone in a group, regardless of their intelligence frame or thinking style, to operate with the same broad set of thinking tools.

Lateral thinking is similar to what others currently call critical or system thinking. It enables us to view a problem from all sides and understand all the alternatives before devising a solution. It requires us to abandon certainty and security, at least for the moment. De Bono's most useful exercise in lateral thinking is called PMI, an acronym for Plus, Minus, and Interesting. Participants are divided into small groups and are asked to evaluate what is good (plus), what is bad (minus), and what is interesting about an idea. In a session with a group of auto manufacturers, for example, De Bono posed the suggestion that all cars should be painted yellow. . . .

[Table 1 on page 105 shows] how the group reacted.

Exercises in lateral thinking work best if each category (good, bad, and interesting) is considered separately and in order when pondering an idea or a problem rather than brainstorming them in the random fashion preferred by conceptual thinkers. Such exercises can be particularly useful when you are floating some new idea or looking for a solution to some problem. They help people focus their perceptions and articulate their reactions and responses. *Common Ground,* a PBS series designed to bring opposing sides together on several controversial issues, used lateral thinking with powerful results. Participants were able to put aside rhetoric and emotion and find they had far more in common than they realized. . . .

We are all, to one degree or another, system thinkers. (I prefer the term system thinking to De Bono's lateral thinking because we are looking at the whole to understand the parts.) We must also combine disparate parts into coherent wholes to put together the puzzles and solve the problems of daily life. A system thinker believes in cooperation and knows that pooling or combining ideas, skills, and experience improves innovation, efficiency, and performance. I think of system thinking as broadscope intelligence and very much like *synergy*, a buzz-word in business in the 1990s. Companies that practiced synergy did so by buying or developing related businesses or by welding their existing units into a more coherent whole.

Table 1   Results of PMI Session: "All Cars Should be Painted Yellow."

Good (Plus)	Bad (Minus)	Interesting
Easier to see on the roads.	Boring.	Interesting to see if shades of yellow arose.
Easier to see at night.	Difficult to recognize your own car.	Interesting to see if people appreciated the safety factor.
No problem in deciding which color you want.	Very difficult to find your car in a parking lot.	Interesting to see whether attitudes toward cars changed.
No waiting to get the color you want.	Easier to steal cars.	Interesting to see if trim acquired a different color.
Easier for the manufacturer.	The abundance of yellow might tire the eyes.	Interesting to see if this were enforceable.
The dealer would need less stock.	Car chases would be difficult for the police.	Interesting to see who would support the suggestion.
It might take the "macho" element out of car ownership.	Accident witnesses would have a harder time.	
Cars would tend to become transport items.	Restriction of your freedom to choose.	
In minor collisions the paint rubbed off onto your car would be the same color.		

Social scientists used system thinking in the 1970s when they began working together to examine the "culture of poverty" as a whole. Edward Deming used it to fine-tune quality processes. The earliest ideas about man and environment as a whole organism represented system thinking. The interrelationship of mind and body in the healing process is another example. When we think about parts of a system, separate from the whole, we cut ourselves off from important information.

System thinking can bridge the gap that sometimes exists between reality and our perception of reality. For example, unproductive workers, falling orders, and sagging profits are indicators of serious problems in any business. Our usual way of thinking may cause us to look at each in isolation. But system thinking helps us understand that all parts of a business or a process are connected, and that when one part is challenged, all the others are as well. We may look for productivity problems on the production line and create new incentives if salespeople are not doing well, but the real "cause" of our problems may be hidden in the system that underlies the entire enterprise. System thinking accepts the inter-relatedness of all things. System thinking is usually the best way to find out what is going on.

System thinking can help all of us understand the zigzags of change. It enables us to see the big picture. From that vantage point we can more easily perceive the changing realities of our work and lives and solve problems. Here are some of the basic characteristics of a system thinker:

- You are physically and intellectually alert.
- You are always wondering how things can be improved.
- You are able to resolve conflict by agreeing to disagree on some points and moving the discussion forward.
- You do not demand perfection from yourself or others.
- You are imaginative and creative.
- You are empathetic and compassionate.
- You are comfortable with chaos.
- You are a nonconformist in one way or another.
- You have a sense of humor.

The future challenges us to question our own minds and how we think, to reexamine our assumptions and see how they connect to the changing realities of our world. Thinking must become a more fluid process; I call it "water logic" because the future will require the development of a fluid, more adaptive level of reaction and response. As humanity evolves, creating ever more complex patterns, the ability to understand, synthesize, and adapt to those patterns will become basic intelligence.

Reprinted with permission of Simon & Schuster Adult Publishing Group from *Thinking in the Future Tense: A Workout for the Mind* by Jennifer James. © 1996 by Jennifer James, Inc.

 ## Vocabulary

As you think about this essay, these definitions may be helpful to you:
1. **consummate**   extremely skilled and accomplished
2. **spatial**   relating to three-dimensional space
3. **conjuring**   imagining

4. **amalgam**   combination of different elements
5. **synergy**   combined action or operation

 ## Discussion Questions

1. In her first paragraph, Jennifer James provides her own definition of intelligence. What is it?
2. What traits seem to be important in Nelson Goodman's expanded concept
   of intelligence?
3. Why are Howard Gardner's eight basic forms of intelligence important in
   broadening our concept of intelligence? Is the form that James adds to Gardner's list different from the others? How?
4. Do you agree with the author's addition of "practical intelligence"? Why?
5. What is "lateral thinking"? How can it be used in problem solving?
6. What are the characteristics of "system thinking," according to the author?
   How can system thinking be used to analyze problem areas?

 ## Suggestions for Your Journal

What does being intelligent mean to you? On which of the eight forms of intelligence do you rate yourself highest? Lowest? Which do you think are most
important for being successful in college? In the real world? Are you intelligent
in some ways that Gardner or James have *not* described?

Learning Styles: They Can Help or Hinder

Al Siebert and Bernadine Gilpin

Al Siebert is a psychologist with more than 20 years of teaching experience in adult education. Bernadine Gilpin started college at age 35 after rearing five children. She has more than 15 years' experience as a teacher, administrator, and counselor.

Siebert and Gilpin believe that understanding how one learns best can help make studying and learning easier. This essay points out how mismatches between teaching and learning styles may cause difficulties and makes suggestions for recognizing and overcoming this common problem.

Researchers wanting to understand all aspects of success in college asked: "Why do some students do well with one instructor but not another?" Their research uncovered a simple truth about academic life: The way some people teach does not always match up with the way other people learn.

Other research looked at why students show wide differences in the time of day and the circumstances best for learning. This research identified an important truth about studying and learning: The learning circumstances best for one person may not be good for another.

Research findings and experience have identified the following important differences in how people learn.

Auditory Versus Visual Styles

Have you ever noticed that someone can read a note you've left him, but the message doesn't get through to his brain? Or that you can tell a person something, but it doesn't register unless you write it down for her? That's because people differ in how information gets into their conscious mind.

Some people learn best by listening. Information doesn't stick well unless they hear it. Other people learn best by reading. They must see something before they believe it and remember it. Some people learn best by doing. What is your natural style?

Do you remember best what is said to you or what you read?
Do you prefer television or newspapers as your source of news?
Would you rather hear an expert talk on a subject or read what the expert has written?
When you purchase new equipment, do you read the instruction manual carefully or do you rarely read manuals?

Is reading the college catalog your main way of learning about your program and classes, or do you merely skim the catalog and go see an advisor who tells you everything you need to know?

Based on your answers to these questions, which learning style do you prefer, auditory or visual?

Everyone learns both ways, of course. It is not an either/or situation. Yet the differences between people are sometimes extreme enough to cause problems. If you have a visual learning style, you operate mainly on the basis of what you read. You may have difficulty with an instructor who believes that telling people what and how to learn is sufficient.

Auditory Learning Style

If you have an auditory style, you will probably do well with an instructor who says everything to learn and do. You may have difficulty with a visually oriented instructor. Such an instructor hands out a written statement about what to do to pass the course without discussing it and assigns textbook material and out-side readings that are never discussed in class.

The solution, if you have an auditory style in a class taught by a visually oriented instructor, is to:

1. Find classmates who will tell you what they learned from the textbook readings.
2. Dictate the main points from the reading assignments and handouts onto cassette tapes and then listen to the tapes.
3. Consciously work at improving your ability to acquire information visually. (Note: For professional help, go to the reading improvement center or the office of disability services at your college.)

Visual Learning Style

If you learn best visually, you may be in trouble with an instructor who doesn't use handouts, emphasizes class discussion, and doesn't write much on the blackboard. The solution with a verbally oriented instructor is to:

1. Take good notes on what the instructor and your classmates say. After class fill in sentences and compare notes with other students.
2. Ask the instructor for suggested articles or books that will let you read the information you need to understand better.
3. Consciously work at listening and remembering what the instructor says. TIP: One woman wrote to us saying that she types her lecture notes immediately after each class.
4. If you are confused about a point, ask the instructor to tell you again and write down what you hear.

External versus Internal Learning Styles

Psychologists have done extensive research on a significant personality variable. It is called the "external and internal *locus of control*."

Externally oriented students believe information when it comes from an authority or expert. Information or suggestions from other sources aren't trusted as accurate.

If you prefer to get the guidance from expert sources and your instructor enjoys being an expert, then you have a good match. The more you need an instructor who tells the class exactly what to learn, the better you will do with this type of instructor. If you need clear guidelines from instructors but take a course from someone who provides little direction, you may flounder. You may be sitting in class waiting for the instructor to tell you what the answer to a problem is, only to have him or her ask the class, "What do you think?" After the class talks for a while, the instructor may refuse to say what the right answer is. He or she might say, "You may be right," or "There is some truth to that."

Some students react negatively to classes in which the instructor encourages discussion and encourages students to develop their own views and answers. These students protest, "I didn't pay good money to sit and listen to a bunch of uninformed people express their opinions. I can get that in the coffee shop." This attitude is legitimate. It is also narrow-minded.

The word *education* means to "draw out of." It does not mean "shovel into." A good education teaches you to think for yourself. It teaches you to ask good questions and then how to find the answers on your own. A good education does not give you a diploma for learning how to seek out an expert for any question you have. It teaches you how to both listen to authorities and come to your own conclusions.

Self-motivated, internally oriented students appreciate an instructor who allows them freedom to follow their own paths. Such students get upset with instructors who tell them exactly what they must learn, and in what way. For them, too much course structure is *abrasive*. They feel handicapped more than helped. Such reactions are legitimate and narrow-minded.

In every field of study, certain basics must be mastered. There are basic terms and concepts that must be understood. There are some techniques fundamental to the mastery of the subject even though the reasons why may not be given.

Being Both Internal and External in Learning

Students who get the most out of school are able to follow the tightly controlled steps used by some teachers and, at the same time, organize their own learning experiences when in a class taught by someone who gives few guidelines. Can you learn to do both?

Differences in Temperament

Isabel Myers and her mother Katharine Briggs developed a test to measure four dimensions of *temperament* identified by psychotherapist Carl Jung. Myers-Briggs tests are probably the most popular personality tests in the country because many people benefit from seeing how differences in temperament explain misunderstandings among people.

This means that differences in *how* you and an instructor think are more important than differences in *what* you think. Here's how the four temperaments influence your learning style.

Extroversion versus Introversion

Instructors and students vary widely in how friendly they want to be and how much emotional distance they need to have. A friendly, *extroverted* instructor enjoys after-class contact with students. He or she will ask students to coffee or out for pizza. If you are similarly friendly, you will have a great year.

If you are a more *introverted* person, however, you may suffer from too much personal attention and closeness. You would much rather have a quiet, tactful instructor who respects your need to be left alone. Such an instructor understands how embarrassing it is to be called on to talk in class or to be openly praised for getting a high score on an exam.

On the other hand, if you are an extroverted person with a more introverted instructor, you may find it puzzling to have him or her pulling away from you after class. After all, what are instructors for if not to be available for students? Yet your desire to be friendly may cause the instructor to stare at you and make excuses to get away. After that, you may feel avoided.

When it comes to studying, the introverted person needs a private, quiet place where everyone stays away. The extroverted person likes to study in the kitchen, in a student lounge, or with classmates. Don't hesitate to tell friends, relatives, and classmates with temperaments different from yours what you need.

Thinking versus Feeling

Descriptions of this dimension of temperament match up closely with left-brain/right-brain research findings. The left brain is where the speech center develops in most humans. The left brain is where you remember words, use logic, and think analytically. It gives you your ability to think rationally and unemotionally. The left brain thinks in a linear fashion. It is time oriented.

The right brain carries your memory for music. You think visually, emotionally, and irrationally in the right brain. It is the source of creativity and intuition. Right-brain thinking follows emotional logic. Using it, you can visualize and think in patterns jumping from one spot in a pattern to another without apparent logic or reason.

If you tend to be left-brained, you will be well matched to an instructor who gives you thorough, unemotional listings of facts, data, analytic explorations, hypotheses, logic, evidence, numbers, definition of terms, and rational conclusions.

If you tend to be left-brained and get an instructor who teaches in a right-brained way, you may find the course to be a bewildering experience. You may experience the instructor as weird, too emotional, disorganized, and a bit nutty.

If you tend to be right-brained with a left-brained teacher, the course will be painful for you. You'll feel like a thirsty person handed a glass of water only to find it is filled with sand.

To resolve personality conflicts such as these, avoid indulging in the attitude, "If only other people would change, my world would be a better place for me." When you have a mismatch, you can try to find someone (perhaps even the instructor) who will translate the material into a form you understand better. More important, however, make an effort to gain more use of your other brain.

The situation may not be easy at first, but it does give you a chance to add another dimension to yourself. And isn't this why you're in school?

You do not have to give up your more natural and preferred way of thinking, feeling, and talking. What you can do is add more to what you already have.

Sensation versus Intuition

Sensation-oriented people like to be sensible. They are guided by experience. Intuitive people like fantasy. They are creative dreamers. According to David Keirsey and Marilyn Bates, authors of *Please Understand Me,* differences on this dimension cause the widest gulf between people.

The sensation-oriented student is practical, wanting facts and evidence. An intuitive instructor can fill the lecture hour with hypothetical explanations, theories, concepts, and a long list of views held by others.

A sensation-oriented instructor gives practical instructions on what to do. An intuitive student wants to know what the underlying theories and concepts are, and asks "but what if?"

What to do about this sort of conflict? Stretch your understanding. Ask for what you need. Try to minimize the judging dimension of the next pair of traits.

Judging Versus Perceiving

If you remember Archie Bunker from the television series "All in the Family," you have seen an excellent example of the judging temperament. Such people make up their minds quickly. They judge others and situations as good or bad, right or wrong.

The perceiving style is to observe without judgment. Such people can watch world events, movies, and sports events without taking sides or having an opinion.

A judgmental style instructor believes the purpose for being in college is to work hard to become qualified for an occupation where hard work will get you ahead. The instructor works hard, expects the same from every student, and privately judges students as good ones or bad ones.

A perceiving instructor looks for ways to make learning fun, tries to minimize office work, and sees all students as learners. This instructor is frustrating for a judging style student who wants serious homework and wants to know how he or she compares to the other students.

Practical Suggestions

What do you do when a teacher is less than ideal? Do you get distressed? Complain?

By now we hope you have realized that finding a really good match between yourself and an instructor does not happen all the time. In fact, if you are an experienced victim, then the college will provide you with many chances to be upset, complain to classmates, and criticize instructors you judge to be imperfect.

As an alternative to being a victim, we have the following suggestions:

1. Before registration ask around to find out about various instructors. If you have a choice between instructors, you'll know which one to choose.
2. Try to get as much out of every course as you can, regardless of who your instructor is or how much the teaching style does not fit your preferred learning style. Be open to try a new way of learning.
3. When you have difficulty understanding what is happening in a course, make an appointment to talk with the instructor. Be prepared to ask for what you want.
4. If you still have problems, go to the office or center that teaches studying and reading skills. The specialists there can be very helpful.

Learn to Appreciate Human Differences

When you experience conflicts with others at school, at work, or in your family, question your attitudes about what other people should be like. If you experience an irritating difference, use that as an opportunity to learn more about human nature. You might as well, because you won't change other people by criticizing them!

We humans are all born with different temperaments and different ways of functioning in life. That is simply the way things work.

Do You Know Where and When?

Several final suggestions: If you grew up in a large family you may study best in a noisy place with lots of people around. Experiment with locations to see what works best for you.

Time of day is another learning style difference. If you are a morning person, get up and study for an hour before others get up. Leave chores for evening when your brain is disengaging. If you are an evening person go ahead and study until one or two in the morning.

The better you know yourself, the more skillfully you will manage your learning style and the easier it will be to succeed in college!

From *The Adult Student's Guide to Survival and Success: Time for College* by Al Siebert and Bernadine Gilpin. Copyright © 1992, Practical Psychology Press. Reprinted by permission.

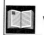 **Vocabulary**

As you think about this essay, these definitions may be helpful to you:
1. **locus of control**   center of self-control, by either internal or external influences
2. **abrasive**   causing irritation

3. **temperament**   characteristic or habitual inclination
4. **extroverted**   being predominantly influenced by what is outside of the self
5. **introverted**   being wholly or predominantly concerned with one's own
   mental life

 Discussion Questions

1. What is a learning style?
2. What is the difference between the auditory and visual style of learning?
3. How does temperament affect your approaches to learning?
4. What aspects of learning does the left brain control? What aspects does the
   right brain control?
5. What four temperaments can influence your learning style? Describe them
   and how they affect the way you learn.

 Suggestions for Your Journal

Analyze how you learn best. Are you more visual or auditory? Have you ever
experienced a class in which the instructor's teaching style did not work with
your best learning style? If so, what happened?

   Do you think a student who does not learn well with a certain teacher's style
should switch instructors or learn to adapt? What suggestions given by the
authors for learning more effectively pertain to you?

The Power of Memory

Regina Hellyer, Carol Robinson, and Phyllis Sherwood

The authors of this essay are English teachers at the Raymond Walter College of the University of Cincinnati. Regina Hellyer is director of the reading program, Carol Robinson teaches English composition, and Phyllis Sherwood is the director of the writing lab.

Everyone forgets something sometimes. And almost everyone wishes he or she could remember more. You probably already have some methods to help you remember. What do you do to jog your memory? The classic (and probably the corniest) way to remember something is to tie a string around your finger. Today Post-It Notes have become a popular means of sparking memory because they are conveniently sized and adhere to most surfaces. All memory begins with the senses because the five senses are the channel through which all information comes. However, although you are bombarded by vast numbers of sights, sounds, touches, tastes, and smells each moment of the day, only certain impressions and information actually go into your short- or long-term memory.

Many people make this complaint: "I have a terrible memory. I just can't remember anything!" Such a statement is not only exaggerated, it is usually untrue. Most people's memories are not bad; they are just not as well trained as they could be. Everyone uses some memory strategies. But whatever memory devices you already use, you may want to add to the power of your memory by adopting some of the following techniques: observation, association, clustering, imaging, and mnemonics.

Observation

Much of your ability to remember hinges on careful observation. *Observation* involves a *conscious* effort to pay attention, be alert, listen attentively, and notice details. If, for example, you have ever lost track of your car in a public parking lot, it was probably because you did not make a conscious effort to pay attention or to notice landmarks. Likewise, you need to employ basic observational skills both in the classroom and in your studying before you can apply any other memory techniques. When you are listening to lectures, taking notes, and studying textbooks, you must make a conscious effort to notice and remember pertinent information. For example, when you are taking notes in class, besides recording the obvious—information on the chalkboard or a *Power Point presentation*—you should be noticing the teacher's body language, his or her vocal emphasis, and transitions and organizational cues. Careful observation of these details allows you to determine what information is of major or minor importance and what you should emphasize in your notes, that is, what is important to remember.

115

Association

The second memory technique, learning by *association,* is based upon a simple principle: Learning something new is always easier if you can associate or connect it with something you already know. For example, if you are just beginning to use a computer, you might not understand what is meant by "windows" until you realize that windows on computers are very similar to windows in buildings: When you look into them, you can see what exists in the computer and in the environment. Or, in a biology class, if you are learning about the structure of neurons in the brain, you might associate one part of the neuron, the dendrites, which grow as you learn new information, with the roots of a tree, which grow when they are watered.

Clustering

Clustering, the process of grouping a large number of ideas into subgroups, is another handy memory device. This technique is based on the fact that you can remember several groups of five or so items more easily than a large number of separate items. If you have thirty items to learn, try to organize them into groups. For example, you might try clustering new terms you have to learn.

Clustering can also be useful as a method for prewriting or organizing an essay or research paper. If your ideas, information, or material cannot be arranged chronologically (relating to time, from first to last) or spatially (relating to area, from top to bottom, side to side, etc.), you can cluster to find categories or groupings that will provide you with a logical method of organization.

Imaging

Imaging, or using a pictorial representation of something, can be an excellent way to remember a fact, process, definition, or concept. For example, most of us know the geographical shape of Italy because its image resembles a boot. However, drawing the geographical outline of Switzerland, Italy's close neighbor to the north, would prove challenging for most people, since its shape does not easily conjure up a picture.

You may already be drawing pictures in your notebooks to reinforce ideas, definitions, or other material you need to learn. If you have not done so yet, try this method with something that you are having trouble remembering. You do not have to be a great artist. Stick figures are fine. These pictures are for your eyes only, so however they look, you will know what the picture is supposed to represent, and the picture will be imprinted on your mind because *you* drew it!

Mnemonics

Mnemonics is a general category of memory devices; mnemonic devices include songs, ditties, and other catchy techniques to help you remember. Mnemonic devices take the form of acronyms, made-up sentences, rhymes or songs, and physical manipulations.

Acronyms

Acronyms are a kind of mnemonic device formed from the first letters of items you are trying to learn. The first letters are arranged to spell a word. People have used acronyms for ages, but in this era of rapidly increasing information, they are becoming more and more prevalent. For example, you are all familiar with Light Amplification by Stimulated Emission of Radiation printers and Light Amplification by Stimulated Emission of Radiation surgery, but you call them laser printers and laser surgery. The acronym *laser* (originally in capital letters) and other words like *radar, sonar,* and *scuba* have become so familiar that you may forget that they were acronyms.

In college, an acronym can act as a trigger to help you remember information. For example, if you have to learn the names of five Great Lakes, it is easy to remember HOMES—standing for Huron, Ontario, Michigan, Erie, and Superior. Likewise, some people remember the colors of the spectrum in their proper order by making each color part of the name "ROY G. BIV" (red, orange, yellow, green, blue, indigo, and violet). Another acronym that is useful to know is SAGE—a "wise" way to remember the four different kinds of context clues: synonyms, antonyms, general sense of the sentence, and examples.

Sentences

Making up sentences or phrases, either nonsensical or serious, can be an effective way of learning and remembering material. The spellings of difficult words can often be learned easily with mnemonics. For instance, saying "A Rat In The House May Eat the Ice Cream" is an easy way to teach a child how to spell *arithmetic* because the sentence is silly (making it memorable), and the first letters of the words, taken together, spell *arithmetic*. For adults, mnemonics can be applied to remember more difficult or confusing spellings. For example, do you spell attendance with an *ance* or *ence*? It's easy to remember the correct spelling if you think of attending a dAnce. Likewise, FeBRuary is a very cold month—brrrr! A sentence mnemonic to learn the letter keys of a standard keyboard on a computer is "The quick brown fox jumped over the lazy dogs." If you type this sentence, you will have practiced using all the letter keys of the three major rows on a standard keyboard.

Jingles or Rhymes

Jingles and rhymes are popular mnemonics because they help you learn through rhythm and sound. Probably the first "learning" song you encountered was the ABC song. Another popular jingle shows how to remember which months have thirty days and which ones have thirty-one. "Thirty days hath September, April, June, and November, all the rest have thirty-one; excepting February alone, which hath but twenty-eight in fine, till leap year gives it twenty-nine."

Another rhyme that you might find useful if you are taking chemistry is "-*ate*, I ate; *ide*, I died." This rhyme helps you remember that cyan*ates* are harmless chemicals, whereas cyan*ides* are extremely poisonous—an important distinction to know.

Physical Techniques

Physical participation can also act as a mnemonic. This can mean simply putting something in a particular place, like putting letters that need to be mailed under your car keys, or acting out a process. Instead of the "Thirty Days" poem for remembering the days in the month, perhaps you learned the knuckle method. This method names the months chronologically, counting January on the first knuckle, February in between, March on the second knuckle, April in between, etc. Knuckle months have thirty-one days; in-between-knuckle months have thirty. Unfortunately, this method does not give you a clue about how many days are in February; you are on your own to figure that out. Nevertheless, this example illustrates that mnemonic devices can include physical components, and the more senses you use to learn something, the more easily you will learn and remember.

Although mnemonic devices made up by others can be very helpful, you may want to make up your own mnemonic devices—you will really own them, and they may be even easier to remember than devices that are provided for you. All the memory techniques described in this essay can help you remember difficult concepts and material that can empower you to be a successful college student.

From *Study Skills for Learning Power.* Copyright 1998. Houghton Mifflin.

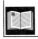 **Vocabulary**

As you think about this essay, these definitions may be helpful to you:
1. **mnemonics**   assisting or intended to assist in memory
2. **acronyms**   an abbreviation formed from initial letters
3. **antonyms**   words of opposite meanings

 Discussion Questions

1. Do you agree with the authors that there is no such thing as a "bad" memory but just an untrained one? Why or why not?
2. The authors suggest you pay attention to the means of nonverbal communication used by your teachers. What important information can you pick up from this?
3. What are the differences between the memory techniques of observation, association, clustering, and imaging? Describe some learning situations where you might use each technique.
4. What mnemonic devices do the authors suggest you use to help you remember? Which ones work best for you? Why?

Suggestions for Your Journal

How would you rate your ability to remember the material required in your courses? Do you use different memory devices in different courses, or do you use the same devices in all courses? Do you use different memory devices in your life outside the classroom than the ones you use in your courses? What steps can you take to improve your memory?

How Do I Find Out What Faculty Are Doing?

Howard K. Schein, Ned S. Laff, and Deborah R. Allen

This essay was written for the *Daily Illini*, the student newspaper at the University of Illinois at Champaign-Urbana, to inform students about how to access faculty resources. The authors are professional academic advisors with wide experience in many areas of higher education.

Faculty members are the moving forces of higher education. You want to pick their brains. You want their ideas, their commentaries on your ideas, and their advice. If you are building a field of study, faculty members are the experts. However, sometimes they don't seem very accessible. How do you find these people, and what do you say once you have located them? Some tips for the curious follow.

Books that list course schedules are academic catalogs. Small gems and good bargains are frequently hidden in the small print. Faculty members teach under their departmental sponsorship, even if their course titles are far afield from their departments' major focuses. International relations may be a natural for a political science department, but at one school, for example, a former ambassador has an appointment in the sociology department. By carefully looking through all course offerings, you may find interesting classes in unexpected places.

Faculty members show off their true interests in upper level courses and in special-topics seminars. Departments go potluck when assigning instructors to introductory courses, so if you want to know who specializes in specific areas, look at upper division and graduate level offerings.

Keep a special eye out for seminar courses, too. Although you may not take courses offered by the specialists of interest for credit, you may be able to sit in on the class. You will find the faculty members' expertise and cross-disciplinary interests in these courses. For instance, when you discover the course in geography of world conflict, your perspective on international relations may take a different bent, especially if your interest is national security policy. You may find that your interest in international relations, when tied to special-topics courses in communications, physics, and economics, makes up an appropriate field of study.

Once you have identified the courses and professors of interest, you need to go through the process of generating a field of study. Suggestions for getting started on planning your tailor-made education follow.

Contact the professors of the identified courses to talk over your interests and expectations for their courses. Get the current course descriptions and look over the reading lists. Ask these professors to identify other people who are working in your areas of interest.

Many departments publish listings of the faculty members' interests. At larger schools, these lists are often part of the promotional package for prospective graduate students. These lists are usually available on departmental Web sites or through the departmental secretary. By the way, the secretary usually knows much more about the faculty's work than most students realize!

Check out all upcoming seminars and lectures. You'll usually hear an informative talk and find out who on campus is involved in your areas of interest.

Once you begin to get a sense of who's doing what, think about how their work fits in with your plans. Then, see these professors during their office hours or write brief e-mails or make quick phone calls to make appointments with them. In your meeting, talk with the faculty member about how to make your program of study substantive. You need to find out if ongoing groups of faculty members and students meet to discuss the topics in which you are interested. They may be meeting through informal lunches, study groups, or Friday afternoon coffee breaks; a faculty member can invite you to these seminars. In your meeting, you can also find out about independent study opportunities with them or their colleagues.

Make use of your elective hours to get into the special-topics courses you've identified, create special-topics courses with the faculty you've discovered, or convince faculty members to lead an independent study project with you. In these special-topics courses, you will be asked to think, apply the tools you have learned, and produce your own work: your education truly begins in these environments. Faculty members are usually willing to teach under such arrangements as long as they know that you are serious.

Find out about ongoing research projects in your areas of interest and try to get involved in these projects. If the lead researchers know that you want to learn and find you to be energetic and able to contribute through good efforts, they'll listen to you. Faculty members won't usually turn away good help. Here's an approach that seems to work: "Professor B, I've been reading some of your articles on international economic development in Latin America. I'm interested in your theory on the interaction of cultural patterns and economic growth. I'd like to work on this problem with you." If you tie into an ongoing research project or independent study, you learn how people define the critical problems in their areas, how they learn to ask the questions to find solutions to those problems, and what it takes to come up with workable answers. Regardless of your field, such skills are critical to your success when you graduate from college.

Keep in mind that you cannot accomplish your goals in a vacuum. You must integrate your current knowledge into your educational plan. You also must increase the amount of information you get and learn to think about how it pertains to you. For example, in addition to reading the major national newspapers and magazines, pick up the trade journals and papers that the professionals read. Don't wait until your senior year to take the initiative to learn outside of class; and if you are a freshman, do it now.

From "Giving Advice to Students," National Academic Advising Association (NACADA) Monograph, No. 11, 2004, pp. 34–35.

Discussion Questions

1. Why do the authors say, "Faculty members are the moving forces of higher education"?
2. How do the authors suggest you use the course catalog to find course offerings that might appeal to you?
3. How can you find faculty members who have expertise in an academic area for which you have an interest? What should you do before making contact?
4. What is the difference between a "major" and a "field of study"? If you would like to put together a "field of study," what are some steps the authors suggest you take?
5. Do you think the authors' suggestions for approaching faculty members are good ones? What other ways would you approach faculty members if you wanted to study with them?

 Suggestions for Your Journal

Describe a positive experience you have had with a faculty member and how it enhanced your academic work. If you have not had a direct, one-to-one contact with a faculty member, how can you initiate one? Have you ever considered asking a faculty member in an area of strong personal interest if you could study or do research with him or her? If so, what was the result?

Distance Education

Michael L. Dertouzos

The late Michael L. Dertouzos is introduced fully at the beginning of his essay on human-centered issues in technology in Unit 5. Briefly, he adds a special perspective on the enduring issues in educating people effectively. It may surprise you to see where he, who was once in effect the webmaster for the World Wide Web, comes down on the issue of distance learning.

Education is the world's most important collaborative human activity. Education is so vital because it defines future society. It's also the only force strong enough to close the expanding jaws of the rich-poor gap. It is natural for people to want to join new information technology with education. Unlike the Agrarian and Industrial Revolutions, which helped learners indirectly by feeding them, transporting them to school, and providing them with electricity, the Information Revolution helps directly, because it deals with the currency of knowledge: information.

Distance education has many faces. It can be used to teach literacy in Africa; provide industrial training and certification to health professionals, maintenance engineers, and other specialists; and offer courses to university and adult populations, as in the case of Britain's Open University. The biggest hope of all, however, is that it be used to interconnect young students with their teachers and peers, forming a new breed of educational communities that straddle space and time. Yet, despite the richness and promise of distance education, there is a dearth of responsible experimentation with its educational approaches. Partly, that's due to the difficulty of measuring objectively how effective a particular approach is. But there is also another reason—a wild-frontier mentality of hope and expectation that these new technologies are bound to help.

In the late 1990s, I attended a meeting where Benjamin Netanyahu, then prime minister of Israel, explained to a group of politicians and computer professionals how he wanted to provide a quarter million of his country's toddlers with interconnected computers. He said, however, he was having trouble funding the project. I turned the tables and asked him why he wanted to do this in the first place. He was stunned, since it should have been obvious—especially to an MIT technologist—that computers are good for learning.

Throughout the world, droves of politicians, led by those in the United States, are repeating the fashionable *mantra* that millions of children in thousands of schools must be interconnected. You can feel their rush: "Isn't it so reasonable and modern to put an emerging technology to work toward the noblest of social goals: the education of our children?"

Not quite.

After 35 years of experimenting with computers in various aspects of learning, the jury is still out with respect to the central question, "Are computers truly effective in learning?" The evidence from numerous studies on whether computers improve the actual learning process is overwhelmingly ... inconclusive.

Certainly, the promise is impressive. Simulators can help teach the kinetic and quantitative skills needed to drive, ski, swim, sail, even operate on humans. Computers can help learners write, compose music, generate designs, and create new objects. Speech understanding machines can be used as literacy tutors teaching adults who feel too embarrassed to fumble along in front of people, to read.

Collaboration at a distance can help teachers and students discuss homework on the Web, debate issues, examine problems, pursue joint projects, and get useful information from other people. At a more ambitious level, collaboration techniques can bridge schools that lack certain teaching specialties with schools that have the right people. Students in different countries can collect information on local customs and then assemble, share, and compare the results.

But potential does not equal actual results. Just to pick one statistic from a pile of evidence, U.S. high school students consistently rank from 12th to 18th, internationally, in physics and math abilities, whereas Asian students rank first. Yet U.S. students have far greater access to computers than their Asian counterparts. What are Asian educators doing, without technology, that American educators would do well to emulate? Another of the many reasons the jury is out is that learning depends critically on what human teachers do best—lighting a fire in a student's heart, nurturing a student, being a role model. None of these attributes is easily conveyed over the Information Marketplace.

So what should we do with this highest form of collaboration? I suggest the same answer I gave to Prime Minister Netanyahu, scaled up here to encompass the world: Let us interconnect students, and experiment with human-centric collaborative education, creatively and widely (in the hundreds of thousands to a few million students), but refrain from deploying it massively (in the hundreds of millions)—at least until the jury reaches some better conclusions. This won't make politicians shine as bright, but our children may shine brighter.

 Vocabulary

As you think about this essay, this definition may be helpful to you:
1. **mantra**   a mystical chant believed to change the world if repeated often enough

Discussion Questions

1. Dertouzos asserts that distance education has many possible strengths but also some limitations. Identify those strengths and weaknesses and add your own ideas to each list. What do you see as the true potential benefits of distance education?
2. What do you see as the future value of distance education for yourself? For others?

 Suggestions for Your Journal

What personal experience have you had with distance education? Was that a good experience for you? Could it have been better? If so, how?

Are We Going to Get Smarter?

Roger C. Schank

Roger C. Schank, a leading researcher in artificial intelligence, is the Distinguished Career Professor in the School of Computer Science at Carnegie Mellon, where he is also chair and chief technology officer for the Department of Cognitive Arts.

Is intelligence an absolute? Does mankind get smarter as time goes by? It depends on what you mean by intelligence, of course. Certainly we are getting more knowledgeable. Or at least it seems that way. While the average child has access to a wealth of information, considerably more than was available to children fifty years ago, there are people who claim that our children are not as well educated as they were fifty years ago and that our schools have failed us.

Today, questions about what it means to be intelligent and what it means to be educated are not at the center of our scientific inquiry, nor are they at the center of our popular discourse. Still we live our lives according to implicitly understood ideas about intelligence and about education. Those ideas will be seriously challenged in the next fifty years.

Over ten years ago, I was asked to join the board of editors of *Encyclopaedia Britannica*. The other members were mostly *octogenarians* and mostly humanists. Because I was both a scientist and much younger than everyone else, most of what I said was met with odd stares. When I asked the board if they would be happy to put out an encyclopedia ten times the size of the current one if the costs involved remained the same, they replied that, no, the current encyclopedia had just the right amount of information. I responded that they would be out of business in ten years if that were their belief. They had no idea what I meant—although I tried to explain the coming of what is now called the World Wide Web. At a later meeting, after having heard me make similar assertions about the future, Clifton Fadiman, a literary hero of the 1940s, responded, "I guess we will all have to accept the fact that minds less well educated than our own will soon be in charge of institutions like the encyclopaedia."

The chairman of the board of the *Encyclopaedia Britannica* at the time was the late Mortimer Adler. He was also responsible for a series called The Great Books of the Western World, which was (and is) sold as a set. These books represent all the great written works of the world's wisdom—according to Adler and his colleagues, anyhow—and the series consisted mostly of books written prior to the twentieth century. I asked Adler whether he thought there might be some new books that could be included, and he replied that most of the important thoughts had already been written down.

This idea, that all the great thoughts have already been thought, has been prevalent in the American idea of education and intelligence for a long time. Here are the admission requirements for Harvard College in 1745:

When any Schollar is able to read Tully or such like clasicall Latin Author *ex temporare,* and make and speake true Latin verse and Prose *Suo (ut aiunt) Marte,* and decline perfectly the paradigms of Nounes and verbes ine the Greeke tongue, then may hee bee admitted into the Colledge, nor shall any claim admission before such qualification.

What the Great Books series and Harvard of 1745 have in common is an underlying assumption that the study of man and his institutions had been sufficiently mastered in ancient times and therefore education required you to be well read and well versed in the thoughts of those who preceded you. An educated person in this view is one who is able to discuss, with *erudition,* a variety of historical, philosophical, and literary topics. Being educated—and therefore being intelligent—has, for the last century and many centuries before that, been about the accumulation of facts, the ability to quote the ideas of others, and a familiarity with certain ideas. Education has meant accumulating information and intelligence has often meant little more in the popular imagination than the ability to show off what one has accumulated.

But what happens when the facts are in the walls?

Fifty years from now, knowledge will be so easy to acquire that one will be able simply to say aloud whatever one wants to know and hear an instantaneous response from the walls—enhanced by a great deal of technology from the walls, of course. Knowing offhand what Freud had to say about the superego won't mean much when you can turn to the nearest appliance and ask what Freud had to say and hear Freud (or someone who looks and sounds a lot like him) saying it and finding five opposing thought leaders from throughout time ready to propose alternative ideas if you want to hear them and discuss them together.

But is intelligence simply the ability to be informed of answers to your questions, or is it the ability to know what questions to ask? As answers become devalued, questions become more valued. We have lived for a very long time in an answer-based society. Signs of it are everywhere: in the television shows that people watch such as *Jeopardy* and *Who Wants to Be a Millionaire?;* in the games that people play, such as Trivial Pursuit; and most of all in school, where answers are king. Increasingly, the chief concern of our schools is testing. School has become a *regimen* for learning answers rather than learning to inquire.

New technologies will change all this. When the pocket calculator was introduced, people asked whether calculators might as well be used in math tests, since from now on such devices would always be available. As a result, math tests began to focus on more substantive issues than long division. The introduction of artificial intelligence into everyday devices will have the same effect. As machines become omnipresent and able to answer questions about whatever concerns us, the values we place on each individual's being a repository of factual knowledge will diminish. The old idea of school, based on the notion that the most knowledgeable person in town had information to impart and the rest of us were forced to sit and memorize that information, will give way to new ideas of knowledge acquisition. Knowledge will no longer be seen as a commodity to be acquired. Anything obtained easily is devalued in society, and it will be the same with knowledge.

What will be valued will be good questions. *Computers can only take you so far,* we will hear people say.

Imagine the following: You're sitting in your living room, talking with your friend, and an issue comes up between you. You turn to the wall for a response. "Who was right?" you demand. The wall points out that it has a number of virtual people available to join your conversation. You choose some characters that you have heard about or conversed with before. A lively discussion ensues. Eventually the limits of the computer's collective knowledge are reached. The walls know no more of relevance. "This, then, is an exciting question!" you exclaim. Knowing a good question makes you ready to enter into a discussion with other live humans interested in similar questions. You tell that to the walls, and suddenly the people interested in such questions—those who have gone beyond the software in the same way that you have—are all there in your living room (virtually). In a world where this is possible, what does it mean to be educated? What does it mean to be intelligent?

To think about the education part of that question, we have to ask what a child's life would be like in that world. Fifty years from now school, as we know it, will have atrophied from lack of interest. Why go to school to learn facts, when virtual experiences are readily available and the world's best teachers are virtually available at any moment? Education will mean—even from the age of two—exploring worlds of interest with intelligent guides available to answer your questions and pose new ones. World upon world will open to the child who is curious. Education in such a society will be a matter of what virtual (and later real) worlds you have entered and how much you have learned to do in those worlds.

To Fadiman's remark quoted above, I responded that minds would not be less well educated, just differently educated. In the world of Clifton Fadiman, an educated mind was one that had been trained at Harvard (or its equivalent) and was conversant with the major ideas in Western thought. His idea of education did not include, for example, being able to program in Java, or understanding the basics of neuroscience. In fifty years, there will still be Harvard, but the value of its *imprimatur* will have been altered tremendously.

Education in its deepest sense has always been about doing, rather than about knowing. Many scholars throughout the years have pointed this out, from Aristotle ("For the things we have to learn before we can do them, we learn by doing them") to Galileo ("You cannot teach a man anything; you can only help him discover it within himself") to A. S. Neill ("I hear and I forget; I see and I remember; I do and I understand") to Einstein ("The only source of knowledge is experience"). Nevertheless, schools have ignored this wisdom and chosen—in the words of John Dewey—to "teach by pouring in."

The virtual schools that will arise to take the place of current institutions will attract students less because of the credentials they bestow than because of the experiences they offer. Since these experiences will be there for the taking when a learner decides to learn, most students will start college long before the age of eighteen. Success in various virtual experiences will encourage us to encounter new ones, much as video games do today. Certifying agencies will worry more about what you can do—what virtual merit badges you have achieved—than what courses you have taken.

Fields of endeavor will create experiences in those fields. Instead of Harvard or Columbia offering courses in physics, physicists from around the world will work with virtual-educational-world designers who will build software to create physics experiences. Those experiences will be available to everyone. The old idea that the smartest people were those who received the best grades from schools that tested them to see how well they had learned the lessons will morph into a notion that the smartest students are the ones who pose questions for the software that have to be sent to humans in order to be answered. Intelligence will mean the ability to reach the limits of an educational experience.

Will we collectively be smarter as a society because of all these innovations? In terms of raw capacity for thought, people are as smart now as they ever were or ever will be. But a brilliant cave dweller who had available to him limited knowledge of the world and limited wisdom from the ages, could work only within the *parameters* of the tools he knew. He may have understood the nature of humans and their institutions as well as the Greeks who followed him. But in any absolute sense he wasn't too smart, because there was so much that he hadn't experienced.

Each generation improves on the experiences it opens up to the next. But a leap of tremendous proportions is coming in the next generation. The fact that we still have teachers and classrooms and textbooks will be almost laughable in fifty years. People will look back at us and ask why it took so long for us to change our notions of education, why we thought SAT scores mattered, or why we thought memorizing answers was a mark of intelligence in any way. The notion that education is about indoctrination by the state—an idea boldly stated in the 1700s and little acknowledged today—will seem scary. The governmental control of information—still popular in some countries and still possible in those countries without computer access—will become an archaic notion. Too much experience will be available too readily and too cheaply to prevent anyone from experiencing anything. Governments will have to give up even imagining that they are in the education business, an area they dominate today, and will be unable to control the broad distribution of virtual experiences in much the way that they are failing to control television and computer access in country after country today.

We will begin to understand in the next fifty years that experience and one's ability to extend its range is the ultimate measure of intelligence and the ultimate expression of freedom. The creation of virtual experience will become a major industry; our homes will be dominated by virtual experiences; our schools will have been replaced by them. What we see today in video games and science fiction movies will become our reality. Today, games like EverQuest attract hundreds of thousands of players, who inhabit virtual worlds in an effort to gain status, form relationships, and acquire various virtual objects. These games are so real to the participants that the virtual objects they employ are for sale (for hefty prices) on online auction sites. Some players of these games have a social life entirely based upon them. In the future, these worlds will become much more sophisticated and even more intertwined with the real world.

It is what we can do, not what we know, that will matter in an educational system based on realistic performance environments. The important intellectual issues will revolve around questions arising from the nature of students' interactions in the virtual educational world.

When educational environments demand questions, ask how questions were obtained, and demand to know the experiences that brought on those questions, then the profound change that computers offer will have been realized. We will all be smarter—a great deal smarter—in the sense that we will not be afraid of new experiences. We will know how to find those experiences and will grow from them. Our minds will be differently educated and our intellectual world will be dominated neither by humanists nor by scientists but by experientialists, those who have been there and have become curious as a result.

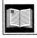 ## Vocabulary

As you think about this essay, these definitions may be helpful to you:
1. **octogenarians**   persons whose age is in the eighties
2. **ex temporare**   extemporaneous
3. **erudition**   extensive knowledge acquired chiefly from books
4. **regimen**   a regular course of action
5. **imprimatur**   a Latin word meaning "let it be printed"; official approval
6. **parameters**   boundaries

 ## Discussion Questions

1. What is the difference between intelligence and knowledge? According to the author, how will our ideas about intelligence and education change in the next 50 years?
2. What does Schank mean when he talks about hearing "an instantaneous response from the walls—enhanced by a great deal of technology from the walls, of course"?
3. Do you agree with Fadiman that all the great thoughts and ideas have already been thought and written down? Why or why not?

4. Schank says school has become a regimen for learning answers rather than learning to inquire. Why does he think that good questions will be valued over answers in the future? Do you agree? Why or Why not?
5. Explain Schank's claim that the smartest students in the future will be those "who pose questions for the software that have to be sent to humans in order to be answered."
6. Is Schank correct when he says that future "governments will have to give up even imagining that they are in the education business"?

 ## Suggestions for Your Journal

Imagine yourself in 50 years, taking part in an educational experience "from the wall" as the author describes it. What area would you be curious about? What are some questions about this topic you would pose for the wall to answer?

How would you feel about conversing with virtual experts in this fashion? Or conversing virtually with others who have the same interest in the topic you do? Would you prefer this method of learning to society's current way of teaching and learning? If so, why? If not, why?

Unit Summary

The writers in this unit describe the learning process from many different perspectives. Because learning is the central mission of the college experience, understanding learning is essential to college success. The readings in this unit have offered an overview of different learning approaches from which every student can benefit.

Summary Questions

1. What specific approaches to learning do the readings in this unit describe? Which ones would you like to experience in more depth? Why?
2. What tasks or strategies described in the readings could you adopt to improve the learning skills needed in your academic work?
3. What implications for your own lifelong learning are suggested in these readings?

Suggested Writing Assignments

1. Write a brief essay describing the advantages and disadvantages of distance learning.
2. Select one reading in this unit and write about how your personal experience has been the same as or different from what the writer describes.
3. Has the use of the Internet influenced how you learn? If so, in what ways?

Suggested Readings

Brown, Neil, and Stuart Keeley. *Asking the Right Questions: A Guide to Critical Thinking.* Upper Saddle River, NJ: Prentice Hall, 2001.

Donald, Janet. *Learning to Think: Disciplinary Perspectives.* San Francisco: Jossey-Bass, 2002.

Goleman, Daniel. *Working with Emotional Intelligence.* New York: Bantam Books, 1998.

Unit 5

What About Technology?

Higher education is in transition, and technology is a major force driving the change. Some colleges are expanding beyond their traditional buildings and campuses into cyberspace in order to reach out to students who want or need to study in nontraditional ways. Technology will not replace colleges, but it is already affecting how we learn. In the next decades, many new information technologies will emerge. As a result, students will experience new and exciting methods of teaching and learning.

As you begin your college experience, you will witness many of these changes. How you adapt to and learn about technology in college will affect how well you later adapt and learn in the workplace. Information technology is changing the nature of jobs and how workers do those jobs. It is projected that by 2010, 90 percent of all workers will be affected.

This unit touches on some interesting facts, applications, and opinions about technology and the influence it has on our lives. Starting with a

The information revolution has changed people's perception of wealth. We originally said that land was wealth. Then we thought it was industrial production. Now we realize it is intellectual capital.

—WALTER WRISTON, FORMER CEO OF CITICORP

comparison between imaginary classes—one at the University of Bologna in 1349 and a second taught via distance learning from a yacht off Vancouver Island in 2003—A. W. Bates and Gary Poole sketch some foreseeable challenges of new educational technology. Steven McDonald deals with practical implications—especially your legal rights and responsibilities—of using the Internet. Rena Palloff and Keith Pratt discuss the characteristics of a successful online student. Ellen Goodman describes her foray into the new technological age by recounting her past experience with old systems. She points out how, much to her sorrow, new technology is changing the way we communicate, or fail to communicate, with each other. Finally, Michael Dertouzos anticipates and explains the need for future technologies to be "human-centric."

The Challenge of Technology

A.W. Bates and Gary Poole

A. W. Bates is director of distance education and technology in the Department of Continuing Studies at the University of British Columbia in Vancouver. Gary Poole is director of the Centre for Teaching and Academic Growth at the University of British Columbia. This reading is from their book *Effective Teaching with Technology in Higher Education,* published in 2003.

Imagine the medieval city of Bologna in 1349. At the university, Professor Ricardus Angelicus is giving a lecture on the differences between the four epistles in the Christian Bible's New Testament, drawing especially on the work of St. Augustine and Thomas Aquinas. The lecture is entirely in Latin. He depends very heavily on the manuscripts collected by the library of the University of Bologna.

Indeed, the session is called a *lecture,* which stems from the Latin word for a "reading," because it is mainly based on readings in Latin from ancient handwritten manuscripts. The philosophical position underpinning the teaching methodology is scholasticism, "training the students to consider a text according to certain pre-established officially approved criteria which are painstakingly and painfully drilled into them" (Manguel 117).

The professor is moving on to the University of Paris at the end of the semester, then will return to his position as a senior administrator in the Vatican in Rome. Later he becomes Bishop of Chichester in England.

There are nine students in the class, and they come from many parts of Europe. They pay a fee directly to the professor. Most are younger sons of nobility or high-ranking clergy, although one or two may also be sons of wealthy merchants. Most are destined for careers in the church or law.

Students are given oral examinations by the professor. The examination contains mainly factual questions around interpretations of the Bible. There is a heavy emphasis on memorization and *rote* learning, as many of the manuscripts are unique or very rare. Also the Roman Catholic Church is anxious that religious texts are interpreted "correctly."

Now let's switch to a small yacht just off the coast of Vancouver Island in Canada in 2003. Roger Boshier, a professor at the University of British Columbia, is online to graduate students in the Masters of Educational Technology program being offered jointly with Tec de Monterrey in Mexico. He is discussing with his students in an online forum the impact of globalization and information technology on national cultures. Roger has been directed to an online article by one of the Australian students and is commenting on it. The session is in English but includes several students from Latin America. An instructor from Tec de Monterrey is offering a similar online discussion forum at the same time in Spanish. Students who are bilingual often switch between the two forums.

The philosophical position underpinning the teaching methodology is *constructivism,* whereby students are encouraged to construct their own meaning through discussion and reflection.

Roger has to return to Vancouver the next day, as he also teaches several on-campus courses, although most of these also have an online component. He will be taking a *sabbatical* next year in New Zealand but plans to continue to teach the Masters in Educational Technology course while away.

He has twenty students in his seminar group, and they are from all over the world. Most are working professionals: teachers in secondary schools or instructors in universities and colleges. Most already have a graduate degree but are taking this program because of the rapid changes occurring in the field. . . .

Which of these two *scenarios* matches most closely your own learning experiences at your university or college? Which of these scenarios would most suit your comfort level (assuming you know Latin)? If Rip van Winkle awoke from his sleep of eight hundred years, would he feel out of place in your typical university or college class?

Our point is not that universities today are old-fashioned. Much has changed and more is changing. We are not suggesting either that newer is better. Does the "modern" scenario challenge the basic values and tenets of higher education? We don't think so. But the two scenarios do indicate the close interrelationship between technological development and the practice of teaching in universities.

We deliberately pitched our first scenario just before the invention of the Gutenberg press. The invention of the mechanical printing press was a product of changing times but further became a major influence on change in society. Information technology, and particularly the Internet, is a similar consequence and cause of major change in our society, including how we teach and learn.

We believe that technology has an important place in university and college teaching, but it needs to be used with care and discrimination. The question then is not, Should we use technology? The questions are: In what contexts and for what purposes is technology appropriate for learning and teaching? What do we need to do to ensure that when we use technology for learning and teaching purposes we use it effectively? . . .

Over the last ten years the Internet has become a major influence on a wide range of activities. It is now used for communications (e-mail, World Wide Web), banking, hotel and travel reservations, entertainment, news, and a host of other applications. The Internet is now an essential feature of work, leisure, and study for many people, and its influence is likely to grow as more and more people are able to access the technology on a global basis.

Its impact on education and training has been as great as on any other area. Web sites provide instant access to data from active volcanoes, Web cameras record events as they happen, and Web databases provide access to a multitude of academic resources. More online courses are becoming available.

Students need to learn how to use technology to seek, organize, analyze, and apply information appropriately. It will become increasingly difficult to accept someone as being fully educated if they do not know how to use the Internet to communicate with other professionals, if they do not know how to find Web sites that will provide relevant and reliable information within their field of study, or if they do not know how to develop their own multimedia reports for communicating their knowledge or research. Therefore, we cannot ignore technology in learning and teaching. The best way to help students understand the strengths—and weaknesses—of technology in their field of study is to use it in teaching.

One frequent criticism of the use of technology in teaching is that we are being driven by a technological *imperative:* we have to use technology because of a blind belief that it is good for us. If we don't agree to the use of technology, we will be considered out of date and may lose our credibility.

Those who challenge the technological imperative do so from a variety of perspectives. Some ask, *What is technology doing to our ways of thinking and understanding?* Those who ask this question usually answer that technology weakens our ability to think rationally or logically. Others go further and suggest that the pressure to use technology in education is a conspiracy by multinational companies and big business to sell technology and hook young people forever into being technology consumers.

Some supporters of the use of technology in teaching believe that there are important educational benefits in using technology but recognize the pressure, especially on senior management, to be fashionable and to have the latest "toys," and they lever that pressure to win support for their technology-based teaching initiatives.

Finally, many postsecondary teachers are aware that whereas technology ought to be able to help them in teaching students, their knowledge of technology is often less than that of their students, and in particular they are unsure of how best to use it to achieve their teaching goals.

Those who believe that technology can play a valuable role in teaching and learning, understand the "technological imperative" arguments. They accept that some of these arguments are valid, but believe that they are insufficient for a blanket denial of the use of technology. We recognize that there is a great deal of hyperbole and exaggeration about the benefits of technology in education. There are pressures from the commercial sector to use technologies for teaching that are based on profit, not educational benefits. And without major changes in the way we work, technology will be time-consuming and require an unreasonable amount of dedication to learn new skills.

Nevertheless, such arguments should not blind us to the genuine benefits technology can bring when used wisely. Pressures for change on the university and college from both within and outside require us to look afresh at how students learn and how teaching is organized and delivered if quality is to be maintained or even improved.

Work Cited

Manguel, Alberto. *A History of Reading.* New York: HarperCollins, 1996.
From A. W. Bates and Gary Poole, *Effective Teaching with Technology in Higher Education,* pp. 3–5 and 8–11. Copyright 2003 John Wiley. This material is used by permission of John Wiley and Sons, Inc.

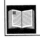 **Vocabulary**

As you think about this essay, these definitions may be helpful to you:
1. **rote**   to learn "by rote" is to learn with the use of memory but little intelligence or understanding.
2. **constructivism**   a philosophy (or system of thinking) in which meaning is not inherent in a word or object but is attached to that word or object ("constructed") by the author or creator
3. **sabbatical**   short for "sabbatical year"; a leave of absence from regular teaching duties, often with pay, granted to professors usually every seventh year, for rest, travel, or research
4. **scenario**   a possible course of action, usually imagined or projected
5. **imperative**   necessary, not to be avoided

 Discussion Questions

1. Compare the two scenarios that these authors use to open their essay. What are the major points of difference? Of similarity?
2. How do Bates and Poole feel about the use of up-to-date technology in college teaching? Do you agree?
3. What benefits do Bates and Poole identify for the use of technology in the classroom?

 Suggestions for Your Journal

It may not be possible for you to imagine yourself back in the University of Bologna in 1349, but try to imagine what it was like to attend school before the advent of the personal computer. If you are 18 or so, talk first with someone old enough to have attended school before, say, 1970. Would you have preferred his or her classroom environment to the one you have now, or do you prefer school in the 21st century?

Have you decided on a future career? For the purpose of your journal, select one and discuss some of the ways that, in your view, college should prepare you for the technological demands of that profession.

Virtual Legality: An Overview of Your Rights and Responsibilities in Cyberspace

Steven J. McDonald

Steven J. McDonald is general counsel for the Rhode Island School of Design. In this essay he discusses legal implications important to those who use the Internet. His focus is especially on college students.

The Internet is a powerful and revolutionary tool for communication— powerful in its ability to reach a global audience and revolutionary in its accessibility to those who formerly were only at the receiving end of mass communications. With access to the Internet, *anyone,* even a preschool child, can now effectively be an international publisher and broadcaster. By posting to Usenet or establishing a Web page, for example, an Internet user can speak to a larger and wider audience than does the *New York Times,* NBC or National Public Radio. Many Internet users, however, do not realize that that is what they are doing.

Not surprisingly, given these facts, the Internet also has a powerful and revolutionary potential for misuse. Such misuse is particularly prevalent on college and university campuses, where free *access* to computing resources is often mistakenly thought to be the equivalent of free *speech,* and where free speech rights are in turn often mistakenly thought to include the right to do whatever is technically possible.

The rights of academic freedom and freedom of expression do apply to the use of college and university computing resources. So, too, however, do the responsibilities and limitations associated with those rights. Thus, legitimate use of institutional computing resources does *not* extend to whatever is technically possible. In addition, while some restrictions are built into the institution's computer operating systems and networks, those restrictions are not the only restrictions on what is permissible. Users of college and university computing resources must abide by all applicable restrictions, whether or not they are built into the operating system or network and whether or not they can be *circumvented* by technical means. Moreover, it is not the responsibility of a college or university to prevent computer users from exceeding those restrictions; rather, it is the computer user's responsibility to know and comply with them. When you're pulled over to the side of the Information Superhighway, "I'm sorry, officer—I didn't realize I was over the speed limit" is not a valid defense.

So just what are the applicable restrictions? The same laws and policies that apply in every other context. "Cyberspace" is not a separate legal jurisdiction, and it is not exempt from the normal requirements of legal and ethical behavior within the college or university community. *A good rule of thumb to keep in mind is that conduct that would be illegal or a violation of institutional policy in the "offline" world will still be illegal or a violation of institutional policy when it occurs online.* Remember, too, that the online world is not limited to your college or university, to the state in which it is located, or even to the United States. *Computer users who engage in electronic communications with persons in other states or countries or on other systems or networks may also be subject to the laws of those other states and countries and the rules and policies of those other systems and networks.*

It is impossible to list and describe every law and policy that applies to the use of college and university computing resources and the Internet—since, by and large, they all do—but the following are some of the ones that most frequently cause problems.

Copyright

Copyright law generally gives authors, artists, composers, and other such creators the exclusive right to copy, distribute, modify, and display their works or to authorize other people to do so. Moreover, their works are protected by copyright law from the very moment that they are created—regardless of whether they are registered with the Copyright Office and regardless of whether they are marked with a copyright notice or symbol (©). That means that virtually every e-mail message, Usenet posting, Web page, or other computer work you have ever created—or seen—is copyrighted. That also means that, if you are not the copyright owner of a particular e-mail message, Usenet posting, Web page, or other computer work, you may not copy, distribute, modify, or display it unless:

- its copyright owner has given you permission to do so, or
- it is in the *"public domain,"* or
- doing so would constitute "fair use," or
- you have an "implied license" to do so.

If none of these exceptions applies, your use of the work constitutes copyright infringement, and you could be liable for as much as $100,000 in damages for each use. In addition, if you reproduce or distribute copies of a copyrighted work having a total retail value of at least $1,000 (which could include, for example, posting a $50 software program on a Web page or newsgroup from which it is downloaded 20 times), your action may also be criminal, even if you do it for free.

It's usually easy to tell whether you have permission to make a particular use of a work: The copyright owner will have told you so expressly, either in writing or orally. However, it is not always so easy to tell whether the work is in the public domain or whether what you want to do constitutes fair use or is covered by an implied license.

Placing a work on the Internet is not the same thing as granting that work to the public domain. Generally speaking, a work found on the Internet, like a work found anywhere else, is in the public domain only if (a) its creator has expressly disclaimed any copyright interest in the work, or (b) it was created by the federal government, or (c) it is very old. Unfortunately, how old a particular work must be to be "in the public domain" depends in part upon when the work was created, in part upon whether and when it was formally published, in part upon whether and when its creator died, and in part on still other factors. Consequently, there is no one specific cutoff date that you can use for all works to determine whether or not they are in the public domain. As a rule of thumb, however, works that were created *and published* before 1923 are now in the public domain. . . . Works that have never been published *might* be in the public domain, but if you don't know for sure, it is best to assume that they are not.

In very general terms, a particular use of a work is considered "fair use" if it involves only a relatively small portion of the work, is for educational or other noncommercial purposes, and is unlikely to interfere with the copyright owner's ability to market the original work. A classic example is quoting a few sentences or paragraphs of a book in a class paper. Other uses may also be fair, but it is almost never fair to use an entire work, and it is not enough that you aren't charging anyone for your particular use. It also is not enough simply to cite your source (though it may be *plagiarism* if you don't).

An implied license may exist if the copyright owner has acted in such a way that it is reasonable for you to assume that you may make a particular use. For example, if you are the moderator of a mailing list and someone sends you a message for that list, it's reasonable to assume that you may post the message to the list, even if its author didn't expressly say that you may do so. The copyright owner can always "revoke" an implied license, however, simply by saying that further use is prohibited.

In addition, facts and ideas cannot be copyrighted. Copyright law protects only the expression of the creator's idea—the specific words or notes or brush-strokes or computer code that the creator used—and not the underlying idea itself. Thus, for example, it is not copyright infringement to state in a history paper that the Declaration of Independence was actually signed on August 2, 1776, or to argue in an English paper that Francis Bacon is the real author of Shakespeare's plays, even though someone else has already done so, as long as you use your own words. (Again, however, if you don't cite your sources, it may still be plagiarism even if you paraphrase.)

Exactly how copyright law applies to the Internet is still not entirely clear, but there are some rules of thumb:

- You *may* look at another person's Web page, even though your computer makes a temporary copy when you do so, but you may not redistribute it or incorporate it into your own Web page without permission, except as fair use may allow.
- You *probably may* quote all or part of another person's Usenet or listserv message in your response to that message, unless the original message says that copying is prohibited.
- You *probably may not* copy and redistribute a private e-mail message you have received without the author's permission, except as fair use may allow.

- You *probably may* print out a single copy of a Web page or of a Usenet, list-serv, or private e-mail message for your own, personal, noncommercial use.
- You *may not* post another person's book, article, graphic, image, music, or other such material on your Web page or use them in your Usenet, list-serv, or private e-mail messages without permission, except as fair use may allow.
- You *may not* download materials from Lexis-Nexis, the Clarinet news service, or other such services and copy or redistribute them without permission, unless the applicable license agreement expressly permits you to do so or unless your particular use would constitute fair use.
- You *may not* copy or redistribute software without permission, unless the applicable license agreement expressly permits you to do so.

Libel

Libel is the "publication" of a false statement of fact that harms another person's reputation. For example, it is libel to say that "John beat up his roommate" or "Mary is a thief" if these statements are not true. If a statement doesn't harm the other person's reputation—for example, "Joe got an 'A' on the test"—it is not libel even if it's false. In addition, a statement of pure opinion—for example, "I don't like John"—cannot be libelous. But you cannot turn a statement of fact into an opinion simply by adding "I think" or "in my opinion" to it. "IMHO [In my honest opinion], John beat up his roommate" is still libelous if John didn't beat up his roommate. If you honestly believed that what you said was true, however, you *might* not be liable if it later turns out that you were wrong.

A libel is "published" whenever it is communicated to a third person. In other words, if you say "Mary is a thief" to anyone other than Mary, you have "published" that libel. That means that almost anything you post or send on the Internet, except an e-mail that you send *only to the person about whom you are talking,* is "published" for purposes of libel law.

A person who has been libeled can sue for whatever damages are caused by the publication of the libel. Since a libel on the Internet could potentially reach millions of people, the damages could be quite large.

A good rule of thumb to follow: If you would be upset if someone else made the same statement about you, think carefully before you send or post that statement to the Internet, because it might be libelous.

Invasion of Privacy

There are a number of different laws that protect the "right to privacy" in a number of different ways. For example, under the Electronic Communications Privacy Act, which is a federal statute, it generally is a crime to intercept someone else's private e-mail message or to look into someone else's private computer account without appropriate authorization. The fact that you may have the technical ability to do so, or that the other person may not have properly safeguarded his or her account, does not mean that you have authorization. If you don't know for sure whether you have authorization, you probably don't.

Invasion of privacy, like libel, is also a *"tort,"* which means that you can also be sued for monetary damages. In addition to the sorts of things prohibited by the Electronic Communications Privacy Act, it can be an invasion of privacy to disclose intensely personal information about another person that that person has chosen not to make public and that the public has no legitimate need or reason to know: for example, the fact that someone has AIDS, if he or she has not revealed that information publicly. Unlike with libel, a statement can be an invasion of privacy even if it is true.

Obscenity, Child Pornography, and "Indecency"

Under both state and federal law, it is a crime to publish, sell, distribute, display, or, in some cases, merely possess obscene materials or child pornography. These laws also apply equally to the Internet, and a number of people have been prosecuted and convicted for violating them in that context.

The line between what is obscene and what is not is hard to draw with any precision—as one Supreme Court Justice said, "I could never succeed in intelligibly" defining obscenity, "[b]ut I know it when I see it"—but the term basically means hardcore pornography that has no literary, artistic, political, or other socially redeeming value. One reason that it is so hard to define obscenity is that it depends in part on local community standards; what is considered obscene in one community may not be considered obscene in another. That makes it particularly difficult to determine whether materials on the Internet are obscene, since such materials are, in a sense, everywhere, and it is therefore not enough that the materials are legal wherever you are. In one case, the operators of a bulletin board service in California posted materials that were not considered obscene there, but [they] were convicted of violating the obscenity statutes in Tennessee when the materials were downloaded there.

Child pornography is the visual depiction of minors engaged in sexually explicit activity. Unlike obscenity, child pornography is illegal regardless of whether it has any literary, artistic, political, or other socially redeeming value.

Sexually oriented materials that do not constitute either obscenity or child pornography generally are legal. Still, it is illegal in most cases to provide such materials to minors, and displaying or sending such materials to people who do not wish to see them may be a violation of your college or university's sexual harassment policy.

"Hacking," "Cracking," and Similar Activities

Under the federal Computer Fraud and Abuse Act, and under a variety of similar other state and federal statutes, it can also be a crime to access or use a computer without authorization, to alter data in a computer without authorization, to transmit computer viruses and "worms" over computer networks, to conduct "e-mail bombing," and to engage in other such activities. Engaging in such activities can also make you liable for monetary damages to any person who is harmed by your activities. Again, the fact that you may have the technical ability to do any of these things, or that another computer owner may not have properly safeguarded his or her computer, does not mean that you have authorization. If you don't know for sure whether you have authorization, you probably don't.

Institutional Policies

Use of college and university computing resources is also normally subject to the institution's rules and regulations—for example, its code of student conduct, policy on academic misconduct, sexual harassment policy, and all other generally applicable institutional policies. In addition, institutional computer use policies often contain the following types of additional, specific prohibitions:

- Institutional computer accounts and passwords may not, under any circumstances, be shared with, or used by, persons other than those to whom they have been assigned by the institution—even family and friends. Users are responsible for all use of their accounts.
- Users must limit their use of institutional computing resources so as not to consume an unreasonable amount of those resources or to interfere with the activity of other users.
- Institutional computing resources are intended for institution-related use and therefore may not be used for personal commercial or business purposes or for other personal gain. Personal use of institutional computing resources for *other* purposes may be permitted when it does not consume a significant amount of those resources, does not interfere with the performance of the user's job or other institutional responsibilities, and is otherwise in compliance with institutional policies.
- Users of institutional computing resources may not state or imply that they are speaking on behalf of the institution and may not use institutional trademarks and logos in connection with their use of those resources without specific authorization to do so.

For Further Information

If you have questions about the legality of your specific use of institutional computing resources, it is best to ask before proceeding. *The resolution of specific legal issues requires an analysis of all the facts and circumstances; the general guidelines in this document do not constitute, and should not be relied upon as, specific legal advice.* You may be able to get general advice (but, again, not specific legal advice) from your academic advisor, from computer lab site managers, or from your institution's computer help desk.

In addition, you can find more information on these and related topics at the following Web sites:

- "Cyberspace Law for Non-Lawyers," which is located at:
  http://www.ssrn.com/update/Isn/cyberspace/lessons.html
- "10 Big Myths About Copyright Explained," which is located at:
  http://www.clari.net/brad/copymyths.html

Reprinted by permission of The Ohio State University Office of Legal Affairs.

 Vocabulary

As you think about this essay, these definitions may be helpful to you:
1. **circumvent**   to get around, evade
2. **public domain**   the legal realm embracing property that belongs to the community at large
3. **plagiarism**   to steal or pass off words or ideas of another as one's own
4. **libel**   defamation of a person by written or presentational means
5. **tort**   a wrongful act that may lead to legal action

 Discussion Questions

1. Why, according to the author, does the Internet have such potential for misuse?
2. How does the author suggest you can judge what is legal or illegal in cyberspace?
3. How do copyright laws affect the Internet?
4. Why is your online "right to privacy" so important?
5. Why are "hacking," "cracking," and similar activities illegal?

 Suggestions for Your Journal

As you think about the legal questions involved in using the Internet, two major issues should be your privacy and your safety as an individual. What steps can you take to protect yourself against identity theft? What practices should you follow consistently in order to be safe from persons who want to take advantage of you in cyberspace?

Who Is the Virtual Student?

Rena M. Palloff and Keith Pratt

Rena M. Palloff and Keith Pratt are faculty members at Capella University, which is an accredited online university. They teach in the School of Education there and have written several books together, including *Building Learning Communities in Cyberspace, Lessons from the Cyberspace Classroom,* and *The Virtual Student,* from which this excerpt is taken.

There is an ongoing debate in the academic world about who is attracted to online learning. It has been assumed that it is predominantly adult learners who take online courses because online learning allows them to continue working full time and attend to their family obligations through the delivery of anytime, anywhere education. The "typical" online student is generally described as being over twenty-five years of age, employed, a caregiver, with some higher education already attained, and equally likely to be either male or female.[1] Recent statistics published by the National Center for Education Statistics (2002) indicate that interest and enrollment in online courses spans all age groups. As of December 31, 1999, 65 percent of those age eighteen or younger had enrolled in an online course, indicating the increasing popularity of virtual high school courses. Fifty-seven percent of those considered to be traditional undergraduates, ages nineteen to twenty-three, had enrolled. Those ages twenty-four to twenty-nine enrolled at a rate of 56 percent, and those thirty and older enrolled at a rate of 63 percent.

Many administrators have embraced online distance learning because they believe it represents a means by which to recruit adult students living some distance away from their campuses. The statistics cited, however, are an indicator that, increasingly, as institutions offer online courses, they attract traditional undergraduates in residence on campus and not the geographically dispersed students administrators anticipated.[2] In addition, with the success of virtual high school programs across the United States, increasing numbers of high school students are making decisions about where they will go to college based on how "wired" the institution is and how many online course offerings it has in its curriculum. High school students who have experienced online learning want to be able to continue to learn this way in college.

It would seem obvious that when students are satisfied with their online courses and programs, they are more likely to be successful and to stick with them. The National Center for Education Statistics (2002) reports that undergraduates who

---

[1] S. D. Gilbert, *How to be a Successful Online Student* (New York: McGraw-Hill, 2001), p. 74.

[2] R. Phipps and J. Merisotis, *What's the Difference?* (Washington, D.C.: Institute for Higher Education Policy, April 1999).

participated in distance learning courses were more satisfied with those courses over face-to-face options 22.7 percent of the time. Forty-seven percent reported liking both distance learning courses and face-to-face courses about the same, and 30 percent were less satisfied with distance learning options.

Student retention in online courses has become a significant issue for administrators as they come to realize that these courses and programs are not inexpensive to create and run. Hardware and software are expensive, as are training, support and faculty pay for course development and delivery. Studies have noted that the very elements that draw students to online classes—convenience in a busy work schedule, ability to continue to attend to family demands—are the elements that interfere with their ability to remain enrolled.[3] Online courses and programs are simply not for everyone. The Illinois Online Network has published a list of qualities that taken together create the profile of the successful virtual student.

Clearly, first and foremost, in order to work virtually, the student needs to have *access to a computer and a modem or high-speed connection and the skills to use them.* Many institutions now publish minimum technology requirements in order for students to complete their online courses. The virtual student needs at least to meet the minimum requirements, if not exceed them, in order to participate online. This is particularly true as we begin to push the limits of *bandwidth* to include elements such as *streaming audio and video.* However, it is important to remember that not all students have access to high-speed connections and are thus less able to access and download streaming media and large graphic files. Furthermore, some students—particularly working adults—may be attempting to access their courses from work and may encounter difficulties with security measures such as *firewalls.* They also have to contend with issues of privacy and confidentiality, conflicts with work time, and copyright and *intellectual property* as they apply to their workplaces.

We recently conducted an online course where this was the case. One student kept sending us e-mails telling us that she could not access the course site. We went through our usual troubleshooting measures with her, asking about the browser she was using and if she had a high-speed connection, and made sure she was typing the correct URL for the course as well as entering her user name and password correctly. It was not until she successfully accessed the course from her home computer that we realized the problem was the firewall installed on the server at her workplace. Luckily, her employer was sympathetic to her needs and was willing to open the firewall to allow her access to her course. However, had she not attempted access from home, we might not have been able to diagnose the problem.

Successful virtual students are *open minded* about sharing personal *details* about their lives, work, and other educational experiences. This is particularly important when we ask online learners to enter into learning communities in

---

[3] S. Carr, "As Distance Learning Comes of Age, the Challenge Is Keeping the Students," *Chronicle of Higher Education,* February 11, 2000.

order to explore course material. Virtual students are able to use their experiences in the learning process and also are able to apply their learning in an ongoing way to their life experiences.

The virtual student is *not hindered by the absence of auditory or visual cues* in the communication process. In fact, he or she may be freed up by the lack of visual barriers that can hinder face-to-face communication. In addition, virtual students feel comfortable expressing themselves and contributing to a discussion through largely text-based means. This does not mean that the virtual student must possess exceptional writing skills to begin online study. Some instructors have found that writing skills improve with ongoing participation in online courses.[4]

Similarly, the virtual student is *self-motivated and self-disciplined*. "With the freedom and flexibility of the online environment comes responsibility. The online process takes a real commitment and discipline to keep up with the flow of the process" (Illinois Online Network, 2002). The virtual student also has the responsibility to communicate to the instructor and others if problems arise. Unlike the face-to-face classroom where the instructor is able to quickly identify who may be having trouble with the course, the signs of a student in trouble online are different but equally obvious.

Virtual students are *willing to commit a significant amount of time to their studies weekly* and do not see the course as the "softer, easier way" to earn credits or a degree. In so doing, they commit to themselves and to the group that they will participate according to the guidelines set out by the instructor or institution. They recognize that if they do not, they are not only minimizing their own chances for success but also limiting the ability of their classmates to get the greatest benefit from the course. Thus, the virtual student is one who *can and does work collaboratively* with fellow learners in order to achieve his or her own learning objectives as well as the objectives set forth in the course.

Virtual students are or can be developed into *critical thinkers*. They recognize that the instructor acts as a facilitator of the online learning process and that in order to have the best online learning experience, they must take charge of that process themselves. This is an "aha" moment that virtual students are bound to have once they embark on the journey of online learning. Engaging in Internet research or following the trail that another student has suggested for supplementing the material in the course helps the student to see that knowledge creation occurs mutually and collaboratively online, leading to increasing critical thinking abilities.

Brookfield notes that ". . . critical thinking is complex and frequently perplexing since it requires the suspension of belief and the jettisoning of assump-

---

[4] P. W. Peterson, "The Debate About Online Learning: Key Issues for Writing Teachers," *Computers and Composition*, 18, no. 4 (2001), pp. 359–370.

tions previously accepted without question. As people strive for clarity in self-understanding, and as they try to change aspects of their lives, the opportunity to discuss these activities is enormously helpful."[5] But it is the student who recognizes—through reflection on the learning that emerges from those activities—that his or her knowledge base and ability to reflect critically is increasing.

The *ability to reflect* is another critical quality for the successful virtual student. Online learning is a transformative experience. The ability to read, reflect, and then respond opens the door to transformative learning; in other words, the student's perspective on what is being studied is transformed.[6] Reflection often takes the form not only of processing the information presented but also exploring the meaning that the material has for the student's life, the changes that may need to be made to accommodate this new learning. It also means questioning where the ideas come from and how they were constructed. Furthermore, in the online classroom, the sharing of reflections transforms not only the individual learner but the group and the instructor as well.

Finally, and probably most importantly, the virtual student *believes that high-quality learning can happen anywhere and anytime, not just in the face-to-face classroom.* He or she does not feel the need to see and hear classmates or instructors in order to learn from them and feels comfortable working in a relatively unstructured setting.

From *The Virtual Student: A Profile and Guide to Working with Online Learners* (San Francisco: Jossey-Bass, 2003) pp. 3–8.

[5] S. D. Brookfield, *Developing Critical Thinkers* (San Francisco: Jossey-Bass, 1987), p. 10.

[6] J. Mezirow, *Fostering Critical Reflection in Adulthood* (San Francisco: Jossey-Bass, 1990).

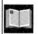 **Vocabulary**

As you think about this essay, these definitions may be helpful to you:

1. **Bandwidth, streaming audio and video, firewalls**   These are terms developed to name features of computer-related technology. Bandwidth relates to the amount of data that can be transmitted in a specified amount of time. Streaming technologies like streaming audio and video depend on having techniques for transferring data so that they can be processed as a steady and continuous stream. A firewall is any system devised to prevent unauthorized access to or from a private network. These definitions and many others related to computer technology are available at Webopedia, a free site on the Internet.

2. **intellectual property**   This concept relates to the notion that just as physical objects can be considered property that belongs to someone, so the product of ideas and creativity can be thought of as intellectual property. For more about this notion, go to the essay "Ideas as Property" by Thomas L. Minnick, pages 170–174 in this book.

Discussion Questions

1. What are the characteristics of a good, or effective, learner in the face-to-face classroom? How many of these characteristics are the same as those listed for a good online learner?
2. Have you ever taken a class online? Characterize that experience by comparing it to some of the good face-to-face classes you have had.
3. In your experience, what are the characteristics of a good online instructor? How might they differ from the characteristics of a good teacher in the face-to-face classroom?
4. What are the advantages and disadvantages of online classes from your current personal perspective? Would you like to attend *all* your course work online?

 Suggestions for Your Journal

How much time do you spend using your computer? Take special note for a few days by maintaining a log of your computer activity. When do you log on? What are your favorite sites? How much time do you spend in each of the following activities: reading the news, blogging (see Webopedia if you need a definition), playing games, talking in chat rooms, and other activities? After you have collected at least several days of data, summarize them (amount of total time, percent in leisure, percent in learning—or whatever categories you choose) and comment about your computer use. Does anything in your study surprise you?

Discuss the dangers of enrolling in an online class. What are they and how might you avoid them? For example, teachers find that the Internet has greatly affected the way students do research—both for better and for worse.

Technology Eliminating Conversation

Ellen Goodman

Ellen Goodman, a columnist whose essays regularly appear in more than 200 newspapers across the country, began her journalistic career as a reporter for *Newsweek* and the *Detroit Free Press*, then joined the *Boston Globe*. She has won a Pulitzer Prize for distinguished commentary and is the author of several books. In this essay she describes her initiation into new telephone technology and how it has affected face-to-face conversation.

We are at lunch when my friend leans over the table to share his latest encounter with telephone technology.

It all began with a voice mail message, which wasn't in itself so startling. But my friend was at his desk when the phone didn't ring. A colleague, it seems, had learned how to dial directly into voice mail—avoiding the middleman, or middle ear, entirely.

Was my friend, a man who *parses* moral dilemmas for a living, insulted that this caller didn't want to speak to the real, live and available him? Were either of us aghast at some new techno-wrinkle of rudeness? Appalled by the state of the art of message-dropping?

No, we were delighted, curious, envious. How on Earth did he do that?

I am old enough to remember black rotary phones, the Model T of this technology. I remember when the telephone was a beloved instrument of conversation. Furthermore, I was raised to believe in courtesy as one of the cardinal virtues.

But we are in the middle of a communications revolution that feels increasingly like guerrilla warfare. Everywhere you turn in this revolution, machines are pointed at you. Today, anyone near a phone can end up feeling like the target of snipers.

Half a dozen years ago when I read that Martha Stewart had something like six or seven voice mail numbers, I was bug-eyed in astonishment. Now I have three voice mails, three e-mails, three fax machines all collecting messages in assorted buildings that are nowhere nearly as well decorated as Martha's, but you get the point.

To understand how the world has changed, think back to the warm and fuzzy telephone ads that once encouraged us to reach out and touch someone. Compare that to my favorite telephone ad of this season. It features Paul Revere in his full midnight ride *regalia* trying to reach John Adams, who is of course screening his calls: "John, John, this is Paul. Pick up. It's important."

In this revolutionary atmosphere, it isn't a new communications weapon that is lusted over by patriots seeking their personal freedom. It's an anti-communications weapon.

We want technology that enhances our ability to not talk to people. We want a personal Star Wars defense system to screen and shoot down, avert and disarm the incoming missives. We long for the ability to be out of touch.

This has created a whole new etiquette called "etiquette be damned." The dirty little secret of corporate America is the number of people for whom phone tag is actually dodgeball. All over the various midtowns of our country, people wait to return calls until they are pretty sure the other person is at lunch. Who hasn't picked up a phone to have a startled caller exhale: "Oh, I just wanted to leave a message"?

Of course, the invasion of the dinner snatchers has created an additional wrinkle. People who know the words to "Solidarity Forever" and are generally sympathetic to the plight of the new working class now greet marketing callers by snarling, "Why don't you give me your home number since you have mine?"

This is now leading to a high-tech arms race, a kind of mutually assured destruction. First you pay to put a phone in your house-office-car. Now you can also pay to keep the calls out.

Just last month, Ameritech announced a service to let customers reject the sort of unwanted telephone calls that come from telemarketers. "Customers are screaming for this," said the company's chief executive officer.

We are also "screaming" for what I would call, in *oxymoronic* fashion, one-way conversations. The linguistic types call this *asynchronous* talk. In that sense the phone is becoming more and more like e-mail. One person leaves a message for the other who leaves a message—look ma, no hands. It's like playing virtual tennis.

But such is the reality of modern life. All the advances have *ratcheted* up the number of "exchanges" we're expected to make until our own circuits are overloaded. Efficiency trumps courtesy. We don't just talk, we use the phone as a drop-off center.

Remember Alexander Graham Bell's first words over the newfangled phone? "Mr. Watson, come here, I want you." What would he say today? "Watson old boy, when you get a minute, have your voice mail call my voice mail."

© 2000 Washington Post Writers Group. Reprinted with permission.

 Vocabulary

As you think about this essay, these definitions may be helpful to you:

1. **parses**   resolves component parts of speech and describes them grammatically; analyzes closely
2. **regalia**   special dress, generally very formal, like an admiral's best uniform or a priest's robes for conducting a high mass
3. **oxymoron**   a figure of speech that combines apparently contradictory or incongruous ideas

4. **asynchronous**   happening at different times
5. **ratcheted**   changed by stages

 ## Discussion Questions

1. How does Ellen Goodman compare her current involvement with technology with her past experiences?
2. What is the "new etiquette" associated with increased telephone technology, according to the author?
3. What does the author mean by "efficiency trumps courtesy"?

 ## Suggestions for Your Journal

Do you make or receive telephone calls when you are driving? Do you notice when other drivers are on the phone? How have such calls changed the quality of your conversations? The use of cellular phones while driving is highly controversial. In many places it is illegal. Take a stand for or against making such telephone activity illegal in the town where you now reside.

Human-Centric Issues in the Information Marketplace

Michael L. Dertouzos

The late Michael Dertouzos was the author of eight books, including *The Unfinished Revolution: Human-Centered Computers and What They Can Do for Us,* from which this essay is taken. Dertouzos joined the MIT faculty in 1964 and became director of the MIT Laboratory for Computer Science in 1974. Under his leadership, it became one of the largest research labs at MIT, with 400 faculty members, graduate students, and research staff. Dertouzos introduced the concept of human-centered computing and, as this essay shows, had a special talent for putting complicated technology into human terms and making it accessible to nontechnical audiences. "We made a big mistake 300 years ago when we separated technology and humanism," Dertouzos said in an interview in *Scientific American.* "It's time to put the two back together."

B y 2010, over a billion people and their computers, along with some 100 billion appliances, will be interconnected. What will they all do? They will buy, sell, and freely exchange information and information services.

Make no mistake: The sharing of information and e-commerce over today's Internet is only the tip of the Information Marketplace iceberg. Take, for example, the "content" that the press and Wall Street were hyperventilating about throughout the late 1990s, in the wake of proposed megamergers like that between America Online and Time Warner. All the content you can imagine—TV, movies, theater, radio, newspapers, magazines, books—accounts for less than 5 percent of the world's industrial economy. On the other hand, a whopping 50 percent of that economy—some $10 trillion—is office work, or, as it used to be called, white-collar work. This includes buy and sell transactions, reviewing mortgage applications, processing insurance forms, dealing with medical information, filling and reviewing millions of government forms, teaching and learning, selling customer services, and a myriad of business-to-business services. That's information work—the processing of information by skilled humans, and secondarily by machines, and the delivery of that work where and when it is needed. This is barely happening over the Internet today, so no one talks about it. But it will be everywhere on tomorrow's Information Marketplace. Human-centric computing must make it easy for people to offer their work across space and time if the Information Marketplace is to reach its full potential.

By 2020, and by my reckoning, some $4 trillion of this information work will flow over the Information Marketplace, shaking up the distribution of labor. Just imagine what 50 million Indians could do to the English-speaking industrial world using their ability to read and write English and offer their office skills, at a distance, for about one-third of what the West pays today. Such a move would have colossal economic consequences, in the redistribution of work, internationally. It would also mark a *poetic comeback* for India, which may then be in a position to exert economic power on a nation like England that taught the Indians English to dominate them. As much as information work will flow from poor to rich, even more will flow from rich to rich—services that will be increasingly delivered via the Net because of speed and convenience. By the time this activity and the electronic commerce in goods level out, the "buy-and-sell" part of the Information Marketplace will grow from some $200 billion in 2000 to some $5 trillion annually, roughly one-fourth of the world industrial economy.

The "free exchange" part of the Information Marketplace will be just as important, because people have as much free time as work time, and they value what they do with it just as much. Already the lives of many people are affected through family e-mail; collaboration, playing, and dating; entertainment through downloading and listening to music and viewing images and videos; accessing information of personal interest; engaging in discussions about litera-ture, hobbies, and social issues; publishing their views; and much more. These uses will grow. When I speak publicly, I always ask those people in the audience who use e-mail to communicate with family members to raise their hands. The ratio, largely invisible in 1995, was consistently over 90 percent in 2000. Many new activities will arise as well that we can't predict today.

Taken together, the monetary and nonmonetary activities of the Information Marketplace, driven by the onrush of faster computers and communications, computerized appliances, mobile gadgets, and portable software, will propel us toward a world overflowing with information and information-related activities. The question is, "How can we build this world so we are ensured of doing more by doing less?" rather than drowning in information overload and computer complexity. Only by throwing out last century's model for computing and adopting—indeed, demanding—a new computing philosophy, a new master plan, that lets people interact naturally, easily, and purposefully with each other and the surrounding physical world.

Human-centric computing will transform today's individual computers, the Internet, and the Web into a true Information Marketplace, where we'll buy, sell, and freely exchange information and information services using systems that will talk with us, do things for us, get the information we want, help us work with other people, and adapt to our individual needs. Indeed, it is these five basic capabilities of computer and communications systems that are the pivotal forces of human-centric computing.

As builders of computer systems start turning these forces into useful tech-nologies, the rest of us who are collectively frustrated by today's computers can accelerate the process by tirelessly repeating the rallying cry of human-centric computing: "Information technology should help people do more by doing less!" If we shout loud enough, *entrepreneurial* companies will make this request their goal. They will recognize the huge, pent-up demand for human-centric sys-tems, and will build them, upstaging the massive computer-communications establishment and shifting the market in their direction.

   Much as we like to tout it, the Information Revolution is not yet here. It started innocently enough in the 1950s with a handful of laboratory curiosities dedicated to mathematical calculations. The 1960s brought time-shared computers, each used in round-robin fashion by tens of people to spread the high computer cost. Universities and other organizations soon discovered that the real benefit was not the money saved but the information shared through e-mail and document transfers within each group sharing a machine. The 1970s brought the Arpanet, which interconnected tens of time-shared machines, mostly at universities; again, this was built to spread computing costs, and again, the real benefit turned out to be expansion of the community that could share information, this time to a few thousand people. The personal computer's arrival in the 1980s made computer power affordable to millions of people who used their machines for office work and for play at home. The Ethernet, which arrived at the same time, made possible the interconnection of hundreds of PCs in local networks, mostly within organizations. The growing demand to bridge together the thousands of these local nets was addressed by the Internet, which had been already developed as a method for interconnecting networks of computers. These changes increased the community of people who could share information through e-mail and file transfers to a few million people. Then, in the 1990s, when networking advances seemed to be leveling out, and it looked like nothing big could possibly happen, the biggest change of all took place—the World Wide Web arrived as a software application for Internetted computers. It hit the steadily growing community of interconnected users with a quantitative and qualitative jolt. Creating and browsing Web sites captivated the world so much that the number of interconnected users shot up to 300 million by the end of the 20th century, as they and the rest of the world began experiencing the awesome socioeconomic potential of the Information Marketplace.

   Unlike the Industrial Revolution, which has run its course, the Information Revolution is still growing. All we have today is several practical activities, an abundance of exciting promises, and a gigantic tangle of complexities, confusions, and fads—to be sure, a revolution in the making, but one that is unfinished. The missing ingredient is human-centric computing. To put it into action requires three big steps: changing the mind-set of users and designers; ensuring that our machines are easier to use and make us more productive; and insisting that new technology reach many more people.

Integrate Computers into Our Lives

The need to change the mind-set of computer users and designers sounds obvious, but we are marching in the opposite direction. Everywhere we turn we hear about almighty "cyberspace"! The hype promises that we will leave our boring lives, don goggles and body suits, and enter some metallic, three-dimensional, multimedia, terabyte-infested, gigahertz-adorned otherworld.

   To which I respond with the technical term: Baloney!

When the Industrial Revolution arrived with its great innovation, the motor, we didn't leave our world to go to some remote motor-space! On the contrary, we brought the motors into our lives, as automobiles, refrigerators, drill presses, and pencil sharpeners. This absorption has been so complete that we refer to all these tools with names that declare their usage, not their "motorness." These innovations led to a major socioeconomic movement precisely because they entered and affected profoundly our everyday lives. People have not changed fundamentally in thousands of years. Technology changes constantly. It's the one that must adapt to us.

That's exactly what will happen with information technology and its gadgets under human-centric computing. The longer we continue to believe that computers will take us to a magical new world, the longer we will delay their natural fusion with our lives, the hallmark of every major movement that aspires to be called a socioeconomic revolution.

Once we change our mind-set in earnest, we will no longer put up with the maddening computer faults we now suffer. And we will be careful about what we accept from the *proselytizers* of technology. No longer will we be seduced by fancy buzzwords like "multimedia," "intelligent agents," "push-versus-pull technologies," "convergence," "broadband," "gigahertz" and "gigabytes," and a few hundred others already with us and yet to come. Instead, we will behave more like we do when we shop for a car: "Rather than tell me how fast the engine turns or whether it has an overhead cam, tell me about how many people it seats comfortably, the gas mileage it gets, and its annual maintenance cost." We must begin asking the same kinds of questions about computers and software: "Rather than tell me about all its gigas of processor speed and memory, tell me how quickly it can find and show me any movie I want to see, or help me find a replacement part for my lawn tractor."

As users, we want to know how much more we can achieve with a given machine or software, and at what effort, compared with what we are doing now. We'll accept quantitative or qualitative answers, as long as they address these kinds of questions. First, we'll be told that computers are different and don't admit to such measures. Nonsense. If we insist, designers and manufacturers will be compelled to respond. As they do, they will gradually adopt the new mind-set too. Eventually, they will be anxious to innovate, develop measures of usefulness, and brag about the real utility their products and services bring, versus that of their competitors.

And when the computers "vanish," as motors did earlier, we'll know the Information Revolution has finished!

Give Us a Gas Pedal and Steering Wheel

The second step toward doing more by doing less is to raise the level of controls we use to interact with our systems, from their current, low, machine level to the higher human level where we operate.

Since computing began, designers and users have been catering to what machines want. Engineers design to suit what the computer, communications system, or peripheral needs. They then throw all the components at the users and expect them to make everything function together. Miraculously, we accept without protest!

As you sit in front of your computer trying to bend it to your wishes, I imagine you trying to control a very early vintage car. Instead of having a steering wheel, brake, and gas pedal, you must wear a ring on each finger. Each ring is connected with pulling cables to levers that control spark advance, fuel mixture, the valve clearance of each cylinder, the angle of each wheel, the tension on each brake drum. What you want to do, at the human level, is go from Boston to New York. But to get there you must operate at the machine level, wiggling all the wires and levers. The prospect is so *harrowing* you would not be willing to undertake the trip. Yet we do it every day when we fire up the computer. We need to replace the low-level controls with the equivalents of the steering wheel, gas pedal, and brake.

Finally, computers will be easier to use and make us more productive if we can stick to a few common and consistent commands to do what we want with information, regardless of where the information resides. It's inconceivable to me that we are still using different commands between operating systems and browsers, just because operating systems work on information that is local to our personal computers while browsers work on distant information that sits on the Web. In both cases we want to do exactly the same things: enter information, see it or hear it, move it around, transform it, use it as a program to accomplish a task, and so on. Human-centric computing requires that we have the same set of commands for both of these cases, as well as for other gadgets and auxiliary systems that, inevitably, do the same things with information. This situation is as ridiculous as using your steering wheel to turn your car on city streets, but having to use the brake pedal to turn the car out in the country. Today's systems not only force us to learn different commands, but also entirely different ways of working each time a system changes or is "upgraded."

Many people confuse wishes with claims. Computer vendors have abused the phrases "ease of use" and "user-friendly." What they usually mean is that you can change a few colors or icons on the screen, which is supposed to give the impression that the system is bending to your commands. Such feeble cosmetics are *tantamount* to painting a smelly trash can in pretty colors to chase away the bad smell. You would be better off if all the multicolor, multimedia bells and whistles were replaced by a thin, noisy pipe, through which you could speak with a wise old man at the other end. Unfortunately, we do not know how to make machines behave intelligently, except in extremely limited contexts. Nor can we create "intelligent agents"—another darling of the spin doctors—that can act in our stead, behaving the way people expect an intelligent surrogate to act. When I say we must improve ease of use and increase productivity, I mean improve the fundamental communication between people and machines, not *wax* commercial about unrealistic desires.

We have complicated things enough. It's time we change our machine-oriented mind-set and invent controls that are much closer to what people want to do. We need the steering wheel, gas pedal, and brake of the Information Age. New technology can help us in this quest.

Reach All People

The third step needed to make computers human-centered and help us finish the Information Revolution is to reach more people. Many more.

At the beginning of the 21st century there were some 300 million people interconnected over the Internet. That big number makes us feel pretty smug. Yet it represents only 5 percent of the world's population. It's scandalous to characterize the Web as "worldwide" when it spans such a tiny portion of humankind. The voices of billions of people in the developing world and the poor regions of the industrial world cannot be heard through anything other than television news tidbits and government information feeds.

If we do nothing, matters will get worse. The rich, who can afford to buy the new technologies, will use them to become increasingly more productive and therefore even richer. The poor will be left standing still. The outcome is inescapable: Left to its own devices, the Information Revolution will increase the gap between rich and poor nations, and between rich and poor people within nations.

This gap is already huge. In the U.S. economy, an average of $3,000 in hardware, software, and related services is spent each year per citizen. In Bangladesh it's $1, according to that country's embassy. I suspect that if I could find an "embassy" representing poor Americans, or the poor of any industrial nation, I would get an equally screeching dissonance between information technology expenditures in the ghetto and the suburbs.

Some people believe the gap will close by itself, because of the growing reach and potential benefits of the Internet. It can't. The poor could have a crack at these benefits if, somehow, they were provided with the communications systems, hardware, software, training, and other help they need to join the club. Absent such help, they can't even get started.

We cannot let this gap widen. It's high time we begin closing it. Not just to be compassionate, but also to avoid the bloodshed that, historically, follows every widening rich-poor gap.

This may sound like a worthwhile social goal, but not something that will necessarily help the rest of us. Not so. First of all, if engineers begin to design computers so simple that they can be used easily by people with limited skills, the machines will be easier to use for everyone! The World Wide Web Consortium is already using this important principle in its Web Accessibility Initiative, which is creating technology to help people with visual, auditory, and other impairments to use the Web. These improvements also make the Web easier to use for people without these limitations. The history of technology shows many more examples like this; whenever designers build utility for the least-skilled user, they enhance utility for all users.

Second, if we can increase the number of people who will benefit from the technologies of information, the productivity of the entire planet will rise. New technologies will not only help the poor become literate, learn how to plant, and take care of their health, but will also help them sell their goods and services over an expanding Information Marketplace. The potential is immense. Companies in developed economies could buy information work from people in less-developed countries at greatly reduced prices, as is now done with manufacturing. Entrepreneurs in developing countries could even help those in developed countries. Imagine a new breed of useful counseling exchanges between the rich people of the West, who are often troubled by depression, divorce, and family problems, and the poor people of the East, who seem to counterbalance lack of money with strong family ties and inner peace: Older, experienced Indian women could spend a lot of time over the Net chatting with Western divorcées, who could benefit from their advice at costs substantially below the psychologist's counseling fee. The lack of time that characterizes Westerners would be counterbalanced by the plentiful time of people in India.

There is little we can do to help people become interconnected except call attention to the disparity. Yet we must not let this important objective be forgotten, for it is essential to our broader quest. We must also persist because the Information Marketplace is huge and largely unexplored. If even a small number of Nepalese or a few inner-city people found a way to become productively interconnected, they would serve as role models to their peers. A timid experiment could turn into a beneficial economic spiral.

From Michael L. Dertouzos, *The Unfinished Revolution: Human-Centered Computers and What They Can Do for Us,* pp. 120–122. Copyright © 2002 by Michael Dertouzos. Reprinted by permission of HarperCollins Publishers, Inc.

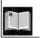 ## Vocabulary

As you think about this essay, these definitions may be helpful to you:
1. **poetic comeback** referring to the idea of "poetic justice," which describes a situation in which vice is punished and virtue rewarded, usually in a manner peculiarly or ironically appropriate
2. **entrepreneurial** acting in the manner of someone who sees an opportunity and takes advantage of it, usually by starting a business
3. **proselytizers** people who attempt to convert others to their point of view or cause; often used about people who attempt to convert others to their own religion
4. **harrowing** from a harrow, which is a farm implement that uses spikes or disks to pulverize the soil; thus, a harrowing experience is harsh and dangerous to its victim
5. **tantamount** equivalent to
6. **wax** to become a specified way

Discussion Questions

1. What does Dertouzos mean by the "Information Marketplace"? How does this concept differ from the Internet and the World Wide Web?
2. Give some examples from this essay to define the idea of human-centric computing. Then suggest some examples out of your own experience with computers.
3. Is it surprising that Michael Dertouzos, who was fluent in understanding the technologies involved in computers and the Web, expresses so much frustration at the lack of human-centric concerns in the delivery of technological services? If so, examine some of your assumptions about technology and technicians in the light of this surprise.
4. What does Dertouzos mean when he says, "Give us a gas pedal and a steering wheel"?
5. The final section of this essay expresses a need to extend the benefits of technology in what amounts to a worldwide social revolution. Dertouzos writes: "The third step needed to make computers human-centered and help us finish the Information Revolution is to reach more people. Many more." What actions would such a step require? Why does Dertouzos believe such actions are necessary?

 ## Suggestions for Your Journal

What is the difference between human intelligence and computer intelligence? Can computers be trained to "think"? If so, on what level?

Two persistent strongly human-centric concerns about computer technologies are that they will lead (1) to loss of individual privacy and (2) to the redistribution of jobs, causing many in developed countries like the United States to face unemployment. Do you share these concerns? If so, what can you do to protect yourself from their negative effects?

Discuss your own experiences with technology. Write about the uses of technology that you expect to take part in.

Unit Summary

The readings in this unit have covered a wide variety of topics and ideas about technology and how it is changing our school, work, and personal lives.

Summary Questions

1. Compare the library in your high school or community with your college library. Which offers the better access to technology? Which is easier to use? What changes might you suggest for your college library, based on your reading in this unit?
2. How has technology influenced your role as a student? How is it different from past generations' experiences?
3. What skills described in this unit's readings can you learn while in college?

Suggested Writing Assignments

1. A major blackout in the northeastern United States showed how dependent Americans are on electricity for their technology. Write an essay in which you assess this dependency: Is it tolerable in a risky world?
2. Visualize the world 25 years from now and write an essay about how you think technology will have changed the college campus and its students' ways of learning.

Suggested Readings

Canter, Lawrence, and Martha Siegel. *How to Make a Fortune on the Information Superhighway: Everyone's Guerrilla Guide to Marketing on the Internet and Other On-Line Services.* New York: Harper Reference, 1994.

Celente, Gerald. *Trends 2000.* New York: Time Warner, 1997.

Dertouzos, Michael. *The Unfinished Revolution.* New York: HarperCollins, 2001.

Levine, John, Carol Baroudi, and Margaret Levine Young. *The Internet for Dummies.* Foster City, CA: IDG Books, 2005.

What Are My Rights and Responsibilities as a Student?

I n many ways, the modern university forms its own community. Like a small town, a university or a college often has its own residential areas, business centers, spaces designed for sports and other recreation, food services including "fast food" options and some that are fancier, centers of government, a hospital or health service center, a security office, and so on. The resemblance is not limited to physical settings, because comparable lines of authority and responsibility can be found in both civil governments (as in villages or towns) and university structures. Like cities, colleges and universities have the authority to establish their own laws—codes of acceptable behavior—and penalties for violating those codes. As well, the state and federal laws apply both to cities and to colleges located within a given state or nation. Each of us is familiar with such laws—those against violence, theft of property, indecent or threatening behavior, excessive noise or other activities that constitute a public nuisance, and the like.

The freedom from work, from restraint, from accountability, wondrous in its inception, becomes banal and counterfeit. Without rules there is no way to say no, and worse, no way to say yes.

—Thomas Farber

Because many new college students are near or at the age when civil laws apply to them in a new way, they need to keep in mind that the older we are, the higher the level of responsibility for our actions the law is likely to expect of us. Some behavior that may be cute from a 2-year-old and merely annoying from a 10-year-old might well be illegal from someone 18 or older. Moreover, the cities and states we live in give us greater freedom when we reach 18 or 21, and with that freedom comes a higher degree of accountability. If you drove your parents' car illegally when you were 13, your parents were usually held responsible (though they may have, in turn, imposed their own regulations on you!), but if at 18 you drive illegally (under the influence of alcohol, for example, or faster than the speed limit allows), it is your own license that will be affected, and your own record that starts accumulating.

Other laws relate specifically to the people who make up the university community. These are generally developed, implemented, and enforced within the university itself. Such laws authorized by a university community usually include the expectation that students, faculty, and staff members will obey and respect the civil laws of their city, state, and nation, but they go further as well. Because a university has special characteristics, its code of prohibited behavior will take its special characteristics into account. We begin Unit 6 with an essay about the special characteristics that make a university unique, "On Academic Freedom" by Halverson and Carter. With that essay to establish the context, the remaining essays in this unit take up the question of your rights and responsibilities as a student member of your college community. Minnick considers one of the ethical dimensions of your role as a student. Like many ethical questions, these essays raise issues that are perennially debatable, for which you may find only provisional answers. C. L. Lindsay discusses how some specific legislation affects you as a student. George Will suggests a change in the emphasis of discussions about these and other ethical issues. All of this is to be expected in a university setting, where the search for truth is constant and the searchers are continually hopeful of better, clearer, wiser answers to such age-old questions as "What is the best way to proceed?" and "How can we make a stronger community?"

On Academic Freedom

William H. Halverson and James R. Carter

William H. Halverson is associate dean emeritus of University College at The Ohio State University. After completing academic studies focused on philosophy, Halverson authored well-known textbooks for college philosophy classes. More recently, he has translated several books from Norwegian into English. James R. Carter, also a philosopher by education, is assistant dean of the College of Arts and Sciences at the University of Louisville. In the following essay, Halverson and Carter define the notion of academic freedom, which is at the heart of a university as established and perpetuated in Western cultures.

People create institutions to serve a variety of purposes that they regard as important. They establish hospitals in order to care for the sick, retail stores to sell goods to consumers, banks to manage transactions involving the exchange of money, radio and TV stations to provide various sorts of program materials to the public, and so on. An institution is a means to an end, a way of doing something that society has decided needs to be done.

The Purpose of a University

What, then, is the purpose for which society has created universities? Why do people spend millions of dollars to build buildings—libraries, laboratories, classrooms, and the like—and additional millions to enable people like us (students, teachers) to occupy those buildings? What is a university for? What is its mission?

Try this: *the unique mission of a university is the discovery, preservation, and dissemination of truth.*

The discovery of truth: that is the heart and soul of the university. You must not think of professors and students as, respectively, those who already know the truth and those who do not. Professors have an edge on students by virtue of having been at the business of learning a bit longer than most students—but they would be the first to tell you, if they are candid, that even after many years of diligent study, their knowledge of the truth is limited, fragmentary, and mixed with error.

Our Common Ignorance

The professor's problem is the problem of human beings generally: we can rarely be certain that what we have learned, what we believe, is the *truth*. For many thousands of years, scholars believed that the earth was flat, and that it was stationary in the center of the universe, and that the sun, the planets, and the stars revolved around it. These beliefs, we now know with a high degree of certainty, were in error. We may be inclined to laugh at those silly people of yesterday who held such childish views. But let us not laugh too loudly, for it is highly likely that among the beliefs you and I hold today are some that will appear as foolish to future generations as the flat-earth theory does to us. Truth and error do not wear labels that enable us easily to distinguish between them.

Our situation, then, may be described as follows. We (that is, all people) hold many opinions, some of which are probably true and some of which are probably false. In addition, there are many matters about which we are totally ignorant, and about which we therefore have no opinions at all. Our task, if we wish to know the truth, is to rid ourselves so far as possible of both ignorance (no opinions) and error (false opinions), to exchange ignorance and error for the truth.

Seeking the Truth

How does one go about this? How does one attempt to determine the truth or falsity of any assertion? Clearly, one must look to the evidence that appears to be relevant to the truth or falsity of that assertion. *Paradoxically, the surest way to establish the truth of an assertion is to try to disprove it.* If there is some evidence in support of an assertion, and if nobody can find any evidence against it after making a reasonable effort to do so, then there is at least some reason to believe that the assertion may be true. Until, of course, some contrary evidence turns up, in which case one has to start all over again.

Thus we arrive at the following *axiom:* one who desires to know the truth concerning any matter must be persuaded by the evidence, and by the evidence alone. Anything or anybody who attempts to compel a conclusion based on anything other than the evidence is to that extent an enemy of truth.

Academic Freedom

Academic freedom is the opportunity to hold opinions based on the best evidence one has and to speak those opinions without fear of reprisal. Academic freedom means free and open discussion, a liberty to read what you want, to debate any issue, to defend new views and reinterpret or criticize old ones in an open forum.

Academic freedom can exist only when two conditions are met. First, it can exist only in a community of open and intelligent individuals who recognize that in principle every legitimate question deserves an answer, and that the legitimacy of question and answer cannot merely be assumed but must be shown capable of withstanding criticism. Second, academic freedom requires that this community make truth its common purpose, and free and open discussion the means to it. Unless both conditions are met, any freedom that there is will be purely accidental, and not very secure.

It is therefore an essential part of this idea to promote and provide for the intellectual development of every member of the academic community. In this community, it is not only those who have already cultivated a high degree of intellectual understanding who have a place. There must also be room for those who are just beginning their intellectual development. Students in each new generation must be allowed their skepticism; they must have time to examine and criticize even the most fundamental, most widely held views. But they in turn must be open to criticism and direction from their teachers and peers.

How does this notion of academic freedom affect your life? The university's need to maintain academic freedom means that *your* freedom to inquire is essential. You cannot be free if there is prejudice in the academic community. The idea of academic freedom requires that the individuals in the university actively help one another through the basic intellectual tactic of challenge and response. In his essay *On Liberty,* John Stuart Mill reminds us of this, and of the unique mission of an academic community, when he writes, "Complete liberty of contradicting and disproving our opinion, is the very condition which justifies us in assuming its truth. . . ."

Enemies of Academic Freedom

Anyone or anything that tends to inhibit free inquiry and discussion concerning any matter, or that attempts to compel a conclusion based on anything other than the relevant evidence, is by definition an enemy of academic freedom. And there are, unfortunately, many such enemies.

Some of these enemies are purely internal, within the individual. They can be rooted out only by great effort on the part of that individual.

One of these is *fear.* The most comfortable opinions to hold are those that we have held the longest, and so we fear the discomfort of abandoning long-held opinions. The most comfortable opinions to hold are those that are widely held by those whose esteem we crave, and so we fear to adopt opinions that we know will be unpopular. A sage once said, "I never learned anything of importance without feeling a sense of loss because of the old and familiar but mistaken view that had to be abandoned." But we are human, and we fear such loss—even though it be for the sake of truth.

Sheer laziness is an enemy of academic freedom. It is easier, it takes less effort, simply to adopt a view that one has heard expressed by someone else than to study the evidence and draw one's own conclusion. But the easy way, unfortunately, is not the best way, for it gives us no basis for distinguishing between opinions that are true and those that are false.

Undue respect for tradition is yet another internal enemy of academic freedom. Indeed, the opinions of one's forebears deserve considerable respect, for they represent the accumulated wisdom of many generations. Still we must not be bound by them, and we must be willing to abandon them if the weight of the available evidence suggests that they are mistaken. For we, too, will pass on a fund of accumulated wisdom to the next generation, and those who receive it have a right to expect of us that it will contain relatively more truth and less error than that with which we began.

Perhaps the more obvious enemies of academic freedom are the external enemies. Every one of us is capable of being such an enemy and probably has in fact acted as one at one time or another. If in the course of a discussion one shouts down a would-be participant instead of allowing him or her to speak, one is playing the enemy. The same is true if one heckles, and so prevents from being heard, a speaker who holds views with which one disagrees. An instructor who uses the threat of a bad grade to compel agreement (or the *appearance* of agreement) with his or her own views is violating the academic freedom of students.

The administrator who denies promotion or *tenure* or a salary increase to an instructor because the instructor advocates views with which the administrator disagrees is violating the academic freedom of that instructor. A citizen who demands the ouster of a faculty member on the grounds that he or she holds views that are "dangerous" or "unorthodox" is asking (usually without realizing it) that academic freedom be abolished.

We repeat: anyone or anything that tends to inhibit free inquiry and discussion concerning any matter, or attempts to compel a conclusion based on anything other than the relevant evidence, is by definition an enemy of academic freedom. That academic freedom has so many enemies, both internal and external, underscores the important fact that the pathway to truth is not an easy one to find or to follow.

Academic freedom, then, is by no means a cloak for nonsense. It does not confer approval upon ideas that are *demonstrably* false, unsupported by evidence, or just downright silly. To the contrary: academic freedom makes it more likely that in due course such ideas will be shown up for what they are, and that views that are supported by the evidence—that is, truth—will prevail. In an institution whose business is the discovery, preservation, and *dissemination* of truth, academic freedom is the *sine qua non*—the "without which nothing," the essential condition in the absence of which it would cease to be a university.

Reprinted by permission of the authors.

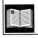 **Vocabulary**

As you think about this essay, these definitions may be helpful to you:

1. **paradoxically**   in a manner seemingly contradictory to common sense and yet perhaps true.
2. **axiom**   a fundamental notion or idea that is assumed to be true
3. **tenure**   used within universities, this term denotes an earned privilege of assured continued employment following a long period—usually seven years—of probation during which a faculty member is evaluated on teaching ability, research productivity, and community service
4. **demonstrably**   capable of being proved, either logically or by reference to the real world

5. **dissemination**   dispersal; thus, universities are said here to exist for spreading the truth (by teaching and publishing, for example), not hiding it

 ## Discussion Questions

1. Identify and explain the paradox in the statement "The surest way to establish the truth of an assertion is to try to disprove it."
2. What, according to Halverson and Carter, are the two necessary conditions without which academic freedom cannot exist?
3. Halverson and Carter argue that "one who desires to know the truth concerning any matter must be persuaded by the evidence, and by the evidence alone." What else are people persuaded by?
4. What, according to Halverson and Carter, are the enemies of academic freedom?
5. How, according to Halverson and Carter, should we regard the opinions we have received from people we respect?

 ## Suggestions for Your Journal

Fear, laziness, and undue respect for tradition—have you ever struggled with these internal enemies of academic freedom? Write a journal entry in which you select one of these and advise a younger friend how to deal with them successfully.

Academic freedom seems to be in conflict with the idea of majority rule. Do you agree? Why or why not?

How does the university differ from other institutions that seem to be, or ought to be, concerned about the truth—churches, for example, or the federal government?

Ideas as Property

Thomas L. Minnick

Thomas L. Minnick, an English teacher who admits to having graded more than 25,000 English composition papers, has served as an expert witness and researcher on issues relating to intellectual property and plagiarism in cases tried in New York, Ohio, and California. In this essay he emphasizes the positive value of ideas and other intellectual creations as property and draws attention to the fact that as property, under the law, ideas can be stolen or mistreated with serious consequences for the thief.

The idea of "property"—that is, something owned by one person or group and therefore *not* owned by anyone else—is among the oldest, most widespread notions that humans share. Even cultures that believe that all things are owned jointly and equally by all members of the society (usually a tribe or clan) also believe that no single individual can claim ownership of those things. For example, because they believe that the land belongs to all, they also regard any individual who claims to own a part of it as violating the property rights of the group. The notions of "thieves" and "theft" depend on the idea of property, since stealing is defined as the act of taking something that does not belong to the thief. The ownership of property is also one of our most important ideas: many of our laws are based on the principle that three rights guaranteed to individuals living in a society are the right to life, the right to liberty, and the right to own property. Thomas Jefferson, writing the Declaration of Independence, paraphrased this already well-established principle when he identified "life, liberty, and the pursuit of happiness" as three *inalienable* rights of Americans.

We take for granted certain categories of property and, along with them, certain kinds of theft or other violations of property rights. For example, if you (or you and your local lending agency together) own a car, then a person who steals your car, drives it carelessly until the fuel is almost gone, then wrecks it, is unquestionably a thief, because he or she has taken your property without your permission and deprived you of it. Even if the car is returned to you no worse for wear, your rights have been violated, and no reasonable person would disagree that a theft has occurred. The same is true if someone takes your watch, your backpack, your pet, or your jacket identifying your favorite sports team. Furthermore, if someone takes your credit card and buys a substantial amount of merchandise in your name, even if the physical merchandise was never yours (and wouldn't fit you anyway), those items have been stolen from you since your property—in this example, your credit line and the dollars from it that will go to pay the bills—has been taken without your knowledge or approval.

Sometimes it may be less clear that *your ideas are your property*, but that is exactly what they are, and the courts recognize them as such. A specialization in legal studies is the field of intellectual property law, which is based on the premise that an idea belongs to the person who created it, and therefore that any profit, financial or otherwise, derived from that idea also belongs to the originator. The theft of ideas takes many forms. Suppose you design and *patent* an important new drug for the treatment of arthritis and, learning of your research, others market that drug under a different name. Unless you and they have entered into a prior agreement about distributing your drug and sharing the profits, their action violates your rights to your intellectual property. Or again, suppose you write a song, both words and music, and someone else, hearing it, decides the words are effective but that the music is not—then adapts your words to new music of their own. Given adequate evidence to establish your claim of prior ownership, you should be able to show that your intellectual property rights have been violated, and you should further be able to claim a monetary award for damages due to the violation of those rights.

Universities, whose defining reason to exist includes the development and teaching of ideas,* have a special stake in the principle that an idea belongs to the person who first conceived it. The integrity of a university depends on a strong belief in this principle, and so universities defend this principle in all they do. For what would a degree from your college or university be worth if students could be caught cheating and nevertheless receive credit for the courses where that offense took place? Undergraduates writing English compositions or research papers for courses in psychology or history, graduate students preparing their master's or doctoral theses, faculty members engaged in leading-edge research—all these participants in the university have a stake in preserving the principle of a creator's right to his or her ideas as property. If they misrepresent themselves as originating ideas that do not belong to them, they are violating the intellectual property rights of others. If they themselves are victims of plagiarists (people who copy their ideas, word-for-word or in paraphrases), then they are deprived of meaningful ownership of what they have created. Even if a particular idea is not worth much money on the open market, the theft of that idea means that the true originator may not receive the *intangible* credit or respect that that idea has earned. So it is essential to the credibility and integrity of a university, and therefore of the degrees that it confers, that it provide the best defense it can for the intellectual property of the members of its community. People who create new ideas should be respected for doing so, and people who claim as theirs those ideas that truly belong to others should be condemned.

Unfortunately, it is part of the nature of ideas that we find it harder to prove ownership of a new idea than, say, of a microwave oven. When someone has stolen your microwave oven, two statements are true: first, you no longer have your microwave, and second, someone else probably does. Ideas are not like that: it is in the nature of ideas that I can tell you my idea, and then you and I both

---

*See the essay "On Academic Freedom" by William H. Halverson and James R. Carter earlier in this unit-ED.

will have it. If I tell you my answer to the third question on our final examination in American history, I will know that answer and so will you. For that matter, I could tell my answer to everyone in our class and we all could produce the same answer on request. And so on: I could tell everyone at my college, or everyone in my state, or everyone in our country, or in the world—and yet I would still have the idea in the same way that I did before, while everyone else also now has it. Moreover, if someone steals your microwave oven, you will probably be able to identify it by brand, size, model number, and condition. If you have had the foresight to mark it as yours—by engraving it with your social security number, for example—then identifying it as your stolen property will be substantially easier. But it is very difficult to mark an idea as yours. Usually the proof of ownership for intellectual property takes the form of a patent or copyright, although it is possible to document prior ownership of an idea in other ways as well.

How can a university protect ideas from thieves? The first step is to make clear to every member of the university that ideas are a kind of property, and that the protection of those ideas really does matter to the well-being of the university. A second step is to teach students at all levels the conventions for acknowledging when they adopt or develop the ideas of someone else. The third is to deal seriously with instances of the theft of ideas, which in an academic setting commonly takes one of two forms—cheating (that is, copying someone else's answers during an examination) and *plagiarism,* the unacknowledged dependence on someone else's ideas in writing, usually in out-of-class assignments. That you are reading this essay is part of your university's effort to make clear that it values and protects ideas as property.

The second step, training in common academic procedures for acknowledging sources, involves learning the accepted forms for footnotes, bibliographies, and citations to other authors in the text of your work. If you have had to write a research paper as a composition exercise in high school or previous college work, then you have probably learned one of the many conventional systems available for acknowledging sources you have used and identifying the specific ideas and language from others that you cite in your own work.[1] What matters is that your reader should be able to tell what ideas are your own original work and what ideas you have adopted or adapted from others. If you quote a section of someone else's writing verbatim, you must enclose the quoted material within quotation marks *and* tell your reader where the original statement appeared. If you rely on someone else's ideas, even if you do not quote them word for word, then a footnote identifying your source and indicating the extent of your indebtedness is appropriate.

---

[1] Perhaps the most widely used guide for authors using footnotes and bibliographies is "Turabian"—which is the shorthand way that writers refer to Kate L. Turabian, *A Manual for Writers of Term Papers, Theses, and Dissertations,* 6th ed. (Chicago: The University of Chicago Press, 1996). Other well-regarded guides of this sort include *MLA Handbook for Writers of Research Papers,* 6th ed. (New York: Modern Language Association, 2003); *The Chicago Manual of Style,* 15th ed. (Chicago: The University of Chicago Press, 2003); and *Publication Manual,* 5th ed. (Washington, D.C.: American Psychological Association, 2001). Your instructor can help you decide among them.

The third step a college or university must take to ensure that ideas are credited to their true creators—namely, dealing seriously with instances of the theft of ideas—will be evident in the ways that instructors and the systems of the university react when a case of cheating or plagiarism is suspected. If an instructor suspects that a student has cheated on a test or copied someone else's essay, the easiest action to take will always be no action at all. But would such a lack of action be the right way to proceed? If cheating or plagiarism mean so little that they can be ignored, then the instructor is contributing to the institution's loss of integrity and the weakening of the degree—of *your* degree. Indeed, by such inaction an instructor would become an accessory to the theft. The right way to proceed is to put the investigation of the facts of the alleged case into the authority of a separate group of people—often called the Honor Board or the Committee on Academic Misconduct. By hearing many cases of this kind, such a group becomes familiar with the kinds of questions that should be pursued, the kinds of evidence that can be gathered, and the appropriate resolution of the incident. Since effective teachers make a commitment to put forth their own best efforts for their students, those teachers may feel a degree of betrayal when a student knowingly tries to misrepresent someone else's work as his or her own. Therefore, it is usually wiser for a neutral party or group to investigate and *adjudicate* a case of suspected misconduct.

Some schools automatically suspend a student who has been found in violation of the rules on cheating or plagiarizing. Such a suspension may be in effect for a term or several terms, and the student will not be permitted to re-enroll until that assigned time period has passed. Other schools dismiss a student permanently for violating the rules of proper academic conduct. The consequences of academic misconduct can be devastating: law schools, medical schools, and the other professional programs available to you may be permanently closed if your record contains a notation about academic misconduct. You need to know what your college considers to be academic misconduct, and you need to know what the penalties for committing such misconduct can be. At many colleges and universities, students are bound by an "honor code" that requires them to notify instructors of any cheating they may be aware of. In such places, the failure to notify an official about suspected misconduct also qualifies as a violation and is grounds for disciplinary action.

Know the relevant policies at your institution, but do not let the seriousness of those policies paralyze you when you start to write an essay or a research paper for one of your classes. Some students ask, with justification, "How can I be sure that my ideas are original? Surely someone else has had almost every idea before me at some time or another. How can I be safe from misconduct accusations?" When you are told to be original, your teacher does not expect that every idea in your essay will be unique in the history of human thought. But a teacher does have the right to expect that *when you knowingly depend* on the thinking of someone else, you will acknowledge that in the conventional way (using quotation marks, footnotes, and a bibliography). You can express your own original turn of thought by seeing an idea in a new light, or combining ideas that you have not read before in the same combination, or by modifying the acknowledged ideas of someone else with critical commentary or new emphasis, and so on. And just to be sure, if you really have any doubts about the originality of your work, talk to your instructor about them before you turn the work in for a grade.[2]

Reprinted by permission of the author.

[2]I am pleased to record my gratitude to my colleagues Professor Sara Garnes and Dean Virginia Gordon for their conversations with me about the topic of this essay.

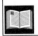 ## Vocabulary

As you think about this essay, these definitions may be helpful to you:
1. **inalienable**   incapable of being surrendered or transferred
2. **patent**   a license securing for an inventor the exclusive right to make, use, or sell an invention for a term of years
3. **intangible**   not capable of being precisely identified; abstract
4. **plagiarism**   stealing or passing off the ideas or words of another as one's own
5. **adjudicate**   to act as judge

 ## Discussion Questions

1. What is the historical basis for ownership of property?
2. How does the author define ideas as property? How do ideas and material property differ?
3. Why is the concept of ideas as property so important in a university setting?
4. What steps can be taken by a university to ensure ideas as property are protected, according to the author?
5. What can happen to a student who is found to have cheated or plagiarized?

 ## Suggestions for Your Journal

Find out and write down in your own words your college's policies and procedures for deciding cases of alleged academic misconduct. This exercise is important so that you know what those policies and procedures are: They identify your responsibilities and your rights. Then comment on whether, in your judgment, those policies are justified and those procedures are fair.

You and the Family Educational Rights and Privacy Act

C. L. Lindsay III

C. L. Lindsay III is the founder and executive director of the Coalition for Student & Academic Rights (CO-STAR). A graduate of Denison University, he completed his law degree at the University of Michigan. This information about the Family Rights and Privacy Act is taken from his book, *The College Student's Guide to the Law* (2005).

Although most of us think of educational records in terms of grades and transcripts, your college has a wealth of other data at their fingertips. Some of it is mundane—payment schedules, housing forms, and so forth. But student files do contain some sensitive materials. And even seemingly benign information needs to be guarded carefully. Identity thieves don't need much—a social security number, for example—to make off with your persona.

There is a federal statute in place that guarantees students a certain level of privacy in such matters. The Family Educational Rights and Privacy Act (FERPA), sometimes called the Buckley Amendment, is the law that governs student records. It gives students the right to inspect and review their records, contest and amend inaccurate records, and control the disclosure of information about them. We'll look at each of these areas in turn and explain the exceptions and caveats that accompany them.

Educational Records Defined

FERPA doesn't protect every piece of paper the school has; it only applies to "educational records" as defined in the act. The rule of thumb: If it personally identifies a specific student, then it's an educational record. This includes transcripts, financial aid records, class schedules, letters of recommendation, and most other things that have a student's name attached to them. The records don't have to be printed on paper. E-mail, electronic records, and even audio recordings count. And they don't have to include the student's actual name. Any mark that identifies the student is good enough. The most common offending collegiate example is the practice of "anonymously" posting grades, where professors list final grades by social security number and tack them to a wall. Since the lists identify the students, they fall under FERPA's purview.

Exempted Records

A few types of records are specifically exempted from FERPA protection. Most significant is directory information. This is "phone book" type of data—name, address, home and local telephone numbers, dates of attendance, major extracurricular activities, and date and place of birth. For student athletes the concept of directory info is a bit expanded. Height, weight, and performance statistics are considered part of their listing. Schools are allowed to disclose all of this information to anyone they please.

Campus law enforcement records are also exempted from the act. So if your name is included in an incident report or some other type of enforcement-related record, it's public. Actual police records are always publicly available, so if your campus security is a commissioned force (or if you get arrested on campus by real cops), the records aren't private.

FERPA also excludes records that are kept in the sole possession of the maker for personal use. For example, if one of your professors commits some comments to paper so that she can grade you later, those notes wouldn't be covered by FERPA. You have no right to inspect or amend them. However, this is only true if she's the only one who ever sees them. If they're ever included in any permanent file or given to any other person, they become *bona fide* educational records and FERPA applies.

Treatment records kept by a campus doctor, counselor, psychiatrist, or any other recognized professional aren't covered by FERPA either. This may seem like a big loophole, but health-related records are covered by the Privacy Rule under the Health Insurance Portability and Accountability Act of 1996 (HIPAA). Much like FERPA, HIPAA guarantees patients the right to inspect and amend their medical records and limits their disclosure.

Finally, information the school gathers about former students isn't covered. So any records created by the school after you graduate fall outside FERPA coverage. "Why would the college keep records about me after I've left?" you might ask. Well, the day after you graduate your school's focus will shift immediately from educating you to trying to squeeze donations out of you. They'll gather all sorts of information to help them gauge how much money you have and how much they can get you to fork over. Even though these files would make for some interesting reading, you have no right to access or amend them. And the school can disclose the information without your consent.

Which Schools and Students?

Like *Title IX*, FERPA applies to all schools that receive any kind of federal aid, so pretty much every school in the country, private or public, must live by FERPA's rules. FERPA rights only vest in students who have actually enrolled in a school. If you've applied to a college but never actually got in or attended, you have no FERPA rights regarding the school's info. And FERPA rights terminate at death. If a student or former student dies, the school can do whatever they please with the remaining records.

Your Right to Inspect and Amend under FERPA

You have the right to inspect all of your educational records—with two exceptions. First, your parents' financial records are off-limits. The forms they've filled out for financial aid and other payment purposes are their business, not yours. Second, you don't have the right to view any confidential letters of recommendation. You've probably already run into this once or twice in your academic career. Recommendation forms usually have a confidentiality statement on them. They say something along the lines of "I openly and freely waive my right to view this recommendation" and have a space for your signature. If you sign on that line, you've waived your FERPA rights.

The Process

Aside from that, you have the right to review and inspect to your heart's content. The process is simple enough. All you have to do is go to your college's student records office or the student affairs office and ask to see your files. There's no specific requirement that the request be made in writing, but if you are serious about getting your hands on your records, it makes sense to submit your request in a letter.

The school then has forty-five days to accommodate you. They can give you either the originals or copies. If there are documents in your file that name other students, the information about them must be *redacted* before the files are given over to you (they have FERPA rights, too).

Inaccurate Records

If something's amiss, you can request that the record be amended to more accurately reflect the truth. Again, you don't have to do this in writing, but you probably should. At this point, the school may just cave and let you amend the file. But if they refuse, you also have a right to a hearing in front of an impartial board. If you prevail at the hearing, then the school has to make the change. If you lose, you still get to add your own statement to the file contesting the contents.

This amendment process is only meant to remedy clerical errors—not the substance that underlies the records themselves. For example, if you got an A in one of your classes but your transcript says you got a B+, then you'd be able to contest under FERPA. On the other hand, if you were awarded a B+, but you think you really deserved an A, you're out of luck—at least as far as your FERPA rights go. You'd have to take that issue up with your professor.

The School's Prohibition on Disclosure

FERPA prohibits any disclosure of your educational records without your written permission. They can't give any identifiable information to your roommates, prospective employers, other schools, the press, or anyone else without your okay. Of course, there are a number of exceptions.

University Employees

The FERPA prohibitions don't apply to disclosure within the campus's professional community. School employees can share student-specific information for educational purposes without prior consent. Without this exception, each professor would have to ask your permission before they reported your final grade to the registrar, your financial aid adviser would have to get consent to discuss your case with a colleague, and so on.

Your Parents

Most parents and legal guardians can access their kids' records. The test is one of legal dependency. If your parents claim you as a dependent on their tax return, then they have the same rights as you. Parental FERPA rights don't replace student rights. They exist in addition to them. So even if you're a legal dependent, you still have all of your FERPA rights. But so do your parents. This means that, just like you, they can inspect and review all of your educational records and consent to their disclosure. So just forget any fantasies about keeping your grades or other school business a secret from Mom and Dad. If push comes to shove, they probably have a right to see your transcript.

Health or Safety Emergencies

If there's a health or safety emergency, FERPA allows colleges and universities to disclose information that's necessary to protect the student in question or others. Personally I can't imagine how this would come up: "There's a flood coming, and the only way to stop it is to release your official transcript." But there it is.

Disciplinary Proceedings

If a student is accused of a violent crime or nonforcible sex offense (date rape and the like), the results of the on-campus disciplinary hearing may be disclosed under certain circumstances. First, the school is allowed to disclose the final results of the hearing, whether guilty or innocent, to the alleged victim. Second, if the student is found guilty, then the school can disclose the name of the student, the violation committed, and the sanction imposed by the school. All other records created in disciplinary hearings are educational records and are given full FERPA protection.

Drug and Alcohol Violations

If a student under the age of twenty-one has violated any drug- or alcohol-related law, the school may notify the legal guardians or parents of the offending student. This exception applies regardless of the dependent status described above.

Subpoenas

If the school is served with a lawful *subpoena* or court order, then they may disclose protected records without the student's permission. Normally, if a university is served with such a subpoena, they'll notify the student before the records are produced. And the court will almost always notify the target of the investigation that a subpoena has been issued. This gives the students a chance to seek an injunctive court order of their own if they wish.

The USA Patriot Act and Student Records

While we're talking about the disclosure of student records, it makes sense to touch on the recently passed antiterrorism laws. As I'm sure you know, the USA PATRIOT ("Uniting and Strengthening America by Providing Appropriate Tools Required to Intercept and Obstruct Terrorism") Act of 2001 was passed by Congress shortly after the September 11 attacks. It amended fifteen federal statutes in an attempt to give law enforcement agencies expanded resources to investigate terrorism.

Although the PATRIOT Act's purpose may have been to "unite and strengthen" America, its effect on civil liberties has been quite the opposite. Many basic constitutional rights were seriously compromised by these laws. Student privacy is no exception. The PATRIOT Act gives the government two new ways to get at your records. And, what's worse, it allows them to invade your privacy without any notice to you at all.

First, FERPA was one of the affected statutes. The PATRIOT Act amendments allow the government access to student records through ex parté court orders (ones that are issued without notice to the adverse party) in connection with the investigation or prosecution of terrorism crimes. Second, the act expanded the government's investigative powers under a law called the Foreign Intelligence Surveillance Act (FISA). Under FISA, government agencies involved in an authorized investigation can get a court order to obtain tangible evidence—including private student records—from colleges and universities. The law mandates that the disclosure be kept a secret.

From *The College Student's Guide to the Law* (Lanham, MD: Taylor Trade, 2005), pp. 111–116.

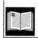 **Vocabulary**

As you think about this essay, these definitions may be helpful to you.
1. **bona fide**   Literally, "in good faith"; without fraud or deceit.
2. **Title IX**   One of the 1972 amendments to the federal Civil Rights Act of 1964. Title IX was the first law prohibiting discrimination on the basis of sex in educational programs. Its most widely known results relate to athletics, since based on Title IX, college and universities needed to provide equity of opportunity for both men and women to athletic teams.
3. **vest**   As a verb, this word primarily means to place designated authority, property, or rights in the control of a person of group. For example, after you work for some organizations for a defined period of time, you may be said to be "vested in the retirement program," which means you have earned the right and expectation to certain property or income.
4. **redacted**   "Redact" is a verb meaning to edit or revise.
5. **subpoena**   A court order requiring the person(s) named in it to appear in court.

Discussion Questions

1. The provisions of FERPA apply to college students. How are these rights different from the rights of students at lower-level institutions, such as high schools? Put another way, how does FERPA make a difference in your life, now that you are a college student?
2. As you understand FERPA, is it a good law?
3. C. L. Lindsay III, the author of this essay, believes that "although the PATRIOT Act's purpose may have been to 'unite and strengthen' America, its effect on civil liberties has been quite the opposite. Many basic constitutional rights were seriously compromised by these laws." From what you know about the changes in your FERPA rights brought about by the USA PATRIOT Act, is Lindsay correct? If so, how does that matter to you?

 Suggestions for Your Journal

Your FERPA rights are only one part of the changes that surround most new college students. Assuming that you are a traditional-age college student (that is, someone who has just finished high school at about the age of 18), what other changes are occurring in your world—especially your life as related to the law?

If you are not a traditional-age college student as defined in question 1, or if you are an international student, FERPA may still affect you but will probably do so in a somewhat different way. For example, many international students are supported by funding managed by their home governments, so they may have to consider obligations to someone other than their parents. How does FERPA matter to you if you are a nontraditional-age or international student?

Please Stop This Talk About Values

George F. Will

George F. Will is a well-known and highly respected conservative columnist and political analyst. In recent years he has been an articulate critic of higher education, arguing on behalf of the "traditional" curriculum that has been under fire for at least the last decade. In this essay, Will takes on a more general ethical issue, urging that writers and teachers focus less on "values" and more on virtues.

Here at Lafayette College in Easton, Pa., as elsewhere in our republic, the birth of which was nobly assisted by the Frenchman for whom the university is named, today's peace and prosperity allow a preoccupation with the problem of teaching what are nowadays called "values." Talk of values is a new, and regrettable, vocabulary for discussing a recurring American concern.

When the Marquis de Lafayette returned to America in 1824, his tour catalyzed the young republic's unease about what it sensed was a decline from the pinnacle of virtue achieved by the Revolutionary generation that was then passing. Then, as now, the nation was feeling its oats economically, was feeling queasy about whether its character was as strong as its economy and, thus, was wondering about whether prosperity constituted progress.

Today it would be progress if everyone would stop talking about values. Instead, let us talk, as the Founding Fathers did, about virtues.

Historian Gertrude Himmelfarb rightly says the ubiquity of talk about values causes us to forget how new such talk is. It began in Britain's 1983 election campaign, when Prime Minister Margaret Thatcher embraced the accusation, which is what it was, that she favored "Victorian values."

Time was, "value" was used mostly as a verb, meaning to esteem. It also was a singular noun, as in "the value of the currency." In today's politics, it is primarily a plural noun, denoting beliefs or attitudes. And Friedrich Nietzsche's *nihilistic* intention—the demoralization of society—is advanced when the word "values" supplants "virtues" in political and ethical discourse. When we move beyond talk about good and evil, we are left with the thin gruel of values-talk.

How very democratic values-talk is: Unlike virtues, everyone has lots of values, as many as they choose. Adolf Hitler had scads of values. George Washington had virtues. Who among those who knew him would have spoken of Washington's "values"?

Values-talk comes naturally to a nonjudgmental age—an age judgmental primarily about the cardinal sin of being judgmental. It is considered broadminded to say, "One person's values are as good as another's."

Values are an equal-opportunity business: They are mere choices. Virtues are habits, difficult to develop and therefore not equally accessible to all. Speaking of virtues rather than values is elitist, offensive to democracy's *egalitarian*, leveling ethos.

181

Which is why talk of virtues should be revived. Alexis de Tocqueville, who toured America not long after Lafayette did, noted that although much is gained by replacing aristocratic with democratic institutions and suppositions, something valuable is often lost: the ability to recognize, and the hunger to honor, *hierarchies* of achievement and character. So democracy requires the cultivation of certain tendencies of aristocracy.

So says Professor Harvey C. Mansfield, Harvard's conservative (who because of his opposition to grade inflation is known there as Harvey "C-minus" Mansfield). He notes that a theme of American literature, *writ large* in the works of Mark Twain, is the effect of democracy on the higher qualities of people. To counter democracy's leveling ethos, universities, Mansfield says, should teach students how to praise.

Students should learn to look up to the heroic—in thought and action, in politics and literature, in science and faith. After all, the few men and women who become heroes do so by looking up and being pulled up by a vision of nobility. Which makes a hero quite unlike a *role model*. A very democratic notion, role model: It is something anyone can successfully emulate.

Here, then, is higher education's special purpose in a democracy: It is to turn young people toward what is high.

A wit has said that in the 19th century, England's ruling class developed the system of elite secondary schools for the purpose of making sure that Byron and Shelley could never happen again. The proper purpose of American higher education is not to serve as a values cafeteria, where young people are encouraged to pick whatever strikes their fancies. Rather, the purpose of higher education for citizens of a democracy should be to help them identify that rarity, excellence in various realms.

These thoughts for commencement season are pertinent to the political season. Whenever you hear politicians speaking of "values," you are in the presence of America's problem, not its solution.

© 2000, The Washington Post Writers Group. Reprinted with permission.

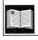 ## Vocabulary

As you think about this essay, these definitions may be helpful to you:
1. **nihilism**   the belief that nothing has meaning or importance
2. **egalitarian**   marked by egalitarianism, the belief that all people should have equal social and political rights
3. **hierarchy**   a group of people arranged by rank or class, often related to political power
4. **writ large**   signified or expressed in a more prominent magnitude, or taken to a higher degree

Discussion Questions

1. What is the fundamental difference that Will draws between values and virtues? What are his best examples of this difference, in your view? Can you suggest other examples?
2. Why does Will refer to Lafayette and Washington in this brief essay?
3. Did Hitler have "values," as Will claims? If so, what might they have been?

 Suggestions for Your Journal

Identify two or three virtues that you believe are important. Do you possess those virtues? If so, give examples that show you have used them in action.

Unit Summary

The essays in this unit focus on ethical values, especially those that relate to institutions of higher education. Halverson, Carter, and Minnick discuss aspects of intellectual honesty as they relate to academic study, and Lindsay explains some important legal issues relating to college students, and Will encourages readers to substitute "virtues" for "values" when talking about ethics.

Summary Questions

1. Do you agree with the essentially intellectual picture of the university that the authors in this unit share? What are some alternative views of the purpose of a university or college education? Can your alternatives fit compatibly with the views these authors offer?
2. An important qualification in most ethical theories is the belief that "ought implies can"—that is, that we cannot be expected to measure up to impossible standards. In the essays in this unit, do any of the authors ask you to do what you cannot reasonably be expected to do?
3. What university courses might you take to further explore the kinds of moral and ethical issues discussed in these essays?

Suggested Writing Assignments

1. Write a short essay connecting your ethical beliefs to those given in one of the essays in this unit. Show how your beliefs significantly differ or coincide with those expressed here.
2. The authors in this unit agree that acts of intellectual dishonesty, like cheating on tests and plagiarizing, are not acceptable at a university. Write a short essay identifying some other forms of behavior that are inappropriate at a university. Suggest a plan for limiting such inappropriate activities.
3. Might you expect your sense of values or virtues to change as you complete an undergraduate degree? Why? How?

Suggested Readings

Emmons, M. L., and R. E. Alberti. *Your Perfect Right.* San Luis Obispo, CA: Impact, 1974.
Lewis, H. *A Question of Values.* New York: Harper & Row, 1990.
Pojman, L. P. *Ethics: Discovering Right and Wrong.* Belmont, CA: Wadsworth, 1990.

What Is Diversity and Why Is It Important?

Just about anyone interested in American higher education can start an argument these days by bringing up the topic of "political correctness." The phrase is highly specific to our time and became important largely because of changes in the way that educators think about how to design a college curriculum.

Before 1980, the question of what to include in a well-designed college program of studies would have had different answers from different scholars, but most of them would have differed only in matters of degree. The questions people asked were "How much science should be required? How many courses of European, English, or American literature should be expected? Should Faulkner receive as much emphasis as Melville?" More recently, debates on the appropriate content of a required curriculum in general studies have grown louder, more political, and nastier. The questions people now tend to raise include "Why have you omitted literature by women and people of color? How can

We reason deeply when we forcibly feel.

—MARY WOLLSTONECRAFT

you prefer courses about the European cultural tradition when students will increasingly need to deal with Asian, African, and Hispanic cultures in their daily lives in the 21st century? Do the courses you propose to require prepare students to improve the world, or just to describe it?" The "gentleman's agreement" (to use a phrase that some would argue expresses the problem) about what to include in a college degree program and how to talk about it is no longer in effect.

Detachment from political considerations used to be thought of, among scholars, as an ideal to be cultivated by educated people. Now many regard such detachment as an illusion and say that every author, teacher, and speaker should begin by identifying his or her political assumptions. So let us say up front that without abandoning the rich history of Western thought, we value diversity and believe that the free expression of diverse points of view is essential to the well-being of a university.

We do not regard that as a predominantly political point of view, though it certainly is a notion with political consequences. On this principle, for example, we oppose all intellectual straitjackets—such as those the Nazis imposed on German universities in the period from their rise to power until the end of World War II, a time when faculty members and students alike suffered imprisonment and death for expressing ideas that were politically incorrect according to the ruling powers of the time. Further, we believe that argument and dissent need to proceed within a civilized framework—that there are reasonable constraints on behavior that all members of a community need to observe and respect. But the essential nature of a university cannot long survive in the presence of restraints on thinking and expressing ideas.

We value diversity of opinions and cultures because the free exchange of ideas is the surest way to expose bad thinking and to find the good. The essay on academic freedom by Halverson and Carter in Unit 6 provides the rationale for this belief.

We also value diversity on the fundamental ground of our shared nature as human beings: We all want to be treated fairly, and we all object to unearned punishments and rewards. So Unit 7 continues with essays in which many individuals speak about why the fact that they are different from the majority—in race, religion, gender, looks, sexual preference—should not disqualify them from the respect accorded to us all in a civilized environment, especially in a free democratic nation. In these essays, students talk about the ways that thoughtless or premeditated comments or other forms of behavior have affected them and made them feel like outsiders. This feeling of alienation is often the motivation that opens the dialogue among diverse groups, a dialogue that is most evident on our campuses perhaps because no other class of institutions is better suited for carrying on just such a dialogue.

Defining dialogue is not an easy task. The sort of dialogue we mean is not merely a conversation. Rather, we intend this term in the way that thinkers such as the 19th-century Catholic philosopher John Henry, Cardinal Newman, and the early 20th-century Jewish teacher Martin Buber have meant it: one person speaking to another, heart to heart, and listening. Universities and colleges offer unequaled opportunities for students to meet others who are different from themselves and to enter into dialogue with them. The goal of dialogue is understanding and connecting with another person, and the result of dialogue is often to understand oneself better through understanding someone else. International students, students from different religions and cultures, students who share your goals in education but may differ from you in almost every other way—these are people worth seeking out for what they can teach you about themselves and about yourself. Dialogue is the means by which we discover and evaluate truth, and diversity is the starting point for dialogue.

Among the most powerful statements of the reasons that America—and especially American universities—needs to keep this dialogue alive will be found in the speech "I Have a Dream," which Reverend Martin Luther King Jr. delivered a few years before his assassination. His vision of a society free at last from judgments based narrowly on the accidents of birth joins in perpetuity such other classic statements of the need for freedom of expression as "Areopagitica," the poet John Milton's defense of a free press, and "On Liberty," philosopher John Stuart Mill's reasoned explanation of the essential character of a free society. To close the unit, Ingram and Parks comment on racial developments since 1963, when King delivered that speech.

Learning from Differences

Richard J. Light

Richard J. Light is professor in the Graduate School of Education and the John F. Kennedy School of Government at Harvard University. He and colleagues interviewed seniors over a ten-year period to develop the information and anecdotes on which he based his 2001 study, *Making the Most of College: Students Speak Their Minds.* This reading suggests that much can be learned from listening to students talk about their college experiences.

The topic of ethnic and racial diversity is a highly charged political issue on many campuses. Students may want to think about how they will approach this issue in their years at college. If their parents attended an American college or university, the modern version will probably be noticeably different. Not just in terms of course coverage, but perhaps most of all in terms of campus atmosphere. What can any student from any background learn from the experience of studying and living and working on campus in this new atmosphere? . . . One key theme is that diversity on campus exerts an impact on learning both in and out of classes. A second theme is that interactions among students often have powerful effects on people from many different backgrounds—not just any one subgroup. A third theme is that while many interactions are positive, some are clearly the opposite. About two-thirds of the examples students give are strikingly positive. Some tell about discussions with fellow students from different racial and ethnic groups that enhance academic learning. Others describe a process of interpersonal growth. Yet several tell of troubling encounters.

Several of the findings are unexpected, at least to me. I did not expect so many students to respond to questions about the educational impact of diversity by describing complex incidents that led simultaneously to academic and personal growth. I did not expect students to identify so many incidents that occur outside of classes, often in residence halls, as the ones they remember most vividly. And I had no idea of the importance of religious life and religious diversity for many undergraduates. Student after student characterizes religious diversity as an especially powerful source of learning. Let us begin with that finding.

Religious Diversity as a Positive Force

When I ask students about the impact of diversity, many bring some aspect of religious diversity into their response. At the outset I focused primarily on racial and ethnic diversity. But I quickly learned that these are intertwined with religion. Understanding the power of students' religious convictions offers some insight into the impact of ethnic diversity.

Religious diversity plays a role in classroom discussions and debates that can serve a powerful educational function. This is most likely to happen when students are able to integrate their religious perspectives into their classes and express them directly. Faculty members who are comfortable inviting and dealing with such comments can capitalize on them to enhance classroom discussion. And students who feel comfortable integrating a spiritual aspect of their life with what may sometimes seem like abstract academic concepts may find that this combination leads to powerful learning.

Why are students so convinced of the educational value of religious diversity? Some report being surprised, taken aback, or even shocked by what other students say in class. Yet when a remark is put into a broader context, such as the context of a religious tradition, it may take on a whole new meaning. Students note that they don't feel they must agree with all religious remarks or observations. Rather, they value the way discussions can be enriched by religious perspectives.

What features do students bring with them when they first arrive on campus? First, if they are religious, regardless of the denomination, they bring a core set of beliefs and traditions. Many bring certain religious rituals that other students may not have encountered before. In classes, such students may interpret literary, historical, or cross-cultural readings in light of their religious upbringing.

And what of students who are not religious? There are many, and, perhaps surprisingly, they show every bit as much enthusiasm for religious diversity as do their more devout friends. Most students who are not religious did not become that way thoughtlessly. They arrived at their views with some reflection. And they are delighted to be informed by fellow students who know more about certain religious traditions. Not proselytized—just informed.

Religious diversity is a bit different from ethnic or other types of diversity among undergraduates. Sara Goldhaber, a student interviewer, concludes from her in-depth interviews with forty religious undergraduates that "given the personal nature of religion, most students learn much more about the religious diversity of their peers through social interactions than they do in class discussions." The students I interviewed echoed this point strongly. And most felt it would be difficult, if not impossible, for the sharing of beliefs and experiences that leads to this personal sort of learning to be built into class discussions. They noted that the nature of classroom discussion at a rigorous college pushes people, understandably, to more academic and abstract conversations and analyses.

Nearly all of the anecdotes students related about learning from religious diversity took place outside of classes. The deeply positive interactions among people of different religions are a striking confirmation of a particular value of a residential college community. Bringing together people from different backgrounds and religions, so that they live together, work together, and play together, leads to an enormous amount of strong positive learning. The evidence is compelling. Goldhaber and I found several kinds of learning from religious diversity.

Reaffirming a Religious Commitment

For some students, living in close proximity to others of different religions, or of no religion at all, leads to reflection and insights that reaffirm their own religious faith. One Catholic student told Goldhaber:

> I have reevaluated my beliefs. The independence of college life and growing intellectually have been the largest influences for me. These things have made me think more critically about my religious beliefs. They are no longer simply the tradition I was brought up in, and all I know to do. Now, at college, there are people of different religions all around me. And some people have chosen the path of no faith. Living and interacting with these people marks an important difference. Simply seeing myself in contrast to other students, and noticing our differences, has made me reconsider and ultimately reaffirm my faith.
>
> Discussions with other students have challenged my beliefs and forced me to explain them. In order to do this well, I have searched for the intellectual bases for my beliefs. I feel I have found them through talking with priests, reading literature, praying, and thinking about issues myself. Part of college is deciding who you are and what you want to be. I think it's the responsibility of every Catholic to seriously consider the priesthood as a vocation. Thinking about this has forced me to think about what is important to me and what drives my life. Friends often come to me to ask about "the Catholic position" on an issue.
>
> For example, in terms of premarital sex, I have learned why the Catholic Church feels it is wrong, rather than just accepting it as dogma. The reasons are both religious and intellectual in basis. Catholics believe that marriage is a sacrament in which man and woman are blessed by God in a special way and only then can engage in sexual intercourse. Also, marriage is a lasting institution, and so sex—as the most intimate expression of physical love—is only appropriate in that context. On other topics, I struggle with the Catholic Church's position, and have questions about the official view. I don't think it is all right to flippantly throw Catholic views out the window, though I do sometimes disagree with the official viewpoint after long consideration of, and struggle over, an issue.

Understanding and Respecting Other Religions

It is natural on a college campus to discuss and examine ideas. And who better to do it with than people who are different from you in some way? When that difference happens to be in religion, students report that they learn a great deal about religions other than their own. Few students have grown up with in-depth knowledge of the customs, traditions, and beliefs of other religions. Living together at college thus provides an ideal environment in which to discuss differing religious perspectives and, even better, to see fellow students practicing their religions. Nearly every student we interviewed expressed respect for fellow students who remain true to their religious traditions even when doing so requires making certain social sacrifices. Seeing friends and colleagues actually implementing customs and beliefs leads to a particularly strong kind of learning.

This theme is brought up repeatedly by students from all religions. It depends heavily on living arrangements, where on a day-to-day basis students from different religious backgrounds and traditions mix and mingle routinely. On a campus where almost any generalization has many exceptions, this learning about different religious traditions seems to be a nearly unanimous feature of residential life.

> I grew up in a Christian community, and had never met anyone Jewish before Harvard. When I moved in with a roommate freshman year who observed the major holidays, I learned a lot about the Jewish tradition. It was eye-opening to see the perspective of a different calendar, rules about food, and observance of holiday traditions.
>
> During Passover, I went with my Jewish roommate and another Christian roommate to an interfaith *Seder* organized by a semi-observant Jew and an Orthodox Jew who were our friends. They invited a Muslim, a Buddhist, a bunch of Christians, and several Jewish friends, so it was a really neat group at the table. We all had the books [Haggadahs], and every time a prayer was read they would go around the table and ask if there was anything similar in our religious traditions.
>
> That was also Holy Week, so I had just come the day before from Good Friday. We had had a similar meal that day to commemorate the Last Supper. I had never really made the connection between the Last Supper and Passover. In Sunday School we had learned that Christ was at a Passover Seder, but if you've never been to one, that means nothing, and is just a trivia fact to pull out. So making connections between these two celebrations, and being with a diverse group of people who were interested in sharing their traditions, was fascinating. It took us hours. We did the entire Passover Seder and in addition all of our interfaith discussions, so we went way longer than the *Hillel* ones did.
>
> That evening gave me an insight into the figure of Christ that I had never really had. I knew he was Jewish, but realizing that he was at the same type of dinner that I had just experienced for the first time helped me to make sense of why all of his apostles were together and drinking wine and eating bread—actually, *matzo*. In the prayer book there's a line the priest says every week during *Eucharist* that quotes Christ saying, "Take, eat, and every time you do this, do this in remembrance of me," or something to that effect. I had never understood that choice of wording. First of all, I thought "this" meant eating in general, and then I realized that it came from the Passover meal, which of course happens only once a year and so had a more special origin.
>
> In addition, I had thought his words were a bit egotistical and should have been ringing alarm bells in the disciples' heads about Christ's coming death. But I realized in the context of the Passover Seder that saying something so important would not be unusual because the rest of the Seder is also of tremendous import. Seeing this special and spiritual meal put Christ's words in a context that made more sense and had new meaning to me. I feel that now I have a whole basis for understanding another religion.

Exploring One's Own Beliefs

The college years are a time of change, introspection, questioning, and exploration of what a student believes in—and religious diversity can help this exploration. One woman spoke to Goldhaber from the midst of this process:

> Everything that I have learned by observing and interacting with my more religious roommates has helped me to decide what is important and not important to me in a belief system, or more generally in a spiritual outlook. I have a specific example.
>
> My observant Protestant roommate got married to a very religious person who wants to be a minister and to participate in religion within a framework that I feel is blatantly sexist. When my roommate was deciding to marry him, I felt very uncomfortable with the idea. Her wedding made me realize that what is important to me in my religious quest is not to find fault with the religions of other people, but rather to interact with people in a loving, caring way. I learned to look past, and to forgive, the aspects of other people's religions and beliefs that I may disagree with.
>
> This process forced me to think hard about what I believe. If I really believe that people carry God within them and are sentient beings, oppression didn't matter. To think that a sexist attitude would oppress people would be to deny the spiritual power of individuals. Yet I am still uncomfortable with this view that I came to, because it commits me to a view of the world that is counterintuitive for me. I am a liberal, and I work to decrease poverty and suffering and oppression in many situations. So it is hard to justify my work while believing in the spiritual framework I just described. I think this all requires a transformation of my perception of suffering, one which I am far from mastering. . . .

Living and Learning Together

When preparing to ask about learning related to students' different ethnic and racial backgrounds, I expected to find that most "academic" learning took place in classes and most "personal" learning happened in interactions outside of classes. Student interviewers predicted that the interviews would confound my expectations. They were right. Learning does not take place in such a partitioned way.

Perhaps because of this crossover between in-class and out-of-class learning, when students interact with fellow students from different racial and ethnic backgrounds in day-to-day living, it makes a strong impression. This finding drives home the importance of creating residential living arrangements that bring students from different backgrounds together, rather than creating separation by racial or ethnic background. If students from different backgrounds live apart from one another, a precious kind of learning may be lost.

Students give myriad examples of such crossovers between in-class learning and residential living, and they characterize them as highlights of their life at college. One striking story comes from a junior:

> I'm an African-American guy who grew up in a pretty middle-class home. I went to an integrated high school. I thought I knew exactly what to expect here at college when I got my freshman roommate mailing. There were going to be four of us—two

white and two black, in a suite with three small bedrooms. So two guys get singles, and two share a bedroom. I wondered how that would work, and expected it might cause some tension. I especially hoped the tension wouldn't be anything racial.

As it turns out, I was completely wrong about what would happen. We quickly resolved the room arrangements by agreeing to split the year with two of us sharing for the first half and the other two sharing for the second half. So that potential dilemma vanished quickly. For the first few weeks the four of all got along quite well.

But it was the connection with our classes that created some tensions. One of my white roommates and I both enrolled in a literature class where we read work by a diverse group of writers. And this was where the academic work and our living together intersected. It made for some difficult moments.

I remember two examples in particular. We read two black authors, and, to say the least, their styles were very different. One was a piece by Imamu Amiri Baraka called "The Toilet." The other was an essay by James Baldwin, written when he lived in Paris. I thought Baraka was a challenging and complex writer, while I was disappointed with Baldwin. My white roommate had exactly the opposite reaction.

Now you could say that this is entirely normal. Why would anyone be surprised that two students would have different takes on two authors? But somehow when we talked about it, we both got very offended. I had assumed he would agree with me, and he had assumed I would agree with him. Then he called the Baraka piece "absolute trash," and I took it as a racial remark. So I clammed up and stopped talking to him. Our relationship became very strained.

Thank goodness for our two other roommates. It was pretty obvious to both of them what was happening. One evening a few days later they just couldn't stand the tension. So when we had our regular weekly "group grousing time" they pressed each of us.

I first realized that evening that if I become angry with a white guy who really is a good guy, it's pretty foolish for me to think he is a racist just because he doesn't like a particular piece of writing by a black man. How would I feel if I told my white roommate I didn't enjoy reading James Joyce, and he accused me of making a racist remark? I would get upset with him, and I think I would be right to get upset with him.

The good news is that the four of us are still living together now, as juniors. And thanks to those awkward moments we had together as freshmen, now I feel completely free to criticize James Michener or James Joyce or Henry James, and my white roommate feels completely free to say what he really thinks about any black author. We even laugh about it now because it's kind of a bond. It's hard for me to advise other people to live together the way our group has done. But I can certainly say that for me, as one guy, the intersection of living arrangement and academic work has been a big learning experience, a big winner.

Another student in his junior year gave the following example to interviewer Anna Fincke:

Freshman year I had one roommate who was black. We became very close friends. We find each other easier to associate with than many other people. Being white, I think having a black roommate freshman year has had an impact on the mix of people I

know. I met people he knew. I don't think that's unusual—any roommate who runs
in a different crowd will bring that. He was from Georgia and had a very strong tradition of African-American culture. He was quite religious and conservative. He really
represents to me some especially interesting, valuable, and worthy aspects of African-
American traditions. In discussions I became aware of some of his struggles and the
circumstances he encounters. Like in my high school there was a considerable rift
between blacks and whites in terms of academics. It's interesting to see how he dealt
with those difficulties.

I don't think anyone comes to college without preconceived notions. They arise
from your life experience. And they always change with your new experiences. The
high school I went to was racially mixed—it was just over half black. The chance to
get to know students of other races here, and have challenging, searching discussions
with them, has raised my confidence in asserting who I am and what I believe, without respect to race. In a small town in Texas, where I'm from, it's easy to fall into certain unfortunate patterns of talking to people of different races. There are certain
formalisms used to smooth over tensions. Now I'm more willing to be direct and
inclined to say what I think is the truth about one issue or another.

For each student, the tone of college life is set early. Much of that tone
depends upon roommates, neighbors, and dorm supervisors. Again, living
arrangements go a long way toward shaping both attitudes and relationships. A
young woman told Sara Goldhaber about an unexpected friendship:

Moving into our dorms freshman year, we all got together the first night in our proc-
tor's room. She had asked us to bring something along that was important to us,
and to introduce it along with ourselves. I had just come back from spending a summer traveling through Eastern Europe and Israel. My object was a pillow. When I was
young, my best friend was an Israeli girl whose family had moved to America for a
few years. That summer I had visited them in Israel. When I left, the younger kids
presented me with a red, heart-shaped pillow they had made. It said in Hebrew,
"Have a safe trip. We love you," and it had all their names on it. It really meant something to me. I thought the pillow was very emblematic of both my relationships with
people and my religious experiences.

Just before my turn, the guy next to me introduced himself as a *Shiite* Muslim
from Pakistan. His object was a necklace with several pendants of *Koranic* verses and a
curved sword. I was stunned. I hadn't ever had direct contact with a Muslim before,
and I had such a historical prejudice and fear of negative interactions between Jews
and Muslims. Shocked and frightened a bit, I went on anyway with what I was going
to say, and explained that I was a religious Jew. He turned to me with a big grin and
said, "Great! It's always hard to find somebody else who doesn't want pepperoni on
their pizza." We became fast friends and it was always a big joke that we could go out
to dinner together, because we had similar dietary restrictions.

Meeting the Muslim guy in my dorm turned Islam into a real religion for me.
After being a fanatical ideal, it became something which real people practiced and
believed in. This experience made me realize the prejudices that I held about religion

in general, and Islam in particular. Before meeting him, I was frankly unwilling to believe that he could keep his Muslim views out of any discussion. I see people make this misguided assumption all the time, because when someone says they are religious, it is easy to jump to the conclusion that that is the only thing which defines them.

Living with students from different backgrounds can actually change behavior. In the spirit of pressing students to go beyond platitudes when talking about the impact of residential living, I asked interviewees to give examples of interactions from their residential living experience that changed their behavior. Two seniors who lived in the same residence hall both told me of a particular incident. It illustrates the power of roommates, the value of choosing wisely, and how residential living experiences can change behavior. One of the seniors described the incident this way:

> Eight of us blocked together. Eight guys. Four of us are white, one is black, three are Asian. We were all just chatting on a weekend afternoon. We had known each other since freshman year. Saw each other practically every day. Didn't expect any big surprises. We feel entirely comfortable with each other.
>
> It was last October. I remember one of the Asian guys asked, "How are you going to handle voting in the November election? Are you going home, or are you going to use an absentee ballot?" All five of us non-Asian guys responded that we hadn't thought about it yet. The truth is that a couple of us might just have let the election slide. We are pretty busy. And since none of us come from cities or towns right near campus, I guess we would have just let this one election pass.
>
> The Asian-American guys became visibly upset. They asked how much we knew about [Daw Aung San Suu Kyi].Two of us knew she was the Burmese woman under house arrest who had won a Nobel Peace Prize while fighting for democracy in Burma. They asked us if we had heard about Wang Dan, who was arrested in China's Tiananmen Square student uprising for democracy. They asked about Wei Jing [Sheng], sitting in jail because of his speaking out and writing for democracy in China. They pressed us how, knowing about these people and what they were risking for the chance to vote, while we were taking so much for granted—how could we just take a pass on voting that year?
>
> Well, it didn't take them long to embarrass us. Big time. They didn't try to rub our noses in it, or anything like that. But they felt strongly about it. They certainly changed our behavior. So the five of us all made a big point of sending away for absentee ballots that very afternoon. And all five of us voted. Now that I think back on that afternoon, it seemed like a small thing at the time. But it really affected me. I bet you I will never pass on another election in my lifetime.

For learning—and behavior change—to take place, students must mix and mingle and interact. Ideally students from different backgrounds should work together to accomplish a common task. Sometimes formally in a classroom. Often less formally outside of classes. The key point is that extensive contact, preferably both inside and outside of class, is what allows students to benefit and learn from ethnic differences on campus—and that residential arrangements can foster this contact in a way that encourages such learning. . . .

In the context of residential living, some students inevitably encounter situations in which they are uncomfortable. This characterizes life at any college. And it was true long before colleges began to strive for diversity in their student bodies. Yet when students from different racial or ethnic backgrounds live together, new kinds of delicate moments and personal interactions inevitably arise. While some of these circumstances can be difficult for students to cope with, students from all backgrounds report that they learn something. Often that something is about themselves.

Several graduating seniors commented on the importance of the simple principle of bringing good will to all personal encounters. For example, a young white woman suggested that one way to enhance good will among people of different backgrounds is to encourage each student to be reflective about himself. Especially when racial or ethnic differences raise a delicate issue or lead to an awkward moment. Inevitably these awkward moments will occur. It is up to each student to transform them into an educational opportunity—a learning experience. When a student is willing to be reflective and assume good will, the results can be powerful.

Reprinted by permission of the publisher. From Richard J. Light, *Making the Most of College: Students Speak Their Minds,* pp. 160–168, 173–180, 185. Cambridge, Mass.: Harvard University Press. Copyright © 2001 by Richard J. Light.

 ## Vocabulary

As you think about this essay, these definitions may be helpful to you:

1. **Seder**   a Jewish home or community service including a ceremonial dinner. This ritual meal is held on the first or first and second evenings of the Passover in commemoration of the exodus from Egypt. The Last Supper of Christian tradition was a Seder on the first night of Passover.
2. **Hillel**   a greatly revered Jewish teacher who lived about the time of Christ. Most campuses with Jewish students also have a gathering place with programs for them, often named in Hillel's memory.
3. **matzo**   the unleavened bread eaten at a Seder and remembered in the Christian communion service
4. **Eucharist**   a Christian sacrament at which bread and wine are taken in remembrance of the Last Supper

5. **Shiite**   One of the major branches of Islam, the religion in which Allah is the one god and Muhammad is His prophet
6. **Koranic**   The Koran is the book of sacred writings accepted by Muslims as revelations made to Muhammad by Allah through the angel Gabriel. Koranic verses are verses from the Koran.

Discussion Questions

1. Most of the examples that Light gives in this reading are positive, even if they do not seem to start out that way. But Light says that "some are clearly the opposite. About two-thirds of the examples students give are strikingly positive. Some tell about discussions with fellow students from different racial and ethnic groups that enhance academic learning. Others describe a process of interpersonal growth. Yet several tell of troubling encounters." Discuss some instances in which dealing with fellow students who are different was either positive or negative.
2. Much of the literature about diversity acknowledges that people need to feel safe in their environment before they can talk about those differences with candor. What needs to be true for an environment to be "safe" for such discussions?
3. Light reports, "Student after student characterizes religious diversity as an especially powerful source of learning." Do you agree? If so, suggest some reasons why this appears to be true.

Suggestions for Your Journal

Most students who live on campus find that they have to make several adjustments to their new college environment. Write about some of the adjustments that you had to confront. Were they routine or difficult?

What kind of difference in others is the hardest for you to come to terms with—religious? ethnic? geographical? racial? sexual orientation? or some other kind? Compare differences that you manage easily with those you find hard to handle.

How Discrimination Works and Why It Matters: Five Personal Statements

Chana Schoenberger, from Bethesda, Maryland, was a high school student when she wrote her comments and published them in *Newsweek*. Joy E. Weeber was a graduate student in a doctoral program in psychology at North Carolina State in Raleigh. Edward A. Delgado-Romero is a psychologist at the University of Florida Counseling Center in Gainesville. Donna M. Talbot coordinates the student affairs graduate programs in the Department of Counselor Education and Counseling Psychology at Western Michigan University, Kalamazoo. And Lisa J. Brandyberry is a senior psychologist and director of adult outpatient and emergency services at Piedmont Behavioral Health Care in Albemarle, North Carolina.

Discussion Questions and Suggestions for Your Journal for these five essays appear on pages 219–220.

Getting to Know about You and Me

Chana Schoenberger

A religious holiday approaches; students at my high school who will be celebrating the holiday prepare a presentation on it for an assembly. The Diversity Committee, which sponsors the assemblies to increase religious awareness, asked me last spring if I would help with the presentation on Passover, the Jewish holiday that *commemorates* the Exodus from Egypt. I was too busy with other things, and I never got around to helping. I didn't realize then how important those presentations really are, or I definitely would have done something.

This summer I was one of 20 teens who spent five weeks at the University of Wisconsin at Superior studying acid rain with a National Science Foundation Young Scholars program. With such a small group in such a small town, we soon became close friends and had a good deal of fun together. We learned about the science of acid rain, went on field trips, found the best and cheapest restaurants in Superior and ate in them frequently to escape the lousy cafeteria food. We were a happy, bonded group.

Represented among us were eight religions: Jewish, Roman Catholic, Muslim, Hindu, Methodist, Mormon, Jehovah's Witness, and Lutheran. It was amazing, given the variety of backgrounds, to see the ignorance of some of the smartest young scholars on the subject of other religions.

On the first day, one girl mentioned that she had nine brothers and sisters. "Oh, are you Mormon?" asked another girl, who I knew was a Mormon herself. The first girl, shocked, replied, "No, I dress normal!" She thought Mormon was the same as Mennonite, and the only thing she knew about either religion was that Mennonites don't, in her opinion, "dress normal."

My friends, ever curious about Judaism, asked me about everything from our basic theology to food preferences. "How come, if Jesus was a Jew, Jews aren't Christian?" my Catholic roommate asked me in all seriousness. Brought up in a small Wisconsin town, she had never met a Jew before, nor had she met people from most of the other "strange" religions (anything but Catholic or mainstream Protestant). Many of the other kids were the same way.

"Do you all still practice animal sacrifices?" a girl from a small town in Minnesota asked me once. I said no, laughed, and pointed out that this was the 20th century, but she had been absolutely serious. The only Jews she knew were the ones from the Bible.

Nobody was deliberately rude or *anti-Semitic,* but I got the feeling that I was representing the entire Jewish people through my actions. I realized that many of my friends would go back to their small towns thinking that all Jews liked Dairy Queen Blizzards and grilled cheese sandwiches. After all, that was true of all the Jews they knew (in most cases, me and the only other Jewish young scholar, period).

The most awful thing for me, however, was not the *benign* ignorance of my friends. Our biology professor had taken us on a field trip to the EPA field site where he worked, and he was telling us about the project he was working on. He said that they had to make sure the EPA got its money's worth from the study—he "wouldn't want them to get Jewed."

I was astounded. The professor had a doctorate, various other degrees and seemed to be a very intelligent man. He apparently had no idea that he had just made an anti-Semitic remark. The other Jewish girl in the group and I debated whether or not to say something to him about it, and although we agreed we would, neither of us ever did. Personally, it made me feel uncomfortable. For a high-school student to tell a professor who taught her class that he was a *bigot* seemed out of place to me, even if he was one.

What scares me about that experience, in fact about my whole visit to Wisconsin, was that I never met a really vicious anti-Semite or a *malignantly* prejudiced person. Many of the people I met had been brought up to think that Jews (or Mormons or any other religion that's not mainstream Christian) were different and that difference was not good.

Difference, in America, is supposed to be good. We are expected—at least, I always thought we were expected—to respect each other's traditions. Respect requires some knowledge about people's backgrounds. Singing Christmas carols as a kid in school did not make me Christian, but it taught me to appreciate beautiful music and someone else's holiday. It's not necessary or desirable for all ethnic groups in America to assimilate into one traditionless mass. Rather, we all need to learn about other cultures so that we can understand one another and not feel threatened by others.

In the little multicultural universe that I live in, it's safe not to worry about explaining the story of Passover because if people don't hear it from me, they'll hear it some other way. Now I realize that's not true everywhere.

Ignorance was the problem I faced this summer. By itself, ignorance is not always a problem, but it leads to misunderstandings, prejudice and hatred.

Many of today's problems involve hatred. If there weren't so much ignorance about other people's backgrounds, would people still hate each other as badly as they do now? Maybe so, but at least that hatred would be based on facts and not flawed beliefs.

I'm now back at school, and I plan to apply for the Diversity Committee. I'm going to get up and tell the whole school about my religion and the tradition I'm proud of. I see now how important it is to celebrate your heritage and to educate others about it. I can no longer take for granted that everyone knows about my religion, or that I know about theirs. People who are suspicious when they find out I'm Jewish usually don't know much about Judaism. I would much prefer them to hate or distrust me because of something I've done, instead of them hating me on the basis of prejudice.

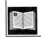 ## Vocabulary

As you think about this essay, these definitions may be helpful to you:
1. **commemorate**   to mark by some ceremony or observation
2. **anti-Semitic**   discriminating against Jews as a religious or racial group
3. **benign**   mild or harmless disposition
4. **bigot**   one who is intolerantly devoted to one's own opinions or prejudices
5. **malignantly**   injuriously, intentionally harmful

What Could I Know of Racism?

Joy E. Weeber

What could I know of racism, being a middle-class, college-educated White woman? What could I know of the pain of being rendered invisible because of a single characteristic? What could I know of having the complexity of myself, a Dutch American from a large extended family living around the world, reduced to that feature which marks me as "different" from the dominant culture? What could I know of being denied entrance to public facilities or required to sit in segregated places because of that characteristic? What could I know of being forced to use a back service entrance, like a second-class citizen? What could I know about being told that if I "work hard enough" I could make it, although getting in the front door for an interview seems an impossibility? What could I know about having to endure painful procedures to make my appearance more acceptable? What could I know of being charged a higher price for services because of the way I look? What could I know about not being able to ride a bus with dignity? What could I know of having a hard time finding a place to live because of housing discrimination or being unable to visit in the homes of my classmates? What could I know of growing up in a society that never portrays my people with positive images in the media, except for those exceptional, inspirational heroes who have more than made it? What could I know of being viewed as less intelligent simply because of the way I look? What could I know of being educated in a segregated school setting, not expected to amount to much and denied opportunities because of it? What could I know of being thought of as less than acceptable because of the way that I speak? What could I know of having to work twice as hard as others just to prove I am as good as they are? What could I know of being viewed as a charity case, rather than one who possesses civil rights?

I can know the pain of all of these things because I am disabled. My disabled brothers and sisters and I experience such acts of discrimination on a daily basis, and the pain these encounters cause is the same pain that racism causes people of color. It is the pain caused by the unconscious beliefs of a society that assumes everyone is, or should be, "normal" (i.e., White and very able-bodied). It is the pain caused by the assumption that everyone should be capable of total independence and "pulling themselves up by their own bootstraps." It is a belief in the superiority of being nondisabled that assumes everyone who is disabled wishes they could be nondisabled—at any cost. In the disability community, we call this "ableism," a form of prejudice and bigotry that marks us as less than those who are nondisabled. In this narrative, I use language the disability community claims in naming its own lived experience. And although it may not be "politically correct," it is meant as a true reflection of how many of us view ourselves and our lives as members of the disability community.

Ableism causes pain because it convinces us that there is something funda-mentally wrong with us, that we are not acceptable just as we are. After all, we are the ones who are "defective," with bodies, speech, hearing, vision and emo-tional or cognitive functioning to be fixed by doctors and therapists. Ableism also causes pain to nondisabled people who are unprepared to deal with their own vulnerability and mortality when accidents and aging require that they do so. I did not understand the pain these attitudes had caused me until I was 35, despite having lived with the effects of polio since I was an infant. Until then, I did not know that I had spent my entire life trying to prove how I had "over-come" my polio, which is no more possible than overcoming being female or African American! I did not understand that these ableist attitudes and acts devalued my body and denied an essential element of who I am.

I only began to understand all of this when I read an essay, "The Myth of the Perfect Body," by Roberta Galler (1984),[1] who also had polio as a child. I felt as if I were reading my own diary! I was not an alien; I had a disability! I was the "supercrip" she wrote about, the defiant opposite of the pathetic cripple I had been made so deathly afraid of being. I had spent enormous amounts of my energy proving how "able" I was, to counter society's belief that I am "unable." I thought I had "passed" as normal in my nondisabled world (despite my crutches and braces), because I was often "complimented" by strangers and friends who "did not think of me as handicapped." Only when I read this woman's words did I begin to understand how my life had been shaped by living with a disabil-ity, even though my family and I had not been able to acknowledge that it existed! Only then did I begin to understand how my sense of self had been con-structed by how my body had been touched, treated, and talked about by those who had been my "caregivers." Only then did I begin to understand how my life had been lived as an outsider, struggling unconsciously for acceptance.

Throughout my childhood, I had successfully resisted sincerely religious strangers' urgings for me to get "healed," people who thought of me as sick and infirm. Although these encounters left me feeling violated and nauseated, I knew I was fine and intact the way I was! Why did they think I was sick? I lived in a tight-knit community that accepted me as a whole person; they did not see me as sick. Not once had I been stopped from living life fully by anyone's low expectations, fear, or lack of imagination in how to change the world to meet my needs. I had been allowed to participate on my terms and discover my own physical limitations. My parents understood the stigma that society places on people with disabilities and were determined to nurture a sense of self that could deflect such negativity.

And yet, at the age of 10, I was marked as "other" by a diagnosis of scoliosis, found to be "defective" with a curving spine and weak leg muscles, and in need of "corrective" surgery. Thus began my searing journey into a medical world

[1] R. Galler, "The Myth of the Perfect Body," in C. Vance (ed.), *Pleasure and Danger: Exploring Female Sexuality* (Boston: Routledge and Kegan Paul, 1984), pp. 165–172.

that would teach me well what it really means to be disabled in this society! It was a world that taught me I was invisible, a defective body part to be talked about as if not connected to a lonely, hurting child. It was a world that taught me I had to be tough to survive, cut off from the emotional support of my family for all but 2 hour visits a week. It was a world that taught me that it was okay for others to inflict pain on me—if their goal was to make me more "normal." This world taught me that what I felt or wanted had nothing to do with what happened to my body, that it was okay to publicly strip children and parade their defects in front of strangers. The result of seven surgeries and innumerable scars was a girl who was numb, disconnected from both body and soul. I was fragmented and lost to a family who had no clue of my inner devastation. The emotional isolation of the hospital followed me home, as I heard in my family's lack of understanding that something was "wrong" with how I responded to life—emotionally, psychologically, spiritually, and politically!

My response to the horror of those years was to make myself outdo everyone, need help from no one, and take care of everyone else's needs. I was constantly proving I was the "exception," not one of those dependent cripples society cannot tolerate. Never mind that I spent my entire adult life struggling with devastating bouts of exhaustion-induced depression—although others only ever saw my bright, cheerful self. Never mind that I was alone, unable to sustain any vital romantic relationships, ever untouchable and independent. I became the angry one who spoke out against social injustice and felt the sexism in our community and family. I was the one who felt the arrogance and violence of racism. I was the one who felt the fragmentation of only seeking spiritual and physical sustenance, while psychological and emotional needs went unacknowledged. Being alone in the hospital, and the thought of seeking the company of those who might share them, never crossed my mind.

At no time did I connect my different ways of perceiving and responding to the world with my experience of living with a disability. I couldn't. There was no disabled person in my world to help me understand that my empathy for those who suffered from injustice or were devalued because of race was rooted in my own experience of being devalued because of my disability. In the 7 years since my first encounter with a disabled person who understood, I have never felt alone. I have come to know the healing of belonging, of being understood without a word in a community of people who validate my feelings. I did not know how fragmented I was, and I needed other disabled people to teach me to love myself wholly! I had needed them to teach me how to embrace that part of myself that society so devalues. I needed them to show me the commonalities between our experiences of ableism and others' experiences of racism. I needed them to give words to the feelings I had never had reflected back to my self in my nondisabled world.

Most of us with disabilities learn to survive alone and silently in our nondisabled families and worlds, never knowing a disability community exists. I was the only disabled person in my family, my community, schools, and my adult social world. As a child, I had learned an aversion to the company of other disabled people because they were associated with being "defective" and stigmatized, and I was neither of those! My only experiences with other disabled people had been in situations in which nondisabled professionals "medicalized" our lives, defining us negatively. I even had my own turn at working in such settings, "helping" others in sheltered workshops and group homes, although always quitting for emotional reasons I only now understand. I had never been in an environment in which disabled people defined themselves in their own terms and celebrated their uniqueness. And now, in the written words and in the company of disabled people, I have found brothers and sisters who are teaching me that there are powerful ways of dealing with the pain of being "other." They are helping me find the words to express what I have always "known" in my body, but had no language to express.

James Baldwin (1972) wrote that "to be liberated from the stigma of blackness by embracing it, is to cease, forever, one's interior argument and collaboration with the authors of one's degradation (p. 190)."[2] It has been my experience that learning to embrace my whole self, disability and all, was not a task I could do alone. I needed the support and guidance of others who not only had lived my experience but also had ceased their internal collaboration with the negative voices of society. It is the same process that bell hooks (1989) speaks of in *Talking Back: Thinking Feminist, Thinking Black*,[3] as the need to "decolonialize" one's mind by rooting out all that does not honor one's own experience. I have found that in addition to decolonializing my mind, I have also needed to decolonialize my body. I have had to cease my interior argument with society's negative messages that I am not as good as everybody else by no longer pushing my body beyond its limits. As I have learned to listen to my body's limits, honoring them as a source of wisdom and strength, I have experienced the healing and liberation of the embrace, and I have begun to thrive.

A most profound way that I have begun to thrive is that I no longer require that I spend most of my energy walking to get around—I have begun to use a scooter for mobility. What an act of liberation—and resistance—this has been! I felt like a bird let out of a cage, the first time I used one! I could go and go and not be exhausted! I was able to fully participate in the conference I was attending, rather that just be dully present. To choose to use a scooter, when I can still walk, flies in the face of all the "wisdom" of those without disabilities. We are taught that to walk, no matter how distorted or exhausting it is, is far more virtuous than using a chair—because it is closer to "normal." Never mind that my galumphing polio-gait twists my muscles into iron-like sinew that only the hardiest of masseuses can "unknot." Never mind that my shoulders and hands, never meant for walking, have their future usefulness limited by 40 years of misuse on crutches. To choose to use a scooter also places me squarely in that stigmatized group of "pitiful unfortunates" who are "confined" to their chairs. It removes me from the ranks of "overcomers," such as Franklin Delano Roosevelt,

[2]J. Baldwin, *No Name in the Street* (New York: Doubleday, 1972).
[3]b. hooks, *Talking Back: Thinking Feminist, Thinking Black* (Boston, Mass.: South End Press, 1989).

Wilma Rudolph, or Helen Keller, whom society mistakenly believes actually "got over" their disabilities. My using a scooter is an act that scares my family. They are afraid that somehow giving up walking will make me give up—period! It makes them think that I am losing ground, becoming dependent on the scooter, when they and society need me to act as if I am strong and virile. Only now that I am embracing my limitations do I know how I spent much life-energy protecting my family from them. I rarely slowed them down or burdened them with feelings they could not understand. Only now can I celebrate my unavoidable need for interdependence in a society that oppresses everyone with its unattainable standard of independence!

Traditionally, families are taught by professionals that their child's disability is an individual functional problem that can only be remedied by individualized medical interventions. And so it remains the focus of many families to adapt their child to a society that needs them to be "normal. "The larger social and cultural oppression that some of those interventions represent is only now being raised by those of us former disabled children who question the extreme and painful measures taken to "fix" us, measures that went beyond what may have been truly needed to ensure our full, unique development. In my scooter, I am choosing now to live by other values—the values of the disability community that require society to adapt to our needs rather than vice versa.

In using my scooter, I experience the full range of the disability experience, including those aspects I avoided when I thought I was "passing" as normal. In my scooter, I experience being denied access to places walking people enter without a thought, because they are inaccessible. In my scooter, I am eligible to use service entrances near stinking dumpsters and seating at public events that is segregated from my walking companions. Seated in my scooter, I am even more invisible to those who could never look the walking-me in the eye—an averted gaze not even required to obliterate my presence. In my scooter, I cannot visit some friends' homes because of stairs or use their bathrooms because of narrow doors. The very cost of my scooter includes a sizable "crip tax"—as the sum of its component parts is far less costly than its hefty price tag in the inflated (and captive) medical equipment market. In my scooter, I don't have full assurance that I will even be able to get on public transportation, much less treated with dignity when I do. In my scooter I feel the insult of those telethon hosts who want to paint my life as pathetic, not livable, unless I am cured. In my scooter, I know that I am viewed as far less able, needing public assistance rather than ramps and power doors to get into job interviews. Although my speech was not affected by polio, my scooter provides further reason to dismiss me, as society dismisses my brothers and sisters who use voice synthesizers to communicate their artistic vision of the world. In my scooter, I am inextricably and unavoidably a member of the disability community, with all the pain and privileges associated with that membership.

I am proud to have found my way home to the disability community. I am now able to "hang out on the porch" and hear stories from the elders of how their visions of equal justice for all took shape, how legislation acknowledging our civil rights was passed. And although it is true that we continue to struggle to define our own lives and live it on our own terms, we have also begun to create a culture that brings us together and celebrates our unique ways of being in the world. I am moved when I hear poetry that speaks my truth and read books that truly reflect my life experiences. I am healed when I see unflinchingly honest performances dealing with the reality and pain caused by ableism. I now know that I have indeed experienced the pain of ableism and I know why I felt the pain of racism when I had words for neither. I now also know the liberating power of embracing my disability and of celebrating who I am because of it.

The Face of Racism

Edward A. Delgado-Romero

When thinking of racism, people might imagine the vision of a hooded Ku Klux Klan member lighting a cross, a "skinhead" wearing swastikas, or an angry lynch mob. However, when I think of racism, one image is clear. I learned about racism in the face of my father. I learned hatred, prejudice, and contempt, and, most important, I learned how to turn that racism inward. After many years of self-reflection and healing, I have just begun to understand how deeply racism has affected my attitudes toward others and toward myself. I have begun to understand that racism works on two fronts. One is the overt and obvious racism of the Klan member. The other is the covert and subtle racism that the victim of overt racism begins to internalize, the racism my father taught me.

My father came to this country seeking to escape the personal demons that had haunted him throughout his life. He saw the United States and New York City as a new opportunity, a new beginning. Part of that beginning was rejecting all the things that he had been. My father sought to reinvent himself as an American. In those days, being an American meant being White (some people might argue that this is still true). My father felt he *was* White, because part of his family was descended from Spaniards. Somehow my father thought being Spanish (and therefore European) was better and of higher status than being a South American or a Colombian, and it was certainly better than being *Indio* or native. Our ancestral records show that the Delgado family was a virtuous family with a long tradition in Spain. However, the only records that remain of my ancestors who were native (South) Americans are a few photographs and some of their physical features that were passed along through "blood."

The United States of America taught my father to hate anyone who was not White. Richard Pryor once observed that the first English word that an immigrant is taught is "nigger." Always a quick learner, my father learned to hate "niggers," "gooks," "spics," "wetbacks," and any other "damn immigrant." However, my father soon found out that he was not excluded from the hatred. After days filled with jokes about "green cards" and "drug dealing," my father would return home to his wife and children, full of pent-up rage. We lived in fear of his anger and his explosiveness. My father tried to transform himself yet felt ambivalent about losing his security. Therefore, we were not allowed to speak Spanish to my father, and my mother was not allowed to learn English. By attempting to separate his children from their culture while denying his wife the chance to acculturate, my father replicated his divided psyche. My mother was forced to be the keeper of the culture and language, which she did with incredible bravery and pride. It was through the courage of my mother that I was eventually able to reconnect with my Latino heritage.

My father's drive to be accepted and to be acceptable knew no bounds. I remember one time as a child, we were driving a long distance to go to a restaurant (which was unusual for us).We sat and ate fried chicken and blueberry pie as my father anxiously waited for the owner of the restaurant to come over and acknowledge him. The owner finally did come over, and I remember how proud my father was to meet "a great American." It was only when I was older that I realized that this man was Georgia politician Lester Maddox. Maddox was one of the fiercest opponents of integration during the civil rights era. He was made infamous by keeping a bucket of ax handles by the door of his restaurant as a reminder of the violence that he had threatened to use against any Black person who would try to integrate his home or business. It shocks me to realize how racism had blinded my father to the fact that his fate as an immigrant and a minority group member in the United States was tied to the fate of other minorities.

As hard as he tried to fit in, my father never really succeeded. Often his physical features, his accent, or his clothes would give him away as being different. My father would react violently when confronted with his failure to become one hundred percent American. For example, during an interview for a promotion, the interviewer asked my father about the "good pot" grown in Colombia. At the time my father laughed it off. However, when he returned home he exploded in rage. These explosions became a daily event. My brother, sister, and I were a captive audience. We had no choice but to listen as he would berate us for being worthless. The angrier he became, the more pressure my father would put on us to "be American." We were wildly successful at being American, which only made my father angrier. As I became a teenager, my father became increasingly competitive with and abusive toward me. The fact that I physically resembled him only made things worse. He saw in me things he could never achieve: I spoke English without an accent, was headed toward college, and I dated Caucasian women exclusively.

I learned racism from my father, and just as he had done, I turned it inward. I came to hate the fact that I was Latino, that my parents spoke with an accent, that my skin, although light for a Latino, was darker than it should be. I wanted to be a White Anglo-American, and for many years, I actually thought I was. During my high school and college years I was in deep denial that I was Latino. I believed that America was a "color blind" society that rewarded people solely on the basis of hard work. I remember my Caucasian high school guidance counselor steering me away from minority scholarships for college and telling me "Ed, you want to get in on your own merit." At the time I believed her, and my "own merit" led to my status as a "token" at a predominantly Caucasian college, thousands of dollars in student loans, and 4 more years of denial.

I remember being deeply embarrassed by Latino music, food, customs, and history. My mother would often talk about her home country with pride and fondness. I used to get angry with her because she was being so "un-American." One time, in an attempt to share her culture with me, my mother gave me an expensive recording of Colombian music. I actually had the nerve to give it back to her because I was ashamed of everything Latino. I was particularly ashamed of my Spanish surname because of the way that my peers could mispronounce it in demeaning ways. I became so used to being called names that often I would participate in using ethnic slurs against myself and other minorities. I remember vividly a Latino varsity football player who was proud that his nickname was "Spic." Having a racial slur as a nickname was a badge of honor; it meant he was accepted. As an enthusiastic participant in the ethnic name-calling, I could continue to deny that I was different. The height of my own denial was when I told a Mexican joke to a priest, who was Mexican. The priest laughed, more out of shock than humor. The joke was, quite literally, on both of us. He confronted me, and pointed out that he was Mexican. As I stood in awkward silence, having offended someone I cared about, something began to awaken within me.

I began to realize that I was an impostor and that there was another side of me that I was denying. Although I felt intimidated and uncomfortable around people of color, there was a depth of connection that was missing in most of my relationships. I struggled to make sense of what I was feeling. My longing for connection with other minorities was first manifested in college through my participation in a fraternity. When I joined the fraternity, the membership was almost exclusively White. However, as I was able to influence member selection, the membership became increasingly diverse. I began to surround myself with other people who could understand what it felt like to be of two worlds and never fully at peace in either one. These were my first steps toward healing the racism that I felt inside.

My cultural explorations coincided with the divorce of my parents. My father eventually left our home and emotionally and financially disowned his family. This split helped me to continue the self-exploration and reclamation of my heritage that had begun in college. I learned about my ancestors, their names, and their lives. I learned my full name and the proper way to pronounce it. I was able to become friends with Latino men and Latina women. I asked my mother to give me back the recording of Colombian music I had refused to take from her and asked her to teach me about her culture. My mother saved up her money and took me on a trip to Colombia. I wish that I could say that I found my "home" in Colombia. I wish that I could say that I reconnected with my ancestors on some deep level. However, in Colombia I felt every bit the foreigner that I was. What I gained from my trip to Colombia was an understanding and appreciation for the enormous sacrifice that my mother had made for her children. In Colombia I realized that I was neither fully Colombian nor fully American. I had to find a way to make sense of my divided identity.

Many of my colleagues in psychology say that therapists enter the profession motivated in part by a need to deal with their own issues. As much as I used to argue that I was the exception to the rule, obviously I was not. In an effort to somehow identify, understand, and deal with my issues, I was drawn to graduate study in counseling psychology. I was offered a lucrative fellowship at a major university. However, only one professor (who later became my adviser and mentor) was honest enough to tell me that it was a minority fellowship. Many of the faculty and students saw the minority fellowship as a way for me to cheat the system because they did not think I was "really" a minority. One student explained his belief that I was not a real minority because I did not speak "broken English." The pressure to fit in and deny that I was different was enormous. I was faced with a choice that reminded me of dealing with my father: stay quiet and accept the status quo of the University and the program (basically "pass" as Caucasian) or assert myself and challenge a culturally oppressive system. I wish I could say that I chose to try to change the system simply because it was the moral or just thing to do. However, I think I chose to fight the system because I was tired of being quiet. Multicultural psychology became my passion and the focus of my career. I have my doubts as to how much I was able to change a deeply entrenched racist, sexist, and homophobic system, but I have no doubt that I underwent tremendous personal and professional growth.

As I progressed through my graduate training and into internship, I found that I surrounded myself with other people who could understand what it was like to face overt and covert racism. I formed a supportive network of friends and colleagues of all colors. At first I felt some animosity toward Caucasian people, but a Caucasian friend once pointed out that all people would benefit from being liberated from racism. I found that the term *liberation* captured the essence of what I was searching for: liberation from hatred and racism and, personally, a liberation from the past. I realized that liberation meant letting go of the intense anger and resentment I felt toward my father. My anger toward my father was like wearing a shrinking suit of armor: Although the anger could make me feel powerful and protected, the anger was not letting me grow and, in fact, was starting to choke me. However, I was concerned that, stripped of my armor, I would lose my motivation to fight racism. I was surprised to find that by liberating myself from my father's legacy, I was able to find peace and that from this peace I could generate more energy and motivation to face racism than I had imagined possible.

As I grow older and consider having my own children, I find myself looking in the mirror to see if I can see my father's face. There have been times when I have been both shocked and disappointed to hear his voice angrily coming out of my mouth or have seen my face contorted with his rage. I was surprised to find out that liberation did not mean I could change the facts of my past or get rid of any influence from my father. However, I gained something even more valuable: I learned that because of my experiences, I can understand why some one would be racist. I can understand what it is like to be both a perpetrator and a victim of racism. I have also come to understand that the answer to fighting racism begins with a moral inventory, a fearless look at oneself. I have come to the conclusion that I can never afford myself the luxury of asking the question "Am I racist?" Rather, I need to continually ask myself, "How racist am I?" As I struggle to deal with the reality of racism in my personal and professional life, I will continue to check my mirror and look for the face of racism.

Personal Narrative of an Asian American's Experience with Racism

Donna M. Talbot

Growing up in New England during the '60s and '70s had its benefits and difficulties. Although the northeast region of the country had larger pockets of people of color and immigrants than most other parts of the United States, the stiffness and arrogance of old money and elitist educational institutions created some inevitable friction among people with greatly diverse cultural backgrounds. It is in this environment (less than 5 miles from a large Air Force base) that I began my identity development, although unknowingly, as a person of color—as an Asian American.

My parents are both naturalized citizens; they were thankful to be in the United States, the land of opportunity and upward mobility. My father is French Canadian and Huron Indian and my mother is 100 percent Japanese. Although my two brothers and I were clearly raised with Japanese values and culture, my mother, our primary caretaker, insisted that we should grow up to be "good American citizens." This was driven by her pride in being a U.S. citizen and her fear of racist acts against us. What she didn't realize was that, despite her wishes, she couldn't help but raise good Japanese American citizens. . . .

Many of my most vivid memories of what I believe to be acts of racism, sexism, and oppression took place in "American institutions," such as schools, social organizations (Moose and Elks Clubs), and church. This fact has largely influenced my decision to become an educator, student affairs practitioner, and counselor; unfortunately, I think these experiences have also influenced my decision to move away from Christianity and to explore other forms of spirituality. In my professional roles, I address my agenda openly—to advocate for oppressed and marginalized populations so that they may not have to be subjected to the same negative experiences that I was.

My first overt experience of racism and recognition that I was "different" took place in school around the third grade. I remember waiting with my classmates in the hallway to go into social studies class. As I was standing there, several boys started to circle me while chanting that their fathers, uncles, and other male relatives had bombed my people. Then, they proceeded to pull up the corners of their eyes with their fingers, so they appeared slanted, and made funny noises like "ching," "chang," and so forth. For me this was extremely confusing because we had all grown up in the same neighborhood; but as I cried in the bathroom and looked in the mirror, it was the first time I cognitively realized that my eyes were different from theirs. Probably the most embarrassing part of this experience for me was that the teacher just stood in the doorway and laughed at the boys taunting me; he never tried to stop them or indicate that they were wrong. From that time on, through most of grade school, I hated myself and my mother for looking and being different.

A few years later, I learned how to be angry toward bias and ignorance. My older brother wanted to play baseball with his friends during the summer. To do that, my parents had to join the local Moose Club so that he could play in their leagues. Because my family would have been classified as "working class poor," this was a major commitment of which my parents were very proud. My father went to the club, completed the paperwork, and paid the application and membership fee. Everything seemed fine for about 2 weeks until we received a call from the membership person at the Moose Club; he explained to my father that the Moose, and other similar clubs, had a policy that prohibited interracial members from joining. The only apology he made was for not catching it sooner!

It wasn't until high school that I started to realize that there were benefits to being different—although I still resented being Asian. Teachers remembered me because I looked so different from my classmates, and the boys liked my long, black, straight hair and clear, olive complexion. Even colleges were interested and pursued this "high achieving" minority student. Although I was encouraged (actually, I was tracked) to take honors math and science courses, I had a strong interest in the social sciences and education. Most people were surprised, even shocked, when I turned down large scholarships from institutions with well-known engineering and computer science programs to go to a small liberal arts college. This marked the second most significant racist, or "classist," event in my educational experience. Early in my senior year, I was the first person in my local public high school ever to be accepted (early decision) to a very prestigious, liberal arts college—Amherst College. Soon, after the word was out that this had happened, I was summoned to the vice principal's office. Being the arrogant young "scholar" I thought I was, I assumed that the vice principal was calling me to give me "strokes" for my accomplishment. Several minutes into the discussion, a dark haze started to crowd my mind as I realized that this was an entirely different conversation than I had anticipated. Very confused and angry, I finally asked the vice principal what, exactly, she was trying to say to me. Her words rang loudly, almost deafeningly, in my ears, "Frankly, Donna, we're not sure you come from the *right kind of family* to be the first to represent our high school at Amherst College." At that point, I remember standing up and announcing that this meeting was over; however, as I was walking out, I suggested that this was a conversation she needed to have with my father. Although there were several other minor attempts to block my efforts to attend Amherst College, they were unsuccessful. I don't think I ever mentioned these incidents to my parents because I didn't want them ever to feel the humiliation that I had. Needless to say, the vice principal never called to have that conversation with my father.

College was an amazing experience for me—every day was a challenge to grow (personally and academically). Toward the end of my sophomore year, I was suspended, with many other Amherst students, for participating in demonstrations and a lock-out of the administration building. During that time, we had an African American dean who believed that the damage from slavery was over and that it was time to eliminate the programs and services that were created in the '60s to assist African American students. Naturally, we just labeled him an "Uncle Tom" and protested these decisions as well as demanded that the college divest its stocks in South Africa. My parents, especially my mother, were very angry with me; they were embarrassed that I would show such blatant disrespect for "authorities" and that I could jeopardize my education. During one of the many scoldings I received for this inappropriate behavior, my mother asked why I always had to be the one to stand up and challenge things, even the issues that didn't apply to me. My response to her was that I had to object twice as loud and twice as often because she wouldn't; either she was going to ride in the boat of change or she would be left behind on the shores of oppression and discontent. This response startled her and, though I didn't know until years later, pushed her into thinking about the role of "activism" and her own multicultural journey.

My faculty adviser at Amherst was a Returned Peace Corps Volunteer (RPCV-Micronesia). As well as turning me on to liberation theology through Freire's (1970) *Pedagogy of the Oppressed,*[1] he also taught me about the "toughest job I ever loved." Three weeks after graduation, despite my parents' hope that I would go to law school, I was on a plane to Ghana, West Africa. Before [I left] for the Peace Corps, friends and family would ask me what I thought about moving to an "uncivilized" country. I thought I knew what they meant, though I had no answers. After several months in my small village in Ghana, my host country friends and colleagues finally felt comfortable enough to ask me what it was like to live in an "uncivilized" country—they were referring to the United States. It suddenly became clear to me that oftentimes we speak the same language, use the same words, and we assume that we all mean the same thing. When my family and friends in the United States used the term "uncivilized" to describe Ghana, they were making comments about the less industrialized nature of the country; when my Ghanaian friends and colleagues called the United States uncivilized, they were referring to the need to lock our doors and to never walk alone at night for fear of our personal safety. This taught me to resist assuming that I understand another person's experience well enough to casually ascribe meaning to his or her words.

When I entered the Peace Corps, I had lofty goals; these idealistic plans soon took a backseat to survival, literally and figuratively. It struck me as humorous, at some point in my service, that I felt less like an outsider here (in Ghana) than I did in my own home country. On one of my many travels across the country, I was stranded on the road without food or shelter as nighttime approached. A young Ghanaian man saw me standing by the road and realized my situation. He invited me home to his village where his family gave me a place to sleep, shared what little food they had, and fetched me drinking and bathing water

[1]P. Freire, *Pedagogy of the Oppressed* (New York: Continuum, 1970).

from a well nearly a mile away. When I was leaving in the morning, I asked if I could give them something for their troubles. They refused my offer, indicating that they did what anyone would do. With this comment, I became extremely embarrassed and uncomfortable as I imagined how this young "Black man" would be treated in the United States if he were stranded by the road. Stimulated by this incident and many other experiences, my time in Ghana was a time of deep introspection and what I now refer to as my "rebirth." Though returning to the States was more traumatic and painful than moving to Ghana, I knew that I had to return because there was work to do here in the United States. . . .

Pain and Perseverance: Perspectives from an Ally

Lisa J. Brandyberry

I grew up as "poor, White, trash" in the middle of the Midwest. The city I lived in was an industrial one—mostly union workers—and always smelled like french fries or rubber. It was mostly White, but there were a fair number of African Americans and Latinos living in various monoracial communities throughout the city. From beginning to end, the schools I went to were integrated, so there is no time I can remember that I didn't know any Black (the term I grew up with) people.

During grade school one of my best friends was Garth, a Black child in my class. We hung around a lot together during lunch hours. I don't remember being upset about the fact that when he and I played together none of my White friends would join us. Some other Black children would come over and join us from time to time. I couldn't have both his friendship and the other White kids' friendships simultaneously.

I felt good around Garth and many of the other Black children. I felt all right around most of the other White children. I was one of few working-class Whites in that particular school. I never had the right clothes because my family shopped at Kmart and hoped for blue-light specials while we were there. My mother gave me haircuts; unfortunately, it wasn't her talent. I was often too loud in my laughter, too crude in my language.

I was also fat, an automatic object of ridicule and harassment for other children. Between being too poor and too fat, there was a lot about me to pick on and many reasons to ostracize me. But, I was never totally rejected. Somehow, something in me was enough to compensate for my "failings," so I always had friends. But with most, if not all, of my White friends, I always knew I was inferior. After the sixth grade, Garth and I were shuffled to different schools, and I didn't think I'd ever see him again.

By my senior year in high school, I had become painfully aware of what made me "inferior" to my classmates. As do many people struggling with internalized oppression, I worked hard to compensate for my failings because I had grown to believe that there was something wrong with me. I worked hard at my classes and did very well; I was always smiling, always willing to do more for others, to laugh at myself when the ridicule would come my way.

My senior year the city closed down one of the other high schools, and the students were bused to different schools. Garth ended up at mine. I saw him one day walking down the hall near my locker, and I started laughing and walking toward him, remembering how good it had felt to have him for a friend. Initially, I thought he didn't recognize me, but he did. He was uncomfortable; he didn't want to be found talking to me. I tried for a few more minutes to talk with him, to find out about what had happened to him. Then I gave up, maybe too soon. After so many years of rejection from others, I was pretty aware of what it felt like to be with someone who didn't want to be with me. We ended with a "see you around" after about 2 minutes of awkwardness. That's the last time I ever spoke to him.

Being a White female, I had learned that my weight was a primary reason for rejection from others, especially males. When Garth seemed not to want to be seen with me, I assumed it was for that reason. I was too fat, too ugly. Who knows? Maybe that was part of it. But now, looking back, I believe it was proba-bly more about race than weight. He had spent the previous 5 years in a pre-dominantly Black school. Who knows how White people had treated him, a Black male adolescent, during those years?

My college life intensified my feelings of being an outsider. I received a schol-arship to a small, private liberal arts college where the majority of the students were wealthy and White. There were a few of us paying for school through schol-arships, jobs, and loans. There were even fewer Black students on campus, but they were there. All the pain I felt growing up being poor and fat was multiplied at this college, but it was there that I got angry about it. Angry about the privi-leges of wealthy people who seemed to believe that it was normal to have more than enough money to go to Europe on vacations, to shop for new clothes every weekend, to have cars at their disposal, to have plenty of leisure time because they weren't trying to fit in a job on top of classes and studying.

I tried reaching out to some of the few Black students on campus and became close with one woman, Doris. I cannot begin to imagine what it was like for a young Black woman from Chicago to have to survive in that small Iowa town. After we had struck up a friendship, she started pushing me to go to Black dance clubs in a nearby city. I initially refused—I didn't even go to White dance clubs. But, eventually, I agreed to go. She took charge of what I was going to wear because I couldn't dress like those "White folks," who dressed down to go out. This was time to go all out with jewelry, makeup, and hairstyles. I remember being very nervous on the long drive to the city, scared about being the only White per-son in the club. I was too embarrassed by this to tell my friend.

Through this experience I got my first taste of being a racial minority. Although this was unpleasant, it was vital in my development. I felt what it was like to have people be angry that I had merely walked into their place, to feel cautious about what I said and how I said it, to feel like a complete outsider, to imagine that everyone in the room must hate me because of my skin color. I am thankful that Doris didn't allow me to disappear into a corner. She pushed me out on the dance floor and pulled me around introducing me to people she knew. By the end of the night I had had a great time, and we went back together several times during the next year.

Graduate school pushed me more than any other experience to really exam-ine myself. I was fortunate to end up in a program that emphasized diversity issues. There were many times it was painful and frightening, because I was challenged to look beyond my "liberal" attitudes to honestly examine myself. I had to go deeper than focusing on all the positive experiences I had had with people of color. I had to examine all the negative messages I had absorbed and determine how much they were still affecting me. I had to learn to see myself as part of the White race, whether I liked it or not.

My family, church, and the media were major influences on me. I went to a church that was entirely White and remember watching how any Black families that would come to visit would have it made clear to them that they weren't welcome. They were treated much like I was when I went to the Black dance club, except they didn't end up having fun and meeting nice people. The stares and whispers didn't end; the shared laughter never started.

I was affected by hearing my brothers talk about "niggers," or more often about "Black bitches." I remember my parents not allowing one of my brothers to go play basketball at a certain court because it wasn't safe around "those" people. I remember my father pointing out what we thought was a garishly painted house and saying "colored" people have no taste. I also remember him making it clear that he didn't want me ever to bring home a Black man. As much as I want to believe I never accepted these attitudes, I know they influenced me and what I believed. I came to believe that "they" were different from "us."

The process of acknowledging what was meant by "us," of owning my own racial heritage, included owning all the history that goes with being White. During this process, the only part of that history I could see was its shame: slavery and genocide of Africans, American Indians, Asians, and Mexicans. There didn't seem to be any horror that wasn't committed in the name of the "manifest destiny" and superiority of European Whites. My reaction was to feel an incredible amount of guilt and shame; I didn't want to be White, didn't want to belong to this group, didn't want to be part of this "us."

Even more painful than that was having to examine how I had benefited from racism. I had to question how I could hold so much anger toward those who were wealthy (or male) because they didn't recognize their privileges but had never acknowledged the privileges I enjoyed from my skin color. It had never crossed my mind that there was a way in which I was privileged. I didn't come from money, I wasn't born beautiful, my family life had been far from perfect, and I had struggled to get where I was.

It wasn't easy to look at the probability that I had struggled less than if I were a person of color. That maybe my White skin had allowed me access to the upper-level college preparatory classes despite being working class, which, in turn, probably increased my test scores, which opened doors to receive academic scholarships and, basically, gave me the opportunity to achieve a level beyond where I was born. I'd like to think that I earned everything I have, but I can no longer tell myself that. I earned some of it, and some of it was very likely given to me because of being White. I have grown to recognize the privileges I receive every day for being White.

It was during this time of feeling overwhelmed with guilt and shame about my race that I worked for a year as the only White person in an all-African American agency. It was not a job I had applied for or wanted; it was a job I was requested (and eventually forced) to accept. I didn't want the job because I was afraid the staff would hate me. I remember talking with my boss about my fears. He was an African American man with whom I'd worked before and who had requested my placement in the position. He never denied that hostility was possible, but he never let me off the hook regarding my responsibility. He made it clear that it was my place to deal with any prejudice directed at me and that he would support me in that process, but that it was something I would have to face. He also reminded me that it was something minorities face on a daily basis. Again, in having to walk through my fear, I enjoyed a wonderful experience. There was only one person who made it clear she didn't want me there, and even she taught me a valuable lesson. She taught me how subtle sabotage can be. I would miss meetings because I never received the memorandum informing me of them. I wouldn't receive phone messages. I'd receive paperwork late or not at all, and I could *feel* her dislike emanating from her. It was through this experience that I learned to be very hesitant to question the experiences of persons of color who feel they are being discriminated against but can't name anything grossly inappropriate.

My professional life has moved me farther in my journey to overcome racism. A large part of that has come from my close work and friendship with an African American lesbian, Jan. We connected immediately when I came to interview and quickly became friends. We have done numerous programs together focusing in general on oppression issues and, often, specifically on race. We have had to struggle together with issues of race more so than any other issue. What has saved our relationship is our willingness to talk about race, to put our "raggedy selves" on the table.

Many of these struggles have come from my desire not to have race separate us and Jan's desire to keep part of her personal space monoracial; that is, sometimes she just wants to hang with the Black folks. Intellectually, I understand this. I sometimes don't want men around because there is a comfort in groups of women that doesn't exist with men present. It has nothing to do with disliking men; it's simply a different vibe that exists. But on a personal level, it continues to hurt. I struggle with feeling rejected, separated because of my skin color, not seen as the person who is Jan's friend but as a representative of the White race. She knows this because we've talked about it at length. She struggles with it as well because she knows it hurts me, but she wants to have her needs met too.

I now understand why I sometimes feel closer to, and more connected with, some people of color than with many White people. My understanding came through viewing oppression as encompassing all the different groups experiencing it. Having been born into a working-class family, I share many cultural dynamics with people of color also born into this economic sphere. It is often difficult for me, and apparently others, to figure out how to separate race from class. My sensitivity to how I've experienced oppression personally, through class, body size, and gender issues, has allowed me to have some sense of perspective on the pain of racism. Finally, my willingness to admit to and name privileges that I experience because of my race seems to afford me some credibility with people of color. . . .

My conclusion, sadly, is that most people of color simply don't expect much from White people. They don't expect us to be open, to have thought about these issues, to have thought about ourselves (rather than them) in terms of these issues, to be working against racism inside and outside of the therapy room. I believe it is my responsibility, as a member of the majority group, to fight racism. As I benefit and derive increased societal rewards from racism's existence, perhaps my voice may reach other White ears that refuse to listen to the voices of people of color. I believe this as passionately as I believe that men must speak to other men about sexism, that heterosexuals must speak to members of their own group about homophobia, and so on.

Those of us committed to being allies must be willing to persevere in this struggle. People of color do not have the option of ignoring racism and its effects; therefore, we must not ignore it either. We must choose to persevere in the face of rejection, criticism, and suspicion from members of majority and minority groups. Not everyone wants Whites to be involved in this struggle, and I understand this lack of trust. But racism is the problem of the racists, not those who are oppressed by it. As a part of the problem group, I must be involved in eliminating the problem itself.

Some say that no one willingly gives up power, and while members of majority groups refuse to see any benefit to themselves for changing the system (personal and institutional), progress will be slow and painful. But when majority group members can see that *their* lives will improve, *their* accomplishments will be seen as more completely due to merit rather than privilege, that the quality of life will improve for all of us, then, perhaps, change will be possible.

 Discussion Questions

1. What do these five personal statements have in common?
2. Each of these essays considers diversity from a different kind of concern. Are they equally important concerns? If you had to rank them, how would you select the one or two that truly matter? If you find you cannot rank them in importance, why not?
3. Do these authors raise issues of political correctness? Or is that too narrow a way of viewing their experiences?
4. What other groups—minority or majority—might put forward similar experiences and draw similar conclusions from them?

5. Federal, state, and local laws now identify specific groups of people as "protected classes." These usually include groups defined by characteristics shared in common such as religion, race, gender, physical disability, and Vietnam-era veteran status. Should these be legally "protected" classes? Explain.

 ## Suggestions for Your Journal

Most of us identify with many different groups. Thus a single individual college student might consider herself a member of all the following: her family, her church, her nationality, her race, her athletic team, her first-year class, her sorority, her armed forces unit, and many more. What groups do you identify with? How have you come to develop that many-faceted sense of identity? Rank those groups in order, from the ones you feel most closely tied to, to the ones that seem most distant to your feelings.

Have you ever felt that others discriminated against you as a member of some group? Write about that feeling and how you dealt with it. Is there a lesson in your personal experience for future action?

A university is a specialized kind of institution. In a journal entry or essay, write about the ways in which the specific character of a university does or should have implications for issues of discrimination.

I Have a Dream

Martin Luther King Jr.

On August 28, 1963, Dr. Martin Luther King Jr. the preeminent civil rights leader in America during the 1950s and 1960s, delivered this speech as the keynote address of the March on Washington for Civil Rights. His widow, Coretta Scott King, said of that occasion: "At that moment, it seemed as if the kingdom of God appeared. But it lasted for only a moment." This speech is one of the enduring documents of 20th-century American history.

I am happy to join with you today in what will go down in history as the greatest demonstration for freedom in the history of our nation.

Five score years ago, a great American, in whose symbolic shadow we stand today, signed the *Emancipation Proclamation*. This momentous decree came as a great beacon light of hope to millions of Negro slaves who had been seared in the flames of withering injustice. It came as a joyous daybreak to end the long night of their captivity.

But one hundred years later, the Negro still is not free; one hundred years later, the life of the Negro is still sadly crippled by the manacles of segregation and the chains of discrimination; one hundred years later, the Negro lives on a lonely island of poverty in the midst of a vast ocean of material prosperity; one hundred years later, the Negro is still *languished* in the corners of American society and finds himself an exile in his own land.

So we've come here today to dramatize a shameful condition. In a sense we've come to our nation's capital to cash a check. When the architects of our republic wrote the magnificent words of the Constitution and the Declaration of Independence, they were signing a *promissory note* to which every American was to fall heir. This note was a promise that all men, yes, black men as well as white men, would be guaranteed the *unalienable* rights of life, liberty, and the pursuit of happiness.

It is obvious today that America has defaulted on this promissory note insofar as her citizens of color are concerned. Instead of honoring this sacred obligation, America has given the Negro people a bad check, a check which has come back marked "insufficient funds." But we refuse to believe that the bank of justice is bankrupt. We refuse to believe that there are insufficient funds in the great vaults of opportunity of this nation. And so we've come to cash this check, a check that will give us upon demand the riches of freedom and the security of justice.

We have also come to this hallowed spot to remind America of the fierce urgency of now. This is no time to engage in the luxury of cooling off or to take the tranquilizing drug of gradualism. Now is the time to make real the promises of democracy; now is the time to rise from the dark and desolate valley of segregation to the sunlit path of racial justice; now is the time to lift our nation from the quicksands of racial injustice to the solid rock of brotherhood; now is the time to make justice a reality for all of God's children. It would be fatal for the nation to overlook the urgency of the moment. This sweltering summer of the Negro's legitimate discontent will not pass until there is an invigorating autumn of freedom and equality.

Nineteen sixty-three is not an end, but a beginning. And those who hope that the Negro needed to blow off steam and will now be content, will have a rude awakening if the nation returns to business as usual.

There will be neither rest nor tranquillity in America until the Negro is granted his citizenship rights. The whirlwinds of revolt will continue to shake the foundations of our nation until the bright day of justice emerges.

But there is something that I must say to my people who stand on the warm threshold which leads into the palace of justice. In the process of gaining our rightful place we must not be guilty of wrongful deeds.

Let us not seek to satisfy our thirst for freedom by drinking from the cup of bitterness and hatred. We must forever conduct our struggle on the high plane of dignity and discipline. We must not allow our creative protest to degenerate into physical violence. Again and again we must rise to the majestic heights of meeting physical force with soul force.

The marvelous new militancy which has engulfed the Negro community must not lead us to a distrust of all white people, for many of our white brothers, as evidenced by their presence here today, have come to realize that their destiny is tied up with our destiny, and they have come to realize that their freedom is inextricably bound to our freedom. We cannot walk alone.

And as we walk, we must make the pledge that we shall always march ahead. We cannot turn back. There are those who are asking the devotees of civil rights, "When will you be satisfied?" We can never be satisfied as long as the Negro is the victim of the unspeakable horrors of police brutality.

We can never be satisfied as long as our bodies, heavy with the fatigue of travel, cannot gain lodging in the motels of the highways and the hotels of the cities. We cannot be satisfied as long as the Negro's basic mobility is from a smaller ghetto to a larger one.

We can never be satisfied as long as our children are stripped of their selfhood and robbed of their dignity by signs stating "for whites only." We cannot be satisfied as long as a Negro in Mississippi cannot vote and a Negro in New York believes he has nothing for which to vote. No, we are not satisfied, and we will not be satisfied until justice rolls down like waters and righteousness like a mighty stream.

I am not unmindful that some of you have come here out of excessive trials and tribulation. Some of you have come fresh from narrow jail cells. Some of you have come from areas where your quest for freedom left you battered by the storms of persecution and staggered by the winds of police brutality. You have been the veterans of creative suffering. Continue to work with the faith that unearned suffering is redemptive.

Go back to Mississippi; go back to Alabama; go back to South Carolina; go back to Georgia; go back to Louisiana; go back to the slums and ghettos of the northern cities, knowing that somehow this situation can and will be changed. Let us not wallow in the valley of despair.

I say to you today, my friends, that even though we must face the difficulties of today and tomorrow, I still have a dream. It is a dream deeply rooted in the American dream. I have a dream that one day this nation will rise up, live out the true meaning of its creed—we hold these truths to be self-evident, that all men are created equal.

I have a dream that one day on the red hills of Georgia, sons of former slaves and sons of former slave-owners will be able to sit down together at the table of brotherhood.

I have a dream that one day, even the state of Mississippi, a state sweltering with the heat of injustice, sweltering with the heat of oppression, will be transformed into an oasis of freedom and justice.

I have a dream my four little children will one day live in a nation where they will be not be judged by the color of their skin but by the content of their character. I have a dream today!

I have a dream that one day, down in Alabama, with its vicious racists, with its governor having his lips dripping with the words of interposition and nullification, that one day, right there in Alabama, little black boys and black girls will be able to join hands with little white boys and white girls as sisters and brothers. I have a dream today!

I have a dream that one day every valley shall be exalted, every hill and mountain shall be made low, the rough places shall be made plain, and the crooked places will be made straight, and the glory of the Lord will be revealed and all flesh shall see it together.

This is our hope. This is the faith that I go back to the South with.

With this faith we will be able to hew out of the mountain of despair a stone of hope. With this faith we will be able to transform the jangling discords of our nation into a beautiful symphony of brotherhood.

With this faith we will be able to work together, to pray together, to struggle together, to go to jail together, to stand up for freedom together, knowing that we will be free one day. This will be the day when all of God's children will be able to sing with new meaning—"my country 'tis of thee; sweet land of liberty; of thee I sing; land where my father died, land of the pilgrim's pride; from every mountainside, let freedom ring"—and if America is to be a great nation, this must become true.

So let freedom ring from the prodigious hilltops of New Hampshire.
Let freedom ring from the mighty mountains of New York.
Let freedom ring from the heightening Alleghenies of Pennsylvania.
Let freedom ring from the snow-capped Rockies of Colorado.
Let freedom ring from the curvaceous slopes of California.
But not only that.

Let freedom ring from Stone Mountain of Georgia.
Let freedom ring from Lookout Mountain of Tennessee.
Let freedom ring from every hill and molehill of Mississippi.
From every mountainside, let freedom ring.

And when we allow freedom to ring, when we let it ring from every village
and every hamlet, from every state and every city, we will be able to speed up
that day when all of God's children—black men and white men, Jews and Gentiles, Protestants and Catholics—will be able to join hands and sing in the words
of the old Negro spiritual, "Free at last, free at last; thank God Almighty, we are
free at last."

 ## Vocabulary

As you think about this essay, these definitions may be helpful to you:
1. **Emancipation Proclamation**   issued by President Abraham Lincoln in
   1862 freeing all slaves in all territory still at war with the Union
2. **languished**   suffering neglect
3. **promissory note**   a pledge to pay a debt; an "I.O.U."
4. **unalienable**   incapable of being surrendered or transferred

 ## Discussion Questions

1. What does King mean by the phrase "the tranquilizing drug of gradualism"?
2. King argues that physical force must be countered by "soul force." What
   does he mean?
3. Using the language of his own time, King speaks of "the Negro." Today's
   authors would probably not use this word. Why?
4. Discuss the ways in which repetition of key words and phrases plays a part
   in making this an effective speech.
5. As a Christian minister, King drew heavily on the language of the Bible,
   which was natural to him. What effect does including such language ("we
   will not be satisfied until justice rolls down like waters and righteousness
   like a mighty stream," "every valley shall be exalted, every hill and mountain
   shall be made low") add to this speech?

Suggestions for Your Journal

Write about the social or political cause for which you would be willing to demonstrate in a public way. In your comments, describe how you came to feel as strongly as you do about this cause.

Martin Luther King Jr. is closely related intellectually and historically to another great social leader, India's Mahatma Gandhi. Both were known for a form of, in King's words, "militant nonviolence." King expressed his admiration for Gandhi by arguing: "We must forever conduct our struggle on the high plane of dignity and discipline. We must not allow our creative protest to degenerate into physical violence." Write an entry in which you agree or disagree with King's statement.

Affirmative Action and Multiculturalism

David Bruce Ingram and Jennifer A. Parks

David Bruce Ingram is a professor of philosophy at Loyola University in Chicago. He is the author of 4 books on philosophy and ethics and 23 books in the area of business ethics. Jennifer A. Parks is an assistant professor of philosophy at Loyola University and the co-director of programs in health-care ethics.

I still get misty-eyed when I read Martin Luther King Jr.'s famous "I Have a Dream" speech, which he delivered in front of the Lincoln Memorial on August 28, 1963, at the height of the Civil Rights Movement. Here's King, dreaming about the day when people in America "will not be judged by the color of their skin but by the content of their character"; when "the jangling discords of our nation will be transformed into a beautiful symphony of brotherhood"; when "black men and white men, Jews and Gentiles, Catholics and Protestants, will be able to join hands and to sing in the words of the old Negro spiritual, 'Free at last, free at last; thank God Almighty, we are free at last.'"

We've come a long way since King delivered those mighty words. We've outlawed segregation and legal discrimination and our society has made tremendous strides in racial healing. But I wonder whether we have gone far enough in eradicating racial injustice and bringing about equal opportunity for all. Blacks as a whole lag far behind whites economically (the typical black family has one-tenth of the assets of a typical white family); they continue to be underrepresented in legislatures and on corporate boards; they have a lower life expectancy and suffer a higher rate of infant mortality; and they continue to face discrimination at all levels of life, from police profiling to discrimination in securing loans and real estate "red-lining."

In Census 2000, the U.S. Government tried to take a nose count of all Americans, including asking each of us to identify what race and ethnicity we belong to. Persons were asked if they are Hispanic or not, and then they were invited to pick one or more (up to six) racial categories that best described them. What was remarkable about this approach was that it recognized that racial identification is not an all-or-nothing affair—none of us, in fact, is racially pure when it comes right down to it. Furthermore, it *tacitly* recognized that race itself is largely a matter of personal preference.

Not so long ago Americans thought that race was an all-or-nothing affair—something fixed in nature, having to do with the blood you inherited from your parents. For example, among whites it was assumed that if you inherited even a drop of "black" blood from, say a great-great-grandparent, then you were totally black. Modern genetics has totally refuted this biological notion of race. A person's racial features express his genetic make-up, which in turn is the product of recombining the genes he inherited from his parents. Depending on how his genes are recombined, persons may or may not look very much like their parents. Genetically speaking, persons who look racially alike are as different as, or more different from, each other than persons who don't look racially alike.

If race doesn't exist in any biological sense, should people still think of themselves racially? Perhaps in an ideal society they wouldn't. Racial distinctions are a modern invention. Prior to the European conquest of the New World, people divided themselves mainly on the basis of religion and culture. Religious and cultural conversion on the part of the heathen/barbarian was almost always possible. The only differences that were regarded as natural were differences between the sexes and, to a far lesser extent, differences between nobles and commoners.

So you see, we didn't always divide the world along racial lines. Racial distinctions were invented to justify the enslavement of Africans and Native Americans by Europeans. Perhaps in an ideal world, differences in skin pigmentation would matter about as much as differences in eye pigmentation.

We often think of cultural differences as forming the basis for ethnic identifications and biological differences as forming the basis for racial identifications. Reality is more complicated than this. Members of the same ethnic group often share overlapping physical features; and members of the same racial group often share overlapping cultural traits. This isn't surprising, since both physical and cultural traits are passed down from generation to generation, the former through genes, the latter through *socialization.*

If race and ethnicity are so closely linked together, then it seems that what applies to one ought to apply to the other. For instance, if we think that an ideal world would be a world without racial distinctions, then it seems that we should also think that an ideal world would be a world without ethnic differences. In fact, if you consider some of the changes that would have to happen in order for racial thinking to disappear, such as complete residential and occupational integration of all races—it becomes clear that these changes would have deep cultural repercussions as well. For many aspects of ethnic culture are also cultivated in relatively tight-knit and geographically bonded racial communities.

This takes us to a very hard question. Is complete racial and ethnic integration a desirable ideal to strive for? We think that racial integration is desirable for fighting racism. However, even after the elimination of legal segregation we see that many blacks prefer to live in black communities because they feel more welcome there. Even after all traces of racism are gone, some blacks may still prefer to live among blacks for cultural reasons. For example, although certain aspects of the African American spiritual tradition can be (and have been) transported into all cultures, the black church as the bedrock of a distinctive black identity can't be. Some blacks might still prefer to live in predominantly black communities in order to preserve this identity.

The problem of integration suggests two ways of fighting discrimination against religious, ethnic, and racial groups:

- anti-racism
- multiculturalism

Anti-racism targets racial segregation, and so promotes the aim of racial integration at all levels of life. It reminds us of our common humanity, and the universal rights we share with all others. Its ideal is that of a raceless society, where physical differences between people are as insignificant as differences in eye color.

Multiculturalism, by contrast, targets cultural domination—or the attempt by a dominant culture to eradicate, assimilate, or otherwise integrate subordinate cultures to the point where they no longer exist as distinct and independent. As a positive agenda, multiculturalism encourages us to respect all cultures as equals. Unlike anti-racism, it sees positive value in preserving and promoting differences, even if this requires granting special exemptions and privileges to minority cultures that are endangered.

So where does affirmative action fit into all this? Affirmative action initially meant actively recruiting qualified minorities—mainly blacks. Good faith recruitment policies didn't work very well, so the government asked businesses to set deadlines for hiring a certain number of blacks. This didn't work very well either, so the government started imposing quotas—a set number or percentage of jobs—that had to be filled by blacks. Along the way, women and other minorities were added to the list of protected classes. Courts have since ruled that the use of affirmative action quotas in college admissions is unconstitutional and that their use in government contracting is highly suspect.

Affirmative action now effectively protects most of the American population. In 1996 the Clinton administration expanded the list of affirmative action beneficiaries of federal contracts to include small businesses owned by women, the disabled, and the socially disadvantaged, in addition to those owned by blacks, Latinos, Indians, Asians, Eskimos, and Native Hawaiians.

In order for affirmative action to be an effective tool for leveling the playing field it must be administered in a way that is sensitive to individual differences in comparative disadvantage. This will be difficult to do, although not entirely impossible. For example, being a woman today is much less of a disadvantage than it was thirty years ago (in fact, women have made the greatest strides in educational and economic advancement of any group and now comprise a solid majority of all students attending institutions of higher education). Being a Native American resident of an impoverished reservation, by contrast, is still (at least in most cases) a very serious disadvantage.

Does affirmative action elevate the less qualified over the better qualified? Yes, if you think that the only relevant qualifications for measuring future job performance are things like where you went to school, what grades you got, and how well you performed on standardized tests. Surely these qualifications matter. The question is, how much?

Pronounced differences in test scores and grades may sometimes predict different levels of job performance. In some cases, grades and test scores might be irrelevant—you don't need to be a literary genius or mathematics whiz to be a good electrician. Other kinds of qualifications—such as speech, appearance, friendliness, and so on—are more subjective, and therefore more prone to racial biases. Experience is an important qualification but it, too, can sometimes mask true ability. And let's not forget that some qualifications are not at all related to future performance. Princeton University admits 40 percent of all admissions applicants whose parents were former students of the university in comparison to just 15 percent of the regular applicant pool. Last but not least, race itself might be a relevant qualification when filling a high-profile post in a Black Studies Program at a university; for typically, such positions involve role modeling and mentoring as well as teaching and research.

Affirmative action is indeed a strategy for "leveling the playing field," but unlike past forms of racial discrimination, it doesn't try to accomplish this by dragging one segment of the population down to the level of oppressed populations. Rather, its aim is positive: to compensate for the continuing effects of sexual and racial discrimination. In other words, its aim is to elevate the oppressed populations to the current, privileged status enjoyed by all the rest.

 ## Vocabulary

As you think about this essay, these definitions may be helpful to you:
1. **tacitly**   expressed silently or understood without the use of words
2. **socialization**   the process of becoming part of a group and fitting in with that group's culture and values

 ## Discussion Questions

1. Ingram and Parks ask what they consider to be "a very hard question"—namely, "Is complete racial and ethnic integration a desirable ideal to strive for?" How do they answer that question? How would you answer it?
2. In your experience, is it true, as Ingram and Parks assert, that "experience is an important qualification but it . . . can sometimes mask true ability"? Give some examples to support your response.
3. Ingram and Parks comment parenthetically that "being a woman today is much less of a disadvantage than it was thirty years ago. In fact, women have made the greatest strides in educational and economic advancement of any

group and now comprise a solid majority of all students attending institutions of higher education." Assuming that this claim is true, identify some reasons that such a considerable change should have happened.

 ## Suggestions for Your Journal

It is difficult for students just entering their college years to imagine what was true of students at the same age 20 or 30 years ago. Interview someone who is at least 20 years older than you are and a college graduate. Summarize their sense of how the world has changed in the intervening years.

Ingram and Parks suggest that there have been improvements related to many of the social problems they talk about and that Dr. Martin Luther King Jr. addressed in his famous 1963 speech, "I Have a Dream." Is there still a need, in your view, for affirmative action programs? How do they affect you personally? How would discontinuing affirmative action affect you?

UNIT SUMMARY

The essays in this unit discuss some of the conditions necessary to ensure that the pursuit of truth, identified in Unit 6 as the defining characteristic of a university, can be carried out by all participants in the university community without interference. Some observers believe that university faculty and students are just trying to be "politically correct" when they acknowledge and try to protect diversity. However, the essays in this unit are not grounded in the relatively recent notion of "political correctness." Instead, these essays address contemporary topics of concern within the framework of a vision of all individuals exercising their freedom to express ideas—a freedom that is essential to, and therefore precious within, the university.

Summary Questions

1. Were you surprised by any of the conclusions that these writers defended? How do they differ from your own current, or previous, beliefs?
2. Can you give examples of finding value in diversity—examples that have made a difference in the way you think or behave?
3. Many people would comment that visions of the future like that presented by Martin Luther King Jr. are attractive and useful as a goal but too idealistic to be realized in a complex society. Do you agree? How might we go about preparing the kind of world that King envisioned in his dream?

Suggested Writing Assignments

1. Do you tend to make judgments about any group of people (for example, a nationality group, a fraternity or sorority, or a religious group) based on membership in that group? If so, write a short essay explaining why you do this. Are there any times when *group* characteristics appropriately outweigh individual character?
2. Have you ever been the object of bigotry? If so, write an essay describing how you were singled out and suggest a plan for responding to such behavior.
3. Whose job is it to ensure that, within a university, people are judged only on the basis of their ability? Write an essay identifying those who need to act on this matter and specify the most important steps they should take.

Suggested Readings

Bowen, William G., and Derek Bok. *The Shape of the River: Long-Term Consequences of Considering Race in College and University Admissions.* Princeton, NJ: Princeton University Press, 1998.

Fisk, E. B. "The Undergraduate Hispanic Experience." Change (May/June 1988), 29–33.

Haley, Alex, and Malcolm X. *The Autobiography of Malcolm X.* New York: Grove Press, 1976.

Halpern, J. M., and L. Nguyen-Hong-Nhiem, eds. *The Far East Comes Near: Autobiographical Accounts of Southeast Asian Students in America.* Amherst: University of Massachusetts Press, 1989.

What Should I Know About Careers?

A ccording to many students, one of the main purposes of acquiring a college degree is to prepare for a career. And yet this process remains a mystery to many students. The concepts of work, job, and career, although often used interchangeably, are very different. Work can be defined as an activity that accomplishes a task. Career is a lifelong process that usually includes many jobs. Work in our culture is often synonymous with one's identity. Even small children are asked what they "want to do" when they grow up. By the time students enter college, many have some idea of general areas of study they might want to explore or pursue. How work is valued by the individual shapes the perceptions of and attitudes about the meaning of a career as the exploration and planning process is engaged.

In their book *Careerism and Intellectualism Among College Students,* Katchadourian and Boli state that there has been an increase in careerism among college students since the late

Our road to success is currently under construction.

—ANONYMOUS

1970s. This trend has been documented in surveys of entering first-year students who indicated that "becoming an authority in my field" and "being well off financially" were of greater importance to them than other non-work-related goals. Students' choices of major have also changed. Whereas students wanting business degrees peaked in the late 1980s, other majors, such as the health professions and computer science, have attracted increasing numbers of students.

Students entering college in the 21st century face a bewildering array of issues concerning their choice of career. Economic shifts, societal and environmental concerns, and the increased complexities of business because of new technologies create a volatile job market. Career-planning professionals encourage students to assess their personal strengths and limitations and base their choices on this knowledge rather than rely on external forces over which they have little control.

The readings in this unit represent a wide array of opinions and attitudes toward work and related issues. Do you expect to "do the work you love" after graduation? If so, Boldt explains how you will be part of a new social movement. Goal setting is difficult for many people but is a critical aspect of career planning. Nicholas Lore provides some specific ways to accomplish this important task. Mary Sherry and Mark Ballard both write about searching for a job. Sherry writes about the process, and Ballard provides some practical insights into how to prepare throughout the college years for the day after graduation.

Peggy Simonsen, looking ahead, points out that traditional career paths no longer dominate the future of new graduates. She describes career patterns for the new century that will require different strategies for success.

All these thought-provoking ideas about work will offer a sense of how important identifying one's work values and purpose is. The college years are a time to explore, gather information, test alternatives, and finally make the first of many career decisions. Although most students approach this process from a very practical perspective, the readings in this unit should also help you think about your personal definition of work and how it will influence your ultimate career decisions.

How to Get There from Here

Nicholas Lore

Nicholas Lore is the founder of Rockport Institute, an international career counseling network that has coached thousands through first-time career and midcareer decisions. He has worked with students, business executives, artists and musicians, government officials, technical people, support staff, and professionals in all fields. Nicholas Lore has been commended for excellence by two U.S. presidents.

I once saw a TV news feature story about two professional golfers. They were the same age, looked alike, had gone to PGA school together, each had 2.2 children, cute wives, were best friends, and had the same stroke average. Two people could not be more alike unless they were twins. One of them had won several major tournaments that year and was raking in high sums of money. The other was working as a golf pro at a country club and had never won anything, even though he had participated in tournaments. The point of the feature story was supposed to be something about the fickle finger of fate. But as they were interviewed, it became evident that there was one big difference between the two golfers. The winning golfer, when asked about his future goals, said his goal was to be the best and most successful golfer in the world. The other fellow said his vision for the future was to make a living playing golf. One had created an extraordinary vision for the future and was going for it 200 percent. The other was happy to putt around in the comfort zone.

It does not make you a better person to have bigger goals. It simply makes life a more exciting game that stretches your very being. You may be happy in the comfort zone. You may just want to have a decent career, 2.2 kids, retire to Florida, and watch TV until one day you don't wake up. If so, I suggest that you really swing out and set some goals that will create an exciting vision for your future. Whatever you want, being clear about your goals makes it much more likely that you will get there.

Principles of Goal Setting

1. Understand that there are three different levels of goals. At the highest level are big comprehensive *meta-goals*. The word *meta* means "transcending or more comprehensive." "These goals usually express large, abstract ideas, like health, contribution, love, ecstasy, pleasure, security, self-expression, prosperity, satisfaction. From these meta-level goals flow *specific goals*. Falling under the broad comprehensive goal of prosperity, you might set specific goals concerning income, saving, investment, retirement, controlling impulse buying, etc. Finally, at the lowest level are the items on your to-do list. Some of these are *action steps*. They are the nitty-gritty, step-by-step plans to make your dreams come true.

Other lower-level goals could be thought of as mileposts. They are markers along the path to completing a project that fulfills a goal. They tell how far down the trail you have gone.

Most people's meta-goals are not something they created. In fact, most of us have had no say in choosing our meta-level goals. Remember that advertising psychologists say that what motivates us is looking good, feeling good, being right, feeling safe, and avoiding pain. With the exception of "being right," these are powerful *motivators* for our nonhuman friends as well. They are already pro- grammed into our internal wiring. If "feeling safe" is a meta-goal, you may have some choice about how to realize this goal, choices about what "safety" means to you, for example. But, you don't have any more choice about the goal itself than you do about your shadow. Like your shadow, meta-goals follow you around everywhere. You can live in the dark and deny they exist, but they will spring forth every time the light shines on you. Many of these higher-level goals will be the same as some of your most important and deepest held values. Once you are consciously aware of the extraordinarily powerful role these meta-goals play in your life, new possibilities arise: perhaps you could start to invent some new ones, alter, transform and even abandon old ones.

The most conscious, evolved people create their own meta-goals rather than just run the software program built into them. For example, Gandhi's nature was deeply sensual, which he abandoned because he thought this meta-goal detracted from his life's purpose. Imagine what people would have thought if he spoke and spun from the grounds of the Himalayan Hedonism Hideaway. When you create a purpose for your life, what you are actually doing is creating the highest form of meta-goal possible. Living from a purpose is essentially surren- dering to a meta-goal that you invented which you elevate to a higher position than the ones already programmed in, and which serves some purpose larger than your self-fulfillment.

2. Make your goals correspond with what you really want. If your goals represent what you think you should want, what would please your parents or your cultural identity but are not authentically your own, you will have great difficulty achieving them. Align your goals with your deepest principles and val- ues and with your most genuine dreams and desires. Wanting something pas- sionately does not necessarily mean you must have it. If you do not have the passion, the desire for something, don't turn it into a goal. Life is short. You don't have time to waste going after things you really don't want.

3. Create goals for every important area of your life. Remember that each part of your life is *interwoven* with everything else. Don't stop with career goals. Create goals for your relationships, your hobby, or your community involve- ment. Make up some health and fitness goals, satisfaction and well-being goals. Parents should not make up goals for their children but should encourage them to become masterful at setting their own goals.

4. Understand that well-founded goals contain some specific ingredients that boost their effectiveness. Fuzziness is the enemy of productivity that moves your goals along to completion. When you are slogging through waist-deep mud along the path to fulfilling a goal, it is amazingly easy to forget why you were in the mud in the first place. All of your goals should be *highly specific.*Whenever possible, make your goals *measurable.*If they are not measurable, how will you be able to tell if you are achieving them? Don't worry about attempting to make your meta-goals measurable. They are usually too abstract to hone into measurability. Goals should have a *definite completion date,* if possible. The whole reason to set goals is to have something specific to shoot for. Goals are an active intention, not a prediction. They focus your energy and direct your attention toward things you desire to accomplish.

5. Write them down. Your brain is a bad place to keep your goals. Goals are more valuable than anything you have, except your health. Your brain is too much like a pocket with many holes in it, too susceptible to hypnotism, *somnambulism,* and storms of uncertainty and doubt to be the best place to store your goals. If you manage a Goals List, you will be able to simply cross off a goal you have accomplished or are abandoning. If you keep your goals in your head, you will have to deal with your psychology and your memory in addition to your goals.

6. Create both short-term and long-term goals. Effective goal setting involves creating a comprehensive life plan as well as deciding what to accomplish next week or tomorrow.

7. Manage your Goals List. Revisit your goals often. At the beginning of each year, go over your long-term goals, create new ones, revise the existing ones, and toss out the ones you decide not to aim for. Go over the goals you set for the year just ending. Complete each goal by marking it done, transferring it to a time in the future, or declaring it complete as it is, even if you failed to get the result you wanted. Go through the same process at the end of every month and every week, focusing on goals you set for those time periods. The most effective people I know complete their Goals List for the day that is ending, create new goals for the next day, and then spend a few minutes looking for ways to improve their efforts tomorrow.

8. Set goals that take you as far as you are willing to stretch to make your wildest dreams come true, but not farther. Most people set goals that do not require much of a stretch. If they wanted to buy a house, they would go after reasonable goals, such as features that fit their price range. Their main criterion is that their goals be sensible, reasonable. If you want a reasonable degree of success and satisfaction, by all means, create reasonable goals. If you want more than that, being reasonable will constantly block your path.

When you come up with a good idea for a possible goal, treat it with respect. Whether it is an idea that solves one of the world's great problems or is just an idea for something wild to do with a friend this weekend, it doesn't matter. Your ideas deserve your respect because they are the output of your internal creative nature. Without them, life would just creep on and on and on. Make a conscious decision about what to do with each idea. Are you going to commit to making it happen, abandon it, delegate it, forget about it, or what? You want your accomplishment cycles to get off to a good start, to be intentional, not accidental.

If you sit down and write out your goals, you will wind up with a nice list. If you want your life to rock and roll, begin to manage the entire cycle of accomplishing those goals. Choosing your future career is a project that is an important part of that accomplishment cycle.

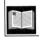 ## Vocabulary

As you think about this essay, these definitions may be helpful to you:
1. **meta-goal**   a goal that is transcending, comprehensive
2. **motivators**   incentives or influences that get you started and keep you going
3. **interwoven**   mixed or blended together
4. **somnambulism**   walking in your sleep

 ## Discussion Questions

1. Are most people aware of the "meta-goals" that influence their lives? How does the author define them? What role do these higher order goals play in one's life?
2. Why is it important to set goals for yourself rather than accept those that others set for you?
3. Why does Lore insist that you write down your goals in specific, measurable terms? Why is setting time limits important?
4. Do you think the suggestions he gives for managing your goals are realistic? How do you manage your goals?
5. Are most of your goals reasonable and sensible? If so, are you satisfied with them? If not, what can you do to stretch them? How flexible are you if you cannot accomplish your goals?

 ## Suggestions for Your Journal

Do you think goal setting is important? Think about what you want to accomplish in your studies one month from now. If you have never written down a short-term goal before, write down one specific, measurable academic goal that you would like to complete in 30 days. What action steps will you need to take to accomplish it? If you are an experienced goal-setter, have you incorporated all of Lore's principles in your experiences? Which of these principles do you need to improve? Do you have difficulty thinking long-term? Why? What specific steps can you take to improve the way you set goals? Do you disagree with any of Lore's activities? If so, explain why.

Doing the Work You Love

Laurence G. Boldt

Laurence G. Boldt is a nationally known writer and career consultant based in the San Francisco Bay Area. He has given speeches and conducted workshops across the country and has been featured in such publications as *Newsweek* and *New Age Journal*.

A powerful new social movement is transforming the way people live and work. For years, virtually invisible to those not directly involved, this movement has been quietly building momentum. Today its impact is no longer in doubt. In recent years, it has become the subject of a spate of newspaper and magazine articles and has been featured in a variety of television and radio programs. Truly grass-roots, this is a social movement without political action committees, paid lobbyists, or effective national or international organization. It is a bottom-up movement in which people are transforming society not by mass political action but by reorienting their own lives. It is a broad-based movement affecting men and women of all ages, races, and socioeconomic backgrounds in many nations.

At the heart of this emerging social movement is a fundamental redefinition of work and success. For a variety of reasons, people's expectations of what their work life can and should be have been dramatically and irrevocably altered in recent years. While throughout most of the twentieth century, work was viewed principally as a means to an end—be it survival, security, status, or power—today it is increasingly being valued on its own terms. More and more people are coming to expect that their experience of work should include meaning, challenge, self-expression, and joy. More and more, people are looking for ways to integrate their values and talents into their everyday experience of work. And more and more, they are finding them—discovering that it really is possible to earn their way in the world without compromising, indeed by celebrating, the promptings of their hearts and souls. The cat is out of the bag and there is no putting it back. The "work-for-love" movement has caught on.

Today, many people are waking up to the need for a new, more conscious approach to work and career. For some, this awakening is coming principally from their internal alarm, from a deep yearning to express their inborn talents, gifts, and abilities. Others are motivated primarily by an external alarm. They feel called to serve humanity, to make a meaningful difference by spreading joy and/or eliminating suffering in the world. For still others, the awakening is coming from the irritating buzz of the snooze alarm—the recognition that the workplace has fundamentally changed and that, as a result, they must assert greater control over their own destinies.

In the final two decades of the twentieth century, the entire landscape of work and career changed dramatically. As the president of a leading executive recruiting firm put it, "The way people approached their careers in the past is history. It will never, never, never return. "These historic changes in the job environment represent the snooze alarm, the final wake-up call to take responsibility and begin shaping your own career destiny. For today's worker, this alarm is ignored at great peril. The chime of the snooze alarm is loud and clear, ringing out: THE WORKPLACE IS CHANGING . . . THE WORKPLACE IS CHANGING . . . THE WORKPLACE IS CHANGING. There are a number of factors driving these changes. We will explore some of the more important ones below.

Globalization: The global marketplace means different things to and for different people. What it means for American workers is that they are in direct competition with data processors in India and Ireland, with manufacturing labor in Mexico and Indonesia, and with technical experts in Korea and Taiwan. Today, those working in low-skilled manufacturing jobs and in related support industries have borne the brunt of the pain associated with the globalization of trade. As the workforce in the developing world continues to become better educated and as technology continues to break down the barriers of distance, college-educated white collar workers can expect to experience in this new century the kinds of job losses that their less-educated blue collar counterparts did in the last two decades of the twentieth.

Merger Mania: Today, big business is more concentrated than ever. In the last twenty years, the banking, insurance, pharmaceutical, media, publishing, transportation, healthcare, utility, and retail industries—to name only a few of the more visible ones—have seen merger on top of merger. Many of these mergers have united companies across international boundaries. For workers, mergers and acquisitions are virtually synonymous with layoffs. Moreover, mergers spark more mergers, which in turn bring even more layoffs. Even companies that manage to avoid being gobbled up by bigger ones feel increased pressure to slash labor costs in order to remain competitive.

The Electronic Revolution: The new electronic technologies are significantly less labor-intensive in manufacturing, management, data collection, and processing than were the old technologies of the industrial era. In some fields, one person with a computer can do the work formerly done by half a dozen. In other fields, new technologies are on their way to replacing some positions altogether. Bank tellers are being replaced with automated tellers; receptionists, with voice mail; gas station attendants, with self-serve and electronic pay-at-the-pump sites. In the early years of the twenty-first century, the electronic revolution is expected to make an even greater impact on middle-management white collar workers.

Out-sourcing: Another trend reshaping the workplace is the rise in temporary, part-time, and independent contractor work. Today, nearly 25 percent of the U. S. workforce, or one in four American workers, is a temporary, part-time, or contract worker. Providing a variety of services to large organizations has been one of the major growth areas for new small business. At the same time, the outsourcing phenomenon has displaced thousands from once-secure jobs within large corporations and will likely continue to do so.

Mass Retail: In many small towns across America, factory outlets and discount superstores have all but eliminated local retailing. In urban centers and small towns throughout America and Europe, large superstores, factory outlets, or franchise chain stores have replaced independent bookstores, hardware stores, office supply stores, grocery stores, barbershops, restaurants, and locally-owned department stores. In many sectors, the small independent retailer is going the way of the small independent farmer. While mass retail has eliminated many small businesses, it has also been a major source of new jobs. Unfortunately, many of these jobs are part-time, low-paying, and not particularly challenging or rewarding.

Coming all at once, these and other trends have in a few short years radically and *inexorably* transformed the American workplace. While echoes from the snooze alarm are sending waves of anxiety and fear throughout the modern workplace, they are also providing the impetus for a variety of creative responses. Fifteen or twenty years ago, the individual with the dream of pursuing a more independent career path looked at the risks involved versus the security of their corporate jobs and decided that they were better off staying where they were. Today, many people are recognizing that it is at least as risky *not* to follow their dreams and begin charting their own destinies. Whether we choose to work for ourselves or for the small business organizations that are providing most of the new jobs, the qualities necessary for success are precisely those that doing the work one loves is likely to possess, namely: self-motivation, a high level of energy, a willingness to learn and grow, and *perseverance*.

While we cannot predict with any certainty how the nature of work will change in the coming century, it seems at this point inevitable that the work-for-love movement will continue to grow. Certainly the three wake-up calls discussed above will go on sounding, and there is every reason to believe that people will go on listening to them. This is truly an exciting time to be alive and one pregnant with possibilities. By making the commitment to follow your heart and do the work you love, you are part of a truly historic social transformation, one that has the potential to make the world a more just, humane, and beautiful place. Best of luck on your quest!

Vocabulary

As you think about this essay, these definitions may be helpful to you:
1. **inexorably**   relentlessly
2. **perseverance**   steadfastness

 ## Discussion Questions

1. How has the fundamental definition of work and success changed in the last 10 or 20 years, according to Boldt?
2. What is the "work-for-love" movement that the author describes?
3. What are some of the societal forces at work prompting a change in attitude toward taking control of one's own destiny?

 ## Suggestions for Your Journal

Record some of your thoughts about your future career. What type of work would you love to do? Is it different from the type of career you are currently preparing for educationally? Discuss how they are the same or different. The author indicates that the qualities necessary for success are self-motivation, a high level of energy, a willingness to learn and grow, and perseverance. Which of these qualities do you have? Which ones do you need to develop further? Do you think Boldt's movement survived the bursting of the dot-com bubble?

Job Search: Chance or Plan?

Mark R. Ballard

Formerly the director of career services in a liberal arts college, Mark R. Ballard is currently director of human resources development at Victoria's Secret Catalogue, where he continues his work in career planning and organizational career development. In this essay, Ballard offers some excellent advice for initiating the job-search process and delineates specific career-planning tasks for each year of student life. He believes his advice, if followed, will generate good job prospects upon graduation.

I want to tell you about Terry—the alumnus who "chanced" his career. His story can provide important insights for your own career planning.

Terry was a popular student in high school, was involved in many activities, and graduated in the top 25 percent of his class. Terry could hardly wait to leave his hometown to become a college student at the university. His academic performance was quite respectable. He could not believe how quickly the years passed. They elapsed so fast that he did not get involved in any structured *co-curricular* activities because he was "too busy" with school, sports, and friends. For spending money, Terry worked, but his employment experience, for the most part, consisted of being a lifeguard during the summers at his hometown pool and a cashier in a fast-food restaurant.

The quarter before Terry was slated to graduate, he decided to visit the Career Services Office. (He remembered hearing about this resource in his freshman orientation class.) Terry eagerly signed up for several on-campus interviews with companies that came to campus to interview students.

Terry bought a suit, had someone prepare a résumé for him, and interviewed with several company representatives. He was confident that he presented himself well in the interviews and would most assuredly get an offer from one of the employers with whom he interviewed. After all, he had never had difficulty finding part-time jobs.

Graduation came and went for Terry. Summer came, and Terry began to panic. Mid-summer, Terry returned to Career Services since the anticipated job offers did not materialize out of his interviews. Terry came back to the office looking for additional companies who were coming on campus to interview students and alumni. But there were none during the summer, since companies who do come to college campuses to interview students generally complete their hiring visits during April. Terry was unaware of this fact since he did not attend the on-campus interviewing orientation session: he was "too busy." Terry left the office disappointed, failing to take advantage of the many other employment resources. He vowed to return "sometime," but he never got around to it.

In the follow-up questionnaire mailed to alumni six months after graduation, we received a letter from Terry. Good news: he had landed a job! Well, maybe not good news. The job, which he stumbled on by "accident," was not the kind of position Terry thought he would land with a college degree. Sadly, his college education would not be fully utilized, and his salary was not comparable to similar college graduates.

Here's the moral of Terry's tale: Finding meaningful employment *commensurate* with one's educational level is not an event that occurs at the end of one's final term in college. It is a process that begins early in one's collegiate career. Making the transition from academics to the work world does not begin with writing a résumé, buying a new suit, or getting that first job interview. It begins with thought, research, and goal setting.

To secure employment upon graduation, begin with the process of self-assessment. As a part of this process, you need to be able to answer such questions as "What do I want to do for work?" and "Where do I want to do it?" In other words, what are your abilities, strengths, assets, gifts, talents? What is it that you are interested in, enjoy, are curious about, are motivated by, or get pleasure from? What are your values—those needs that you want satisfied by your work (recognition, independence, money, prestige, social status, uncovering knowledge)? What are the job tasks or activities of the careers that you are considering, the types of organizations that employ individuals in these occupations, the job outlook/forecast, salary ranges, entrance requirements, and lifestyle issues associated with the vocations you are considering? What are the steps necessary to undertake the decision-making process related to your career? Do you know where to go to find out how to write a résumé, interview for job offers, and to learn strategies to find jobs? If you can answer these questions, you will increase your prospects for success in the job search.

As an entering student, you may find it easy to say: "I'll deal with those job-related questions and issues during my senior year, or when I'm ready to graduate." "It's too early now." "I don't have time." "I'm just a freshman." "I'll figure it out. After all, I figured out how to apply to and get accepted to college."

But consider the following. Suppose you were to interview today for the job of your dreams, and the interviewer said to you, "Tell me about yourself and why you want this job. You have thirty minutes. I'll begin timing when you begin talking." How would you respond? What would you say? That is a common opening statement for an employer to make in a job interview.

To land the job of your dreams, you will first need to know about yourself. Do not confuse starting the process with implementing your career decision. You don't need to choose a career now, just to begin to think about, and to get actively involved in, the process during your early years of college. That way, early in your senior year, you can reflect on the self-assessment and the career exploration tasks that you addressed and the career decision that you made early in your college years. Your senior year is also the time for you to focus attention on *transitional* issues that will take you from academics to the work world, or on to graduate or professional school. Career planning is working through the many tasks associated with finding employment through planning—rather than through chance.

Career planning is the developmental, systematic process of

1. learning about yourself (for example, your interests, abilities, and values);
2. identifying occupations that correspond to your assessment of self;
3. exploring the occupations that you are considering;
4. selecting an occupation to pursue;
5. readying yourself for the job search process (resume and application letter writing, job interview skill development, job finding techniques and strategy knowledge); and
6. securing satisfying employment.

Does it seem that the process of career planning could be simplified by proceeding directly to step six—finding a job upon graduation? If so, remember Terry. That is exactly what he did. He jumped into the job search without establishing the foundation of the first five stages. He landed a job, but a job in the ranks of the underemployed, and that can have *ramifications* for a lifetime.

Your career process will be easier if you fully use the career planning and placement services provided at your university. There, staff members can help you answer the all too familiar question, "What can I do with a major in . . . ?" and assist you in finding purposeful, gratifying employment.

As a career services professional, I have worked with thousands of students, employers, and alumni. When I survey employers and alumni for their perspective on how students can best prepare themselves to make the transition from academics to the work world, they usually give five recommendations for students entering college.

1. Choose a major in a subject that interests you—one that really gets you excited. Do not rely on your parents, peers, or counselors to make the choice for you regarding your academic major or the occupation to pursue. Make the decision yourself. As a related note, given the difficulty of predicting which skills will be in demand even five years from now, not to mention in a lifetime, your best career preparation is one that emphasizes broad skills (for example, social, communication, analytical, logical, leadership, human relations), intellectual curiosity, and knowledge of how to learn.
2. Strive for a rigorous academic program and high grades. Yes, grades are important to employers. Job candidates are often rejected from interviews due to low GPAs.
3. Develop your leadership, communication, human relations, and time management skills by taking active roles of responsibility in student organizations and activities. This involvement will provide you with an opportunity to put knowledge from the classroom into practice.
4. Get career-related experience prior to graduation (through part-time positions, *cooperative education,* internships, and volunteer work). The benefits of such experience go well beyond making money. You will have a chance to

sample a variety of jobs and work settings, make valuable contacts with professionals for future networking, develop self-confidence, and gain insight when choosing elective courses in your academic program.
5. Use the career planning and placement services on campus early in your academic experience to help you with your career decision making and your job search. By doing so, you can get a head start on your employment future.

You can take the above recommendations a step further by following a year-by-year plan for your job search. Use this scheme as a general strategy to increase the likelihood of your landing the job of your dreams upon graduation.

As a Freshman . . .

The goal of your freshman year should be to learn as much as you can about yourself and the relationship this information has to careers. Consider the following:

In your academic course work, use the required general education courses and other college courses to help you explore your potential. You might wish to take courses and explore subjects that have always been of interest to you but that you never before had an opportunity to take.

Visit the career services office (sometimes referred to as the Placement Office) on your campus and get acquainted with the services and resources of that office. Your academic adviser can direct you to the right place.

Explore your interests, abilities, and values. Identify appropriate career choices by using the computerized career guidance systems (DISCOVER and SIGI-Plus are two that are commonly available), looking up career information on the Internet, meeting with a staff member of the career services office for a career counseling session, attending any career awareness workshops offered on campus, and sharing your goals with your academic adviser.

Find out about cooperative education and internship opportunities through your intended college of graduation.

Analyze job descriptions in the career services office and ask yourself how these positions fit with your identity profile.

Begin investigating and getting involved in at least one of the student organizations and activities on campus to develop your leadership, communication, human relations, and time management skills.

Find a summer job that will provide you with an opportunity to learn or refine skills that will be attractive to a prospective employer (e.g., communication, responsibility, ethical decision making, and human relations—learning to work with individuals of differing backgrounds).

As a Sophomore . . .

During your sophomore year, your goal should be to concentrate on identifying careers that appeal to you and to begin testing them out.

Use the Internet and the career books and other references in the career office and elsewhere on campus to research career options.

Learn to begin the process of informational interviewing—contacting and talking with people employed in fields you are considering. For example, if you are interested in chemistry, dietetics, or nutrition as a major, consider conducting an informational interview with a nutritional researcher at an area business or hospital. Career services staff members can help you identify professionals working in occupations that are of interest to you.

Take active roles of responsibility in clubs, organizations, and activities.

Cultivate relationships with faculty, counselors, and others who can help in answering questions that relate to careers and the relationship of course work to careers.

Take time to attend the "career days" held on campus and in the area. These events provide you with the opportunity to meet representatives from major U.S. organizations. Be sure to ask about cooperative education and internship opportunities.

Find out about summer internships and cooperative education opportunities through the career services office.

Begin developing a résumé as well as job interviewing skills. Workshops on these topics are conducted regularly through many career services offices.

As a Junior . . .

During your junior year, your goal should be to obtain career-related experience.

Prepare for the job search by attending workshops and individual counseling sessions on résumé writing, application letter writing, job search strategies, and interviewing skills. Look up Web sites that can increase your understanding of these important skills.

Develop a network of contacts in the field of your choice through continued informational interviewing, involvement in professional associations, and cooperative education or internships.

Continue to attend the "career days" held on the campus and in the area. Continue to ask the company representatives about internships and cooperative education opportunities.

Research job leads and make initial contacts early in winter for sources of possible employment that have some relationship to your tentative career choice. Gather letters of recommendation written on your behalf from past employers, current employers, professors, teaching associates—professionals who can vouch for your skills and abilities. Open a credentials file if your career services office has such a service.

As a Senior . . .

Your senior year is the culmination of your college education and is the launching pad for your future. Your goal is to secure satisfying employment or to get accepted to graduate or professional school if your career interest indicates the need for an advanced degree.

Learn the procedures for interviewing with the various career placement offices on campus should you wish to interview with organizations that come on campus to interview graduating students.

Research the organizations with which you wish to interview by using the Internet and the career services office's company literature libraries.

Attend "career day" events that are held on the campus and in the area and actively participate by distributing résumés to the company representatives and telling them about who you are and the type of position you are seeking.

Interview for jobs during the year with employers who come on campus through the career services office. Note: they are not likely to be there during the summer. (Remember Terry's disappointment?)

Continue collecting letters of recommendation written on your behalf by people who can attest to your skills and abilities. Keep these letters on file in your college's career services office.

Explore, in consultation with career services personnel, other strategies to find employment for your field of interest, such as using the many job listings on the Internet and those postings in your career services offices, enrolling in national employment databases, and learning the process of networking (getting involved with professionals in the field you wish to enter and learning where the hidden job market is). **The best job search strategy is to use a variety of job search strategies simultaneously; do not rely solely on one strategy to find employment.**

Choosing a career and finding a professional job take a lot of time and effort. You need to find out as much as you can about what interests you, what you do well, and what you want out of life. Even after you have decided on your career direction, you will find a wide range of job options available to you. There may be occupations that you have never even heard of that would suit your education, interests, values, and abilities perfectly. It is important to find out about them as early as possible. By waiting too long to begin proper planning and preparation for a successful career, you run the risk of embarking on the job search scene unaware of what field to pursue, getting frustrated, giving in, giving up, and taking any job you are offered.

The staff members of your career services office can help you with every phase of the career planning and employment process. It is not a magical, quick process, and the staff will not find a job for you. What you can expect, however, are informed professionals who will guide your career decision making and your job search process.

The valuable information you will receive from these offices will prove beneficial to you for the rest of your life. Make a commitment to get a head start on your career. Visit your career services office today. You owe it to yourself.

Reprinted by permission of the author.

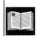 **Vocabulary**

As you think about this essay, these definitions may be helpful to you:
1. **co-curricular** being outside of but complementary to the regular curriculum
2. **commensurate** equal in measure or extent
3. **transitional** in the process of passing from one state, stage, or place to another
4. **ramifications** consequences or outgrowths
5. **cooperative education** a program that combines academic studies with actual work experience

 Discussion Questions

1. What is the first important step in the job-search process, according to Ballard?
2. What would you tell an employer about yourself in 30 minutes during a job interview?
3. What are the six steps that Ballard outlines to systematically begin the career-planning process?
4. What type of work experiences can students engage in prior to graduation?
5. What are some strategies students can use during their first year to enhance the career-planning process? As sophomores? Juniors? Seniors?

 Suggestions for Your Journal

Describe your dream job. Where would it be? What tasks would you be involved with all day? How would it fulfill your work values? How would it affect your family? How could it affect your lifestyle? Paint a picture of what a typical day would be like.

Which of the tasks or activities on Ballard's list for the first-year college student have you accomplished? What specific steps can you take to complete them by the end of the year?

Discuss the differences between the practical suggestions for career planning in this reading and the ones suggested by Burtchaell in Unit 3. How can you accomplish both?

Postgraduate Paralysis

Mary Sherry

Mary Sherry owns a firm that publishes research reports for architects and real estate developers. In this essay, which first appeared in *Newsweek* magazine, Sherry offers a parent's perspective on an offspring's job search. When she realized her daughter was looking for a career, not a job, her perspective on how to help changed.

Thousands of college graduates took their diplomas this year in fear or even embarrassment. They were not proud of themselves, nor eager to take on the real world. Instead, they thought of themselves as failures. These are the graduates who have not been offered fat salaries and generous benefits. They are the ones who won't be going to work as lawyers, investment bankers and engineers. They have taken the right courses, gotten good grades and gone through some on-campus job interviews. But because they weren't offered the perfect job—no, that exciting career—seemingly guaranteed to all those who make the right moves, they are sitting at home, victims of postgraduate paralysis.

This may come as a surprise to anyone who has read about the fabulous job offers tendered to recent graduates. However, those of us who are parents of children in this age group know that such offers are relatively rare and that many liberal-arts students graduate with the belief that the work world may not have a place for them.

Consider my daughter; she graduated from college with a degree in economics two years ago. She was offered a job by a *recruiter* who came to her campus—but it was with a trucking firm in South Carolina, as a dispatch-management trainee. She turned it down. It was her parents' first clue that she had a problem.

It seems economists don't work for trucking firms. Nor do Midwestern children want to live in the South before they become arthritic. Yet even at home in Minneapolis, our daughter couldn't seem to find anything to apply for. Her father told her to make the rounds of the personnel agencies. But she was so horrified by the *demeaning* atmosphere at one that she refused to visit any others.

Then one day, when she was looking at the Sunday paper and complaining that there was nothing in it, I told her that there had to be something. "Look at this," I commanded. "And this! And this!" I circled a number of jobs in the first two columns I skimmed. But Maureen protested: "I don't want to be an administrative assistant."

It was then that her father and I realized that she had been looking in the paper for a career, not a job. And ever since, we have watched the children of friends suffer from this same *delusion*. No one, it seems, has told them that a career is an *evolutionary* process.

When I graduated from college 25 years ago, I never expected to find a job that was in itself a career. In those days, we were told we knew nothing, but that upon graduation we would have the tools to learn. And learn we did—on the job. I began by doing grunt work in the customer-service department at *National Geographic* magazine. In due time, I wound up with a career, indeed, owning and running a firm that publishes research reports for architects and real-estate developers.

Apparently, schools have changed their approach. Today's students are told they know everything in order to succeed in a career. Career talk often begins in seventh grade or earlier, and the career is offered as the reward one receives upon graduation. No one is satisfied with this system. Businesses complain that they get new graduates who are unhappy with anything less than high-level, decision-making jobs as their first assignments. And parents are shocked that the child without a job can graduate traumatized by the fear of rejection.

As I see it, parents are a principal cause of the problem. Who among us hasn't thought, "What's wrong with that kid?" when we hear that a recent college graduate is a checker at a grocery store because "he can't find a job." At the same time, how many of us can put the screws on a recruiter's reject and convince him that he must abandon his idea of a career and take up the idea of finding work?

This is a distasteful task, especially when we have shipped our children off to expensive colleges, believing that simply by footing the tuition bill we are making them economically secure. The kids believe this, too, but the reality is that when they graduate, they are no more prepared for careers than we were.

Entry-level positions: It is not a disgrace to go out and pound the pavement. I used just this expression the other day with a friend of my son who, though he had graduated in December with a degree in philosophy, has not yet found a job. He had never heard the saying before. He is bright, personable and would do well in almost any kind of business. But he complains that he can't find work in the want ads—he has not visited any personnel agencies—and so he talks about going to law school instead. He was crushed by not having been recruited before graduation.

Which brings me back to my daughter. After some yelling and screaming by her parents, she did make the rounds of *headhunters* and found one who specialized in entry-level positions. This gentleman was wonderful; he helped her assess her skills and prepared her for interviews. She also read the newspapers and answered different types of ads. Not surprisingly, she got many responses. After a few weeks she had the exhilarating experience of having three job offers at once. Two were the products of answering newspaper ads and one came through the headhunter's efforts. She landed an excellent position as an insurance underwriter—a job she didn't even know existed when she graduated.

Happy in her job, Maureen also fell in love; and when she began to look for employment in Chicago where she and her husband will live, she needed no help from her parents. She was confident and aggressive. She used headhunters, the want ads, her friends and ours. She had a new resource—business contacts.

Yet as she was typing letters one day, I offered some sympathy about how hard it is to hunt for a job.

"It's OK, Mom," she said. "This isn't like the first time. Now I know how to look for a job!"

And she found one as a senior underwriter. She'll make more money and more decisions.

It's beginning to look like a career.

From Mary Sherry, "Postgraduate Paralysis," from *Newsweek,* July 11, 1998. Reprinted by permission of the author.

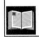 **Vocabulary**

As you think about this essay, these definitions may be helpful to you:
1. **recruiter**   a representative of a company or organization who is seeking to secure the services of or hire individuals to work for that organization
2. **demeaning**   degrading
3. **delusion**   something that is falsely believed
4. **evolutionary**   characterized by a process of change in a certain direction
5. **headhunters**   paid recruiters of personnel

 Discussion Questions

1. Why do some students feel like failures if they do not have a job at graduation, according to Sherry?
2. How did Sherry's daughter approach the job-search process?
3. What is the difference between a job and a career?
4. What advice does Sherry give for finding entry-level jobs? Do you agree?
5. How did Sherry's daughter finally find her first job? Subsequent jobs?

 Suggestions for Your Journal

Do you know any college graduates who are still searching for a job? If so, what have you learned from their experiences?

What type of entry-level job are you preparing for when you graduate? What kinds of experiences (such as internships, volunteer work, co-op or work experiences) would enhance your chances of getting the job you desire? What resources exist on your campus to help you obtain these experiences? What other steps can you take to make yourself more marketable when you graduate?

Career Patterns for the 21st Century

Peggy Simonsen

Peggy Simonsen is president of Career Directions, Incorporated. She designs and implements career development and performance management systems and training for corporations. Simonsen is a nationally prominent speaker and frequent contributor to numerous journals and newsletters. In this essay she describes the career patterns that will emerge in the new century and how these will be different from old ways of thinking about career patterns.

Up is not the only way.
—Beverly Kaye

Managing your career strategically in the new century requires new ways of thinking. . . . A variety of career patterns are evolving. There may be flatter, team-based environments where expectations of upward progression are limited and limiting. A career pattern driven by internal choice rather than external structure will be the most valuable to individuals and will therefore add the most value to the employing organization. Newer employees in organizations today recognize this and aren't as likely as their predecessors to create careers based on incompatible structures or outdated expectations and reward systems. As one employee learning new ways to think about careers said, "You mean it's OK not to want to move up?"

Portfolio Careers

The career pattern most different from the traditional upward career path is that of the *portfolio* career, such as freelance writer. Not employed by a single organization, a freelance writer might have regular assignments with one publication, occasional articles published by others, and some consulting work creating PR campaigns or brochures. In addition, he or she might write and lay out a newsletter and perhaps take on a large one-time assignment to create a policy manual. This writer would be creating a portfolio of work he or she has done.

Today, portfolio careers have expanded to encompass more than one field. Sometimes used to build expertise while planning a career change, the portfolio career can give more autonomy, time, freedom, and opportunity for creativity and diverse activities. People with portfolio careers might be managing a traditional assignment in a large organization while building a small business on the side. An engineer might prefer to work for a job shop, taking on assignments that last from six months to two years, building a variety of experience, and having the freedom to leave when the project is completed or gets too routine. Someone with a love for a field that doesn't pay well might add another type of work to add more income, without giving up the work he or she loves. . . .

254

Portfolio careers might be driven by *"contingency* work"—that is, employment by a company as long as necessary, but not full-time, permanent employment. To remain flexible and avoid creating new bureaucracies, down-sized companies are increasingly using contingency workforces. For a person wanting to hold on to the work patterns of the twentieth century, contingency work seems like a step down the ladder, with no chance for advancement and typically no company-paid benefits. However, for individuals who choose to build portfolio careers, the advantages are autonomy in selecting assignments, variety of work, time freedom, higher hourly pay than for the same work that is salaried, and the chance to build a greater *repertoire* of skills.

This career pattern requires individuals to recognize that they must market their capabilities. They need to be aware of the value of their skills in the marketplace and present themselves as people who can solve others' problems. While this may sound like the essentials of a job search, it must become a regular course of action for a successful portfolio career.

Lifestyle-Driven Careers

Women balancing family and work have been the primary practitioners of lifestyle-driven careers. Taking the primary responsibility for raising children, the wife and mother would work at a part-time job that wouldn't interfere with her home responsibilities. This career pattern is evolving and becoming a choice for men, too. With more two-career households, many couples are finding themselves with little time to build and enjoy their life together and with their families. Others have strong outside interests or *avocations,* so they want to balance their workloads to allow time for these. Still others find their lives out of balance because of excessive work demands after organizational downsizing. People are insisting that work be a subset of life, not all of it. So individuals are making choices about careers on the basis of life needs. The labor shortage gives individuals some leverage by causing employers to create more flexible policies and practices. Companies are recognizing the value of lifestyle-friendly policies, especially when retention of educated and skilled workers is a goal. But organizations are also recognizing that a culture of support for individuals—making work time more satisfying and less stressful—makes good business sense. . . .

Research on career motivation shows that lifestyle-driven careers are the fastest-growing pattern. People with this motivation say career is important, but more important for career decisions is having a balanced, fully satisfying life. The demands of many work environments make a lifestyle-driven career pattern difficult to implement.

Emerging workers, who may be willing to work eighty-hour weeks to meet critical deadlines, expect reciprocation and a break when the crisis passes. Without loyalty to an organization, they will pack up and leave when work demands become unreasonable.

Mature employees, who have lived through downsizing changes—and perhaps personal burnout from excessive time and work demands—often feel less commitment to their work and talk about leaving. Some are too risk-averse to take action to leave, but their work is likely to suffer. These are the people who need to take action, for their own good and that of their employers. Employers who don't recognize the validity of a lifestyle-driven career pattern will lose good people.

Linear Careers

Linear careers are the closest to the traditional career path. However, linear careers in the twenty-first century are not likely to be with only one organization. Rather than going to work for a good company and expecting to be employed for life, employees will avoid much of the frustration experienced upon reaching a level in the organization beyond which they cannot move. Individuals who expect to move up in responsibility and compensation in the future will change organizations when they reach a plateau or growth slows. People managing their careers strategically will not have the expectation that a linear career can happen in one organization. They will be more *proactive* to make it happen.

Organizations will still need leaders willing to take on greater responsibility. They will need to build commitment to the company's success. But they won't be able to take this commitment for granted, assuming loyalty at all costs. The mutual benefits of shared responsibility for organizational development and career success will be recognized by both organizations and employees.

Even today, after excessive downsizing, many organizations are recognizing the need for succession planning and workforce planning. They recognize the disruptive nature of constantly hiring from outside instead of developing from within. There is a growing trend to design systems to develop competencies in internal candidates for assignments as they become available.

Conversely, individuals cannot assume that length of service alone will determine career progression. They must constantly add value, build networks, and overcome barriers to their development. People who will build successful linear careers will take a broader, organizational perspective rather than a personally driven perspective. With flatter organizations, self-directed teams, and therefore fewer management positions, promotions will rarely occur through a person's being in the right place at the right time. They will more likely be based on proven ability to lead. People who fit this career pattern are motivated by achievement, power, and ambition and are willing to pay the dues necessary to achieve success the way they define it. . . .

Expert Careers

Perhaps the only recognized alternative to moving up in the past was the role of individual contributor who chose not to become a manager. A career pattern that has existed forever but often was not valued in traditional organizations is that of the expert. I say "not valued" because rarely was a skilled expert compensated as well as a mediocre manager. The whole structure was designed to support linear careers, so people who turned down promotions because they preferred their technical tasks often felt like second-class citizens. As technology demanded expertise, some organizations created dual-ladder career paths to reward people who were individual contributors, not managers. However, most dual-ladder models still rewarded upward paths—for example, from junior engineer to senior engineer to group leader to project manager.

A few organizations whose success depended on superior individual contributions created rewards for exceptional outcomes, such as patents, scientific breakthroughs, journalistic awards, and record-breaking sales records. This latter pattern will continue into the next century. Led by young firms, without the baggage of the old corporations (especially compensation systems), the expert career pattern is coming into its own. People are rewarded with stock, profit sharing, or substantial bonuses when the project is completed successfully, not because it is the end of the year. Hard work and capability are not only valued, they drive the organization's success. As organizations require fewer managers but need all the state-of-the-art skill they can get, this career pattern may become predominant.

If an expert career pattern is right for you, it will require continuously developing your expertise. It will mean running fast to keep abreast of changes in your profession. The very traits that drive individuals to become experts might frustrate them when the work is changing so fast that it is impossible to maintain an expected level of expertise. It certainly is not a career pattern that allows one to slack off and trade on previous successes, as it might have been in an era of slow change. People whose career pattern is based on expertise need passion for their work, desire always to learn more, ambition to make significant contributions to their fields, and satisfaction from their technical competence. ("Technical" here means task specific, not necessarily electronic. An editor has technical competence in language use; a sales representative has technical competence in both the sales process and the products he or she sells.)

Like a linear career, an expert career probably will not happen in just one organization. It is up to individuals not only to manage their own growth in the field but also to be proactive about the environment in which the work is performed. The company might sell off the division that requires their particular set of skills and knowledge, so while the work doesn't change, the employer does. Technology might suddenly move a generation ahead, leaving experts' work obsolete or declining in value. Or the employer might not choose to move forward in technology, so experts might need to leave in order to continue growing in their areas of expertise. Organizational priorities might change in response to market demands, leaving a previously valued area of expertise now less important—and therefore with fewer resources to support the work. Expert employees might realize the unique nature of their expertise and decide to create their own organizations, to specialize in the work they have been paid to do as employees. While expertise may be seen as a career pattern out of the past, the circumstances in which it is applied will be more dynamic in the future. . . .

Managing your career strategically might mean recognizing the contribution you make and the satisfaction you derive from being an expert at what you do—and turning down a promotion. It is possible to take on management responsibilities and still maintain expertise, but the focus changes. In our fast-changing environments, it is hard enough to maintain expertise without having it be secondary to getting work done through others, but some highly competent individuals manage both roles well. . . .

Sequential Careers

A growing approach to managing your career strategically is the choice of a sequential career. Rather than involving simultaneous career activities, as in the portfolio career, in a sequential career one role ends before another is launched. As people retire from a primary career earlier in life, and as life expectancy is extended, the twenty-first century will see more sequential career patterns. In some cases, the second career is less demanding or not as well compensated as the first, but often it is just different.

We are seeing a substantial increase in the number of people choosing sequential careers because of the decline of the old career patterns. People who bought into the concept of a job for life—even if it was one they didn't choose or want to be in—are suddenly free to make other choices. Either because their job ended or because the paradigm changed and they are thinking about work differently, many are changing careers at midlife or beyond. Some have the opportunity for an early-retirement severance package, which leaves them with the financial base to make choices that are based on fit rather than compensation. Some who have been in the business environment are choosing new work in the not-for-profit sector, intentionally choosing to make income and lifestyle changes. . . .

Younger people are purposely building sequential careers because of the variety they allow. They work in one field for a while, building a level of competence or experience, and then when the challenge begins to wane they decide to pursue work in another area of interest. As long as they move from strength and not from unsatisfactory performance, the building of a sequential career is not seen as negative. Sometimes they move to completely different areas for the sake of new experience, which typically requires starting in a lower-paying job than the one they left. To avoid stepping back, sequential career builders often move to a related area where their background is valued, though not a direct contribution to the new field. For example, a financial analyst in a sales department who knows the company's products moves into a sales support position, then into marketing with another company, and finally into strategic planning, each time adding new skills and experience to her work history.

Sequential career builders may not stay long enough at one organization to build a strong reputation for expertise or to position themselves for promotions, but that isn't what's driving them. Change, variety, and challenge are their drivers, and they definitely don't want linear careers. However, it's important to distinguish between a successful sequential career and job-hopping. A sequential career is successful if the person attains some expertise, competence, and acknowledgment in each job. Young people, particularly, may go from one field to another without gaining any expertise. Then they find themselves at the age of thirty without a portfolio of well-honed skills and with an image of moving away from unsuccessful attempts. In some cases, they even turn down promotions, which might have been important for moving into higher-level situations. . . .

Entrepreneurial Careers

Some people seem to be born entrepreneurs. Creative, independent, driven by their own goals and passions, they need the autonomy of their own companies. These types have always existed, so what is different now? The career patterns we've discussed are enabling entrepreneurial types to start their own businesses in different ways:

- Portfolio careers, where people juggle paid employment with a fledgling business—perhaps in the same field, perhaps in a new area
- Lifestyle-driven careers, where some start their own businesses to get more time flexibility, or to reduce a commute, or to be less tied to a demanding environment
- Linear careers, when the move up has been derailed or a plateau has been reached; capable women who have hit the glass ceiling in a large organization often opt to start a business where their leadership skills can be maximized
- Expert careers, where people feel they can use their expertise better with fewer limitations in their own businesses, or where the expertise is no longer needed by an employer and so a former employee becomes self-employed to provide the same service or product to the market
- Sequential careers, where an entrepreneurial drive has been squelched for security reasons and now can emerge as the next career

Obviously, not all entrepreneurs are from the same mold—if they were they wouldn't be entrepreneurs. But there are some whose very nature is entrepreneurial. They are risk-taking, goal-oriented, creative, hard-driving, persevering, competitive, and challenge-driven. . . .

Not all entrepreneurs are driven to start more than one business. Some land at the helm by happenstance (as when they inherit a family business) and make a commitment to grow the business over many years. Some entrepreneurial people never start a business at all but become equity partners in small, already established operations, where they contribute to growth and success. These aren't people who need structure and a predictable paycheck; they can create their own systems and take financial risks because of the potential payoffs.

Many new companies in the field of technology are launched because their founders have the expertise and because they can be so much more responsive to market opportunities than old, bureaucratic organizations.

Increasingly, larger organizations are recognizing the value of entrepreneurial traits to innovation and creative problem solving inside the company. Gifford Pinchot (1985)[1] calls this "intrapreneuring": the company provides the equivalent of venture capital, and a small group of employees creates a business plan for an innovative product or service to be developed in-house and brought to market.

Pluralistic Career Cultures

With the old "employment contract" an artifact of the twentieth century, something is needed to replace the way we define careers. Instead of shifting from the old, relatively stable structure to one of free-form *pandemonium,* organizations will need to recognize and support multiple career patterns. Brousseau, Driver, Eneroth, and Larsson[2] make a plea for organizations to adopt a pluralistic approach to career management and to develop a pluralistic career culture as a way to cope with change and the diverse needs of organizations and people. Encouraging and including a variety of career patterns can realign individuals and organizations.

We can hope that in the coming century, both individuals and organizations will value a variety of career patterns. Individuals will need to know which types of careers are appropriate for them at any point in time, and organizational practices will reward those patterns that serve their purposes and keep the company on track to achieve business goals. Today only slightly more than half of all work options are derivatives of traditional work arrangements (that is, full-time positions at the same workplace for a long time).The variety will expand as the new century grows. . . .

[1]G. Pinchot III, *Intrapreneuring: Why You Don't Have to Leave the Corporation to Become an Entrepreneur* (New York: HarperCollins, 1985).

[2]K. Brousseau et al. (1996),"Career Pandemonium: Realigning Organizations and Individuals, " *Academy of Management Executives,* 10(4), 53.

 Vocabulary

As you think about this essay, these definitions may be helpful to you:
1. **portfolio**   a selection of representative work
2. **contingency**   the state of happening by chance or unforeseen causes
3. **repertoire**   a supply of materials, skills, or devices

4. **avocation**   a hobby or occupation pursued for enjoyment
5. **proactive**   taking the initiative
6. **pandemonium**   wild disorder

 ## Discussion Questions

1. In what ways do these new career patterns differ from the old, more traditional ones?
2. What, according to Simonsen, are the characteristics of the "lifestyle" career pattern?
3. How do modern linear careers differ from those in the past?
4. Why might an "expert" career pattern be difficult to maintain in work that changes rapidly?
5. Why are younger people purposely building sequential careers, according to Simonsen?

 ## Suggestions for Your Journal

How do you define "career"? Will you want to change careers often, or will you feel more secure working in the same career for a long time? Which of the six career patterns that Simonson describes appeals the most to you?

What reward systems are most important to you? How would your choice of career pattern provide the rewards you desire? How do your current ideas about your education fit into what you most desire in a career?

UNIT SUMMARY

The readings in this unit provide a wide variety of opinions about work and workers. Reflect on your own ideas about your place in the work world and how these writers have added to your understanding of its complexities and challenges.

Summary Questions

1. Responding to a recent poll, younger workers indicated that they care more about job satisfaction than job security. How do you think that knowing this might influence what employers offer new workers?
2. Describe how you have searched for a job in the past and the differences having a college degree might make in the way you will search for a job in the future.
3. How do you think the American workplace has changed in the last 20 years? How will your work life be different from that of your parents? How will these differences, if any, affect your life in a way different from theirs?

Suggested Writing Assignments

1. The readings in this unit explore several beliefs, attitudes, and perspectives about work. Select one and write a brief essay on why the ideas in this reading agree or disagree with your own ideas about work.
2. Write a brief essay on what you want in your future career (e.g., independence, creativity, security, high salary) and why these work values are essential to you.
3. Write a brief essay about how you are currently approaching the choice of academic major and career field and what you still need to do in order to make an initial decision or confirm one you have already made.

Suggested Readings

Gardner, Howard. *Intelligence Reframed—Multiple Intelligences for the 21st Century.* New York: Basic Books, 1999.

Gordon, Virginia, and Susan Sears. *Selecting a College Major: Exploration and Decision Making.* Upper Saddle River, NJ: Prentice Hall, 2004.

Michelozzi, Betty N. *Coming Alive from Nine to Five.* Mountain View, CA: Mayfield, 2000.

Terkel, Studs. *Working.* New York: Pantheon, 1974.

Life After College: Future Success or Future Shock?

Imagine the day you will be wearing a cap and gown and receiving the diploma that attests to your status as a college graduate. What does the future hold for you? Several readings in previous units offered visions of the future from different perspectives. These can stimulate your thinking about what you might hope to accomplish during your college years so that your college education can prepare you for both the workplace and your life in general.

In Unit 1, several authors described the value of a college education and emphasized the importance of taking advantage of the opportunities offered through the experience of higher education. You were asked to examine your reasons for being in college and how these might affect your initial goals for the college experience itself. The beginning of your college life is a good time to set some tentative goals to reach by the day you are ordained a college graduate. Through your college career, you will want to broaden those goals to

Climb high

Climb far

Your goal the sky

Your aim the star.

—INSCRIPTION ON JOHNS HOPKINS HOSPITAL

MEMORIAL STEPS

include specific actions to prepare for the future lifestyle you desire. Some of your ideas might change very much.

You will also want to set goals related to the type of work you want to do and the type of worker you want to become. These should take into account both the type of job and quality of work life you hope to obtain after college. Thoughtful planning now can also improve your effectiveness as a worker later in life.

During the college years many foundational skills and personal competencies can be acquired and practiced, usually in a nonthreatening environment. The quality of your life after college will depend on how well you take advantage of the opportunities presented to you during your college years.

The essay by Edmund Pellegrino was a commencement address in which the speaker distinguished receiving a baccalaureate degree from being educated. Arthur Levine and Jeanette Cureton compare the current generation of college students with those of the past and suggest four attributes today's students need to possess to live successfully in the new century. Mel Levine discusses the transition from school to being a "startup adult." He lists some issues individuals might face *after* graduation. The reading by Neil Howe and William Strauss describes their vision of the Millennial Generation, who they insist might be the next great one. Christopher Reeve urges college students to maintain their integrity "in a culture that has devalued it" and describes how his injury helped him live a more "conscious" life.

In addition to discussing these issues in class and writing about them in your journal, you might want to talk to family, friends, and others to whom you look for guidance. Examining what is important to you now and in the future is a first step in setting thoughtful, realistic goals for your life after college. Don't wait until the day you march down the graduation aisle to consider who you are and where you want to be when that day arrives.

Having a Degree and Being Educated

Edmund D. Pellegrino, M.D.

Edmund D. Pellegrino is professor emeritus of medicine and medical ethics at Georgetown University. This essay was a commencement address given by Dr. Pellegrino at Wilkes College.

Few humans live completely free of illusions. Reality is sometimes just too harsh to bear without them. But comforting as they can be, some illusions are too dangerous to be harbored for very long. Eventually they must meet the test of reality—or we slip into psychosis.

I want to examine a prevalent illusion with you today—one to which you are most susceptible at this moment, namely, that *having* a degree is the same as *being* educated. It is a bit *gauche,* I admit, to ask embarrassing questions at a time of celebration. But your personal happiness and the world you create depend on how well your illusion is brought into focus. And this *emboldens* me to intrude briefly on the satisfaction you justly feel with your academic accomplishment.

The degree you receive today is only a certificate of exposure, not a guarantee of infection. Some may have caught the virus of education, others only a mild case, and still others may be totally immune. To which category do you belong? Should you care? How can you tell?

The illusion of an education has always plagued the honest person. It is particularly seductive in a technological society like ours. We intermingle education with training, and liberal with professional studies, so intimately that they are hard to disentangle. We reward specific skills in politics, sports, business, and academia. We exalt those who can *do* something—those who are experts.

It becomes easy to forget that free and civilized societies are not built on information alone. Primitive and despotic societies have their experts too! Computers and animals can be trained to store and retrieve information, to learn, and even to out-perform us. What they can never do is direct the wise use of their information. They are imprisoned by their programmers and their own expertise. The more intensive that expertise, the more it cages them; the less they can function outside its restricted perimeter.

In a technological society experts proliferate like toadstools on a damp lawn. Some are genuine. Others are quick studies specializing in the predigestion of other people's thoughts. They crowd the TV screens, the radio waves, the printed page, eager to tell us what to believe and how to live—from sex and politics to religion and international affairs. They manufacture our culture, give us our opinions and our conversational *gambits.*

Now that you have a degree in something, you are in danger of stepping quietly into the cage of your own expertise—leaving everything else to the other experts. Whether they are genuine or phony makes little difference. If you do, you sacrifice the most precious endowment of an education—the freedom to make up your own mind—to be an authentic person. Knowledge, as Santayana said, is recognition of something absent. It is a salutation—not an embrace—a beginning, not an end.

You cannot predict when you will be brutally confronted by the falsity of your illusion like the juror who was interviewed following a recent murder trial. He was responding to one of those *puerile* how-does-it-feel questions that is the trademark of the telecaster's *vacuity*. "Being a juror was a terrible thing," he said. "I had to think like I never thought before. . . . I had to understand words like justice and truth. . . . Why do they make people like us judges?"

This is the pathetic lament of a sincere, sympathetic, but uneducated man. He was surely an expert in something but he could not grapple with the kind of question that separates humans from animals and computers. Justice and truth are awesome questions indeed. But who should answer those questions? Is being a juror another specialty? Do we need a degree in justice and truth? Does not a civilized and democratic society depend upon some common comprehension of what these words mean?

These same questions underlie every important public and private decision— from genetic engineering to nuclear proliferation, from prolonging human life to industrial pollution. They determine *how* we should use our expert knowl-edge, *whether* we should use it, and *for what* purposes. The welfare of the nation and the world depend on our capacity to think straight and act rightly—not on the amount of information we have amassed.

To be a juror, to be a person, to live with satisfaction, requires more than a trained mind—it requires an educated one, a mind that does not parrot other men's opinions or values but frames its own, a mind that can resist the poten-tial tyranny of experts, one that can read, write, speak, manipulate symbols, argue, and judge, and whose imagination is as free as its reason.

These attributes are not synonymous with simple exposure to what is *euphemistically* called an education in the humanities or liberal arts, even when these are genuine—as often they are not. That belief only piles one illusion upon another. Rather than courses taken, or degrees conferred, the true tests of an educated mind are in its operations. Let me suggest some questions that indi-cate whether your mind operates like an educated one—no matter what your major may have been.

First, have you learned how to learn without your teacher? Can you work up a new subject, find the information, separate the relevant from the trivial, and express it in your own language? Can you discern which are your teacher's thoughts and which are your own? Your first freedom must be from the subtle despotism of even a great teacher's ideas.

Second, can you ask critical questions, no matter what subject is before you— those questions that expose a line of argument, evaluate the claims being made upon you, the evidence adduced, the logic employed? Can you sift fact from opinion, the plausible from the proven, the rhetorical from the logical? Can you use skepticism as a constructive tool and not as a refuge for intellectual sloth?

Do you apply the same critical rigor to your own thoughts and actions? Or are you merely rearranging your prejudices when you think you are thinking?

Third, do you really understand what you are reading, what people are saying, what words they are using? Is your own language clear, concrete, and concise? Are you acquainted with the literature of your own language—with its structure and nuance?

Fourth, are your actions your own—based in an understanding and commitment to values you can defend? Can you discern the value conflicts underlying personal and public choices and distinguish what is a compromise to principle and what is not? Is your approach to moral judgments reasoned or emotional? When all the facts are in, when the facts are doubtful and action must be taken, can you choose wisely, prudently, and reasonably?

Fifth, can you form your own reasoned judgments about works of art— whether a novel, sonata, sculpture, or painting? Or are you enslaved by the critic, the book reviewer, and the "opinion makers" vacillating with their fads and pretentiousness? Artists try to evoke experiences in us, to transform us as humans. Is your imagination free enough to respond sensitively, or are you among the multitude of those who demand the explicitness of violence, pornography, dialogue—that is the sure sign of a dead imagination and an impoverished creativity?

Sixth, are your political opinions of the same order as your school and athletic loyalties—rooting for your side and ignoring the issues and ideas your side propounds? Free societies need independent voters who look at issues and not labels, who will be loyal to their ideals, not just to parties and factions. Do you make your insight as an expert the measure of social need? There is no illusion more fatal to good government!

If you can answer yes to some of these indicators, then you have imbibed the essence of a liberal education, one which assures that your actions are under the direction of your thought, that you are your own person, no matter what courses you took and what degree you receive today. You will also have achieved what is hoped for you:

> Education is thought of as not just imparting the knowledge of a professional discipline, but also as demonstrating a certain way of life—a way of life which is humane and thoughtful, yet also critical and above all rational.

If your answers are mostly negative (and I hope they are not), then you are in danger of harboring an illusion—one that is dangerous to you and society. The paradox is that the expert too has need of an educated mind. Professional and technical people make value decisions daily. To protect those whose values they affect, to counter the distorted pride of mere information, to use their capabilities for humane ends, experts too must reflect critically on what they do. The liberal arts, precisely because they are not specialties, are the indispensable accoutrements of any mind that claims to be human.

There are two kinds of freedom without which we cannot lead truly human lives. One kind is political and it is guaranteed by the Bill of Rights. The other is intellectual and spiritual and is guaranteed by an education that liberates the mind. Political freedom assures that we can express our opinions freely; a liberal education assures that the opinions we express are free. Each depends so much on the other that to threaten one is to threaten the other.

This is why I vex you with such a serious topic on this very happy occasion. The matter is too important for indifference or comfortable illusions. My hope is that by nettling you a bit I can prevent what is now a harmless illusion from becoming a delusion—firm, fixed belief, impervious either to experience or reason.

May I remind you in closing that the people who made our nation, who endowed it with the practical wisdom that distinguished its history, were people without formal degrees. One of the best among them, Abraham Lincoln, went so far as to say: "No policy that does not rest upon philosophical public opinion can be permanently maintained." Philosophical public opinion is not the work of information or expertise but of an educated mind, one that matches the aim of Wilkes to impart a way of life that is ". . . humane and thoughtful, yet also critical and above all rational."

T. S. Eliot, in his poem "The Dry Salvages," said: "We have had the experience of an education—I hope you have not missed the meaning." You have had the experience of an education—I hope you have not missed the meaning.

Reprinted by permission of the author.

 ## Vocabulary

As you think about this essay, these definitions may be helpful to you:
1. **gauche**   (pronounced gōsh) lacking social experience or grace
2. **embolden**   to instill with boldness or courage
3. **gambits**   in this essay, remarks intended to start a conversation or make a telling point
4. **puerile**   childish
5. **vacuity**   the state of being empty or lacking content
6. **euphemistically**   substituting an agreeable or inoffensive expression for one that may offend or suggest something unpleasant

 ## Discussion Questions

1. Why does Dr. Pellegrino think it is an illusion that having a degree and being educated are the same?
2. What is an uneducated person, according to Pellegrino?
3. How does Pellegrino define "knowledge"?

4. List six ways that, according to Pellegrino, the mind works. To which ones can you answer yes?
5. What are the two kinds of freedom needed to live "truly human lives," according to Pellegrino?

 ## Suggestions for Your Journal

How do you view a college degree? As a piece of paper that can get you a job or as a symbol of the years when you learned to become "educated"? What is your definition of being educated? Do you think it is important to think about how an educated mind works? Why?

What are some specific actions you can take to master the six ways the mind of an educated person operates during your college career? When you graduate, how will you, as Pellegrino states, use your knowledge "to think straight and act rightly," not just use the information you have accumulated in your mind?

A Time of Discontinuity

Arthur Levine and Jeanette S. Cureton

Arthur Levine is president and professor of education at Teachers College, Columbia University. Jeanette S. Cureton is an academic researcher, formerly of the Harvard Graduate School of Education. This reading is taken from the authors' 1998 book, *When Hope and Fear Collide: A Portrait of Today's College Student.*

There are rare times in the history of a society in which rapid and profound change occurs. The change is so broad and so deep that the routine and ordinary cycles of readjustment cease. There is a sharp break between the old and the new. It is a time of *discontinuity*. In the history of this country, there have been two such break points.

The first was the Industrial Revolution, which began in earnest in the first decades of the nineteenth century. It brought about a transformation in the United States from an agricultural to an industrial society. For those who lived through it, everything appeared to be in flux. The nation's economy was turbulent and uncertain, with wide swings both up and down. New technologies with the capacity to remake the nation's daily life, ranging from steamboats and canals to railroads and mechanized factories, were burgeoning. Old industries were dying, and new industries were being born. Demographics were shifting dramatically as the population moved west and south, from rural to urban areas. Large numbers of immigrants, with relatively little formal education, were coming to America. All of the country's major social institutions—church, family, government, work, and media—were being transformed. Reflecting on the vastness of the changes, Henry Adams concluded that "the old universe was thrown into the ash heap and a new one created."

Adams's assessment was very close to the mark. The effects of industrialization have been well documented. Among the consequences are family disorganization, *attenuation* of kinship ties, and a splintering of connections between generations. Mate selection and marital patterns are retarded. Gender roles change. Homogeneity gives way to heterogeneity. Apathy and alienation grow. New and higher literacy levels are required to function in society, causing sharp differentiation in the wealth and status of the populace. Mass communication expands, and isolation within society declines. Interest groups and associations multiply. . . .

The second break point or time of discontinuity is occurring now. The United States is currently undergoing profound demographic, economic, global, and technological change. Demographically, the U.S. population is aging, changing color, coming from other countries, and redistributing itself across the country at astounding rates. . . .

270

For today's college students, this world of change dominates their lives. The cycles of community and individualism have given way to a world of unceasing, unknowable change.

This reality is compounded by the enormous size of the population attending college today. As a consequence, the benefit of a college education has diminished. When only a small proportion of an age group graduates from college, they are virtually guaranteed the best jobs a society offers. When the majority attend college, this is no longer possible. The guarantee of the best jobs expires along with the guarantee of any job. In short, the students who attended college at the turn of the century were shopping at the educational equivalent of Tiffany's. Today's undergraduates are at something much more akin to Kmart. The multiplication in size of the college student population means they are subject to exactly the same social forces as the rest of the nation's population. A smaller, more *elite* group might have been protected from the waves of change crashing upon the rest of the country. The college *cohort* is simply too large today to be sheltered in any fashion. . . .

The consequence of rapid social change and shifting conditions in higher education today is a generation straddling two worlds, one dying and another being born. Each makes competing and conflicting demands on today's college generation; they are torn between both. A dying world makes them want security, and a world being born makes urgent their call for change. In the same fashion, pragmatism wrestles with idealism, doing well with doing good, and fear with hope. They are, above all else, a transitional generation, not unlike the young people of Henry Adams's day, and they are experiencing the same symptoms as did those who lived through the Industrial Revolution.

Education for a Transitional Generation

As a group, current undergraduates might be described as having the following characteristics. They are

- Frightened
- Demanding of change
- Desirous of security
- Disenchanted with politics and the nation's social institutions
- Bifurcated in political attitudes between left and right; the middle is shrinking
- Liberal in social attitudes
- Socially conscious and active
- Consumer oriented
- Locally rather than globally focused
- Sexually active, but socially isolated
- Heavy users of alcohol
- Hardworking
- Tired

- Diverse and divided
- Weak in basic skills and able to learn best in ways different from how their professors teach
- Pragmatic, career oriented, and committed to doing well
- Idealistic, altruistic, and committed to doing good
- Optimistic about their personal futures
- Optimistic about our collective future
- Desperately committed to preserving the American dream

This generation is no better and no worse than any other generation, but, like every other generation before, it is unique. As a result, this generation requires a unique brand of education that will enable it to attain its personal dreams and to serve the society it must lead. The education we offered to previous generations, whether successful or not, will not work for these students. They are different, and their times are different. Above all, current undergraduates are in need of an education that provides them with the following four things.

Hope

The first is hope. When we speak about hope, we do not mean the flabby or groundless, rosy-eyed, Pollyannaish brand. Rather, we mean the kind of conviction that allows a person to rise each morning and face the new day. It is the stuff Shakespeare talked of when he wrote, "True hope is swift and flies with swallow's wings; / Kings it makes gods, and meaner creatures kings" (*Richard III* 5.2.23). Current students profess to being optimistic about the future; but that optimism is frail.

By way of example, in the course of our research we talked with a student who told us she was majoring in business. We asked how she liked it. She said she hated it. We asked what she would rather be majoring in. She said dance. We asked, Why not major in dance? She looked at us the way one would look at a dumb younger sibling and said, "Rich is nice. Poor is not nice. I want nice," and she walked off. We had no answer that day, but over time we have thought about that student a lot. She gave up all of her dreams to study a subject she hated. If she follows a career that flows from her major, she will probably dislike that too. The saddest, saddest part of the story is that she did not have to make the choice she did. This student may not have become a professional dancer, but she could manage a dance company, or be a dance teacher, or a critic, or perhaps operate a store selling dance equipment. The tragedy of the story is not that she made a bad selection. It is that the young woman gave up her hope. It was so tenuous that she dared not hold onto it. . . .

Responsibility

The second *attribute* is responsibility. Despite all we said about the adversities this generation is facing, current college students are still among the most fortunate people in the world. They owe something to others. Indeed, they are more involved in service activities than their predecessors, but at the same time they are not convinced that they can both do good and do well. Many feel that when it comes to security and responsibility, a choice must be made.

At a New England liberal arts college, all first-year students were required to participate in an exercise called "Freshman Inquiry." Students were required to prepare an essay talking about what they had learned and not learned in college so far, their hopes and aspirations for the future, and how they planned to use the remainder of their college education. After the essay was written, each student met with a panel composed of a faculty member, an administrator, and a fellow student to discuss it. One student submitted an essay to a panel, saying when she grew up she wanted to be CEO of a multinational corporation, become a U.S. senator, head a foundation that provided scholarships for college students, and work for nuclear disarmament. The student was asked what she needed out of college to accomplish all this. After a little thought, she answered, "A killer instinct." Her listeners sought clarification. She said this meant the ability to step on people or walk over them when necessary to get what she wanted. She was asked about altruism. This time she asked for clarification, and the word was defined for her. She said that was not part of her game plan. The panel reminded her of her desire to work for nuclear arms control. Surely that was altruistic. She told the panel they did not get it: "If there were a nuclear war, I would not get to be CEO of a multinational corporation." Three years later, the student graduated, plans and opinions intact. Her grades were high, and several years later she was attending one of the nation's better business schools. All of her dreams may come true, but one is forced to conclude that her college experience was inadequate. It never taught her about responsibility, what she had an obligation to do for others.

Appreciation of Differences

The third attribute is understanding and appreciation of differences. Today's undergraduates are living in a world in which differences are multiplying and change is the norm, but they attend colleges that are often segregated on the basis of differences and where relationships between diverse populations are strained. . . . It is imperative that college students learn to recognize, respect, and accept their differences.

Efficacy

The final attribute is efficacy, that is, a sense that one can make a difference. Here again, current undergraduates affirmed this belief at the highest rates recorded in a quarter-century. . . . It brings to mind a group we met at a well-known liberal arts college. The college had created a special program for its most outstanding seniors to prepare them for the nation's most prestigious graduate fellowships. Levine [a co-author of this essay] was asked to talk to the students about leadership. After a few minutes of watching the students squirming in their seats, looking out the windows, and staring at their watches, he concluded the talk was not going well.

He told the group what he suspected; they agreed. They traded hypotheses back and forth about what had gone wrong. Finally, one student said, "Life is short. This leadership stuff is bullshit. We could not make a difference even if we wanted to." Levine took a quick poll of the group to see how many agreed with the student. Twenty-two out of twenty-five hands went up.

Today's students need to believe that they can make a difference. Not every one of them will become president of the United States, but each of them will touch scores of lives far more directly and tangibly—family, friends, neighbors, and coworkers. For ill or for good, in each of those lives students will make a difference. They need to be convinced that making a difference is their birthright. They should not give it away. No one can take it away. . . .

From Arthur Levine and Jeanette S. Cureton, *When Hope and Fear Collide.* Copyright © 1998 Jossey-Bass, Inc. This material was used by permission of John Wiley and Sons, Inc.

 ## Vocabulary

As you think about this essay, these definitions may be helpful to you:
1. **discontinuity**   lack of continuity or cohesion
2. **attenuation**   weakening
3. **elite**   a powerful minority group
4. **cohort**   in statistics, a group of individuals having a great deal in common
5. **attribute**   an inherent characteristic

 ## Discussion Questions

1. According to the authors, what are the two periods in history when pro-found change occurred? What do these two periods have in common?
2. Why do the authors claim the benefit of a college education has diminished?
3. Do you agree with the authors' description of current undergraduates? Why or why not?
4. What four attributes must a college education provide? Do you agree these are the most important for the future? Why or why not?
5. What can college students do to make sure they will "make a difference"?

Suggestions for Your Journal

Are you feeling the "time of discontinuity" that the authors describe? If so, in what way? Do you think you are getting a Tiffany or a Kmart education? Why? What would you add to or subtract from the list of characteristics that these authors attribute to current undergraduates? Do you personally believe that you can make a difference in the world? Do you really want to? Why or why not?

Here Life Comes

Mel Levine

Mel Levine, M.D., is professor of pediatrics at the University of North Carolina Medical School and director of its Clinical Center for the Study of Development and Learning. He is the founder and co-chair of All Kinds of Minds, a nonprofit institute for the understanding of differences in learning.

Lives flow with heavy undercurrents, much like the open sea; they *undulate* through well-timed waves, such as the preschool period, adolescence, and the so-called golden years of late life. Each arriving era brings its special challenges and opportunities, along with its unique stresses and pressures. A person may or may not be equipped to ride the next wave, to manage the requirements—obvious and hidden—of his or her latest time of life.

A particularly challenging period is the opening stages of a life at work, the school-to-career years, a time that, although rarely thought of as distinct, may be one of the roughest to traverse. These are the startup years, a pivotal time that claims more than its share of unsuspecting victims. In fact, most people are better prepared for their retirement than they are for the startup of their working lives! For some the startup years commence at age sixteen or seventeen, upon their dropping out of high school. For others the startup years may not begin until age twenty-nine, following a residency in plastic surgery.

Many individuals in and around their twenties come to feel abandoned and anguished. They start to question their self-worth, and they are prone to some awful mistakes in their choice of career or in the ways they perform as novices on the job. They suffer from an affliction I call work-life unreadiness, which may have its onset right after high school, in college, during the job search, or during the early phases of a job or a career.

The length of the startup period varies from just a few years to a decade or more of uncertainty and justified anguish. Some emerging adults take longer to start up a stable work life than do others. Some never stop starting; they can't move ahead toward a career because of repeated false starts or because they keep changing course. They start up and stall out! Others feel *stymied* in their work choices, while some of their friends effortlessly and expediently move into job roles that fit them as snugly as their favorite athletic socks.

Clearly, work life is not one's only life! Family life, perhaps spiritual life, sex life, social life, along with assorted other slices of life, operate in concert and sometimes in conflict with work life. To a large extent people are what they do. But we must remember that life at work is influenced by and influences numerous facets of day-to-day existence.

The culture of the modern world affords multiple ways to get lost or ambushed along the work-life trail. More than ever before, young adults are apt to confront job descriptions that are strikingly different from those familiar to elder members of their families. Role models within a family are an endangered species. Even if a young person breaks into the identical occupation as his mother or father, the chances are that its current routines and requirements look nothing like those his parents faced. Practicing medicine or law or tending to the family farm is a whole different ball game these days. Meanwhile, new adults have to face an economic world as *unfathomable* as it is unpredictable.

In their book *Quarterlife Crisis,* Alexandra Robbins and Abby Wilner make the observation, "The whirlwind of new responsibilities, new liberties, and new choices can be entirely overwhelming for someone who has just emerged from the shelter of twenty years of schooling." Startup adults may be totally unprepared for some of the bracing realities of early work life. Some matters they need to consider:

- They are accumulating experience at school and work—no matter what kind of work they're doing. That means it's better to work than be unemployed and have to contend with the costly stigma of being "inexperienced," a common reason for being turned down for a good job.
- Parents are often good sounding boards, if they can be asked not to preach or dispense too much glib, oversimplified advice.
- People should never feel they can't backtrack. Poor decisions are always reversible. Life is full of trials and errors; no one should let an error put the brakes on their forward motion. A startup adult can learn from taking a wrong road.
- Startup adults should never give up on their passions. They should keep finding ways to get where they want to be, namely, getting paid to do things that they love.
- Startup adults have to realize that there is no work entitlement. Their boss doesn't owe them anything, and he is not losing sleep worrying about their self-esteem. But they are being watched, and they need to perform as if they are being scored on their performances. Being impressive actually can be fun.
- Early in a career, it is a good idea to explore diverse roles within a field. That means that a person who wants to become a screenwriter and is having trouble selling her scripts should consider a job as an associate producer or assistant casting director—a job that might eventually lead right back to screenplay writing or branch out into something else worthwhile within the movie world. Early insistence upon a particular role can be counterproductive.
- It is important for startup adults to keep sniffing out the connections between what they are doing and what ultimately they hope to be doing. A person might say, "Eventually I'd like to manage a restaurant; working in this coffeehouse is teaching me a lot about customer service, and I'm observing closely how my superior operates; she's terrific." By the way, such connections are very effectively mentioned during a job interview.
- Everyone should have some well-thought-out alternative plans and then be ready to change course when an excellent opportunity presents itself that fits with someone's overall career aspirations. It is hazardous to wait around

for such golden chances and foolhardy to get so stuck on a plan that potential windfalls are missed.

The French philosopher Jean-Paul Sartre once wrote, "Il faut choisir, vivre ou raconter"—in English, "One must choose whether to live one's life or tell it." That advice suggests another *formidable* challenge faced by startup adults. People have to live a life that's right for them, not an existence that *sounds* right. The world is replete with posers, folks of all ages, who are telling their lives rather than living them. A startup adult needs to be especially careful to avoid making important choices solely because a choice would embellish a "cool" story. Although it can be tempting to try to emerge as a *charismatic* character in one's own biography, there has to be more to life than that. The best success stories are about people who have refused to be anyone but themselves.

 ## Vocabulary

As you think about this essay, these definitions may be helpful to you.
1. **undulate**   to move in a wavy or flowing manner
2. **stymied**   presenting an obstacle
3. **unfathomable**   impossible to comprehend
4. **formidable**   having qualities that discourage approach
5. **charismatic**   a magnetic charm or appeal

 ## Discussion Questions

1. Why, according to Levine, can the "school-to-work" life stage be one of the most difficult to traverse? Do you agree with him?
2. Why might some "startup" adults be unprepared for the realities of early work life? What can they do to be better prepared?
3. What does Levine say about work entitlement? Do you agree with his stance? If not, why not?
4. Why should we explore diverse opportunities within an occupational field early in our careers? Give some examples of alternatives in the general career field you would like to pursue.
5. How does Levine describe the difference between an existence that *sounds* right and living a life that *is* right? Discuss the implications of each of these existences as they influence a "startup" adult.

Suggestions for Your Journal

What advice that Levine gives in this essay makes the most sense for you? Have you ever experienced the feelings of a "startup" adult that Levine describes? When and how? Are you "living" your life or "telling" it? If you are "telling" it, how can you change?

The Next Great Generation

Neil Howe and William Strauss

Neil Howe and William Strauss, the authors of *Generations, 13th Gen,* and *The Fourth Turning*, write and lecture frequently on generational issues. They host active discussions with readers (at www.millennialsrising.com and www.fourthturning.com) and run LifeCourse Associates, a strategic-planning consulting firm.

"We're the Millennial Generation," asserts 17-year-old Tyler Hudgens of McLean, Virginia. "We're special, one of a kind. It's our turn, our time to shine."

"Kids Today," answers the "buzz" page in *Newsweek.* "They're just no good. No hardships + no cause = boredom, anger, and idiocy."

Who's right—Tyler Hudgens, or *Newsweek*?

Until very recently, the public has been accustomed to nonstop media chatter about bad kids—from mass murderers, hate criminals, and binge drinkers to test failers, test cheaters, drug users, and just all-around spoiled brats. To believe the news, you'd suppose our schools are full of kids who can't read in the classroom, shoot one another in the hallways, spend their loose change on tongue rings, and couldn't care less who runs the country. According to a national survey, barely one adult in three thinks that today's kids, once grown, will make the world a better place.

As for Miss Hudgens, where could she look to find allies? She won't find them among hard-line culture warriors, whose agenda for moral renewal feeds on the supposed *depravities* of youth, nor among those on the other side, whose plans for expansive government depend upon youth's supposed pathologies. She won't find them in business, which has learned how to target the hard youth edge so well that it would rather avoid the risk of trying anything new. Only among Tyler's teenage peers will she find an unwavering optimism to match her own. Even there, one can imagine a well-trained note of irony: *We're special? Oh. And on whose planet?*

Yet, the central message is that *Newsweek* is wrong and Hudgens is right.

A new generation is rising.

Meet the Millennials, born in or after 1982—the "Babies on Board" of the early Reagan years, the "Have You Hugged Your Child Today?" sixth graders of the early Clinton years, the teens of Columbine, and the much-touted high school classes of the new century, now invading the nation's campuses.

As a group, Millennials are unlike any other youth generation in living memory. They are more numerous, more affluent, better educated, and more ethnically diverse. More important, they are beginning to manifest a wide array of positive social habits that older Americans no longer associate with youth, including a new focus on teamwork, achievement, modesty, and good conduct.

Only a few years from now, this can-do youth revolution will overwhelm the cynics and pessimists. Over the next decade, the Millennial Generations will entirely recast the image of youth from downbeat and alienated to upbeat and engaged—with potentially *seismic* consequences for America.

Look closely at the dramatic changes now unfolding in the attitudes and behaviors of today's youth, the 18-and-unders of the new century. The evidence is overwhelming—and just starting to attract notice. In the spring of 2000 newsweekly magazines with "good news" youth stories marked a possible turning of the media tide.

That's not all. When you fit these changes into the broader rhythms of American history, you can get a good idea of what kind of adult generation the Millennials are likely to become. You can foresee their future hopes and fears, strengths and weaknesses, as they rise to adulthood and, in time, to power. You can understand how today's kids are on track to become a powerhouse generation, full of technology planners, community shapers, institution builders, and world leaders, perhaps destined to dominate the twenty-first century like today's fading and ennobled G.I. Generation dominated the twentieth. Indeed, Millennials have a solid chance to become America's next great generation, as celebrated for their collective deeds a hundred years from now as the generation of John Kennedy, Ronald Reagan, Joe DiMaggio, and Jimmy Stewart is celebrated today.

By that time, no one will recall the *Newsweek*-styled cynical barbs that greeted Tyler Hudgens as she, along with millions of other young people, began setting a new tone for America. And by that time, perhaps Miss Hudgens's sunny opinion of her generation will be widely shared, reinforced by the enduring memories of heroic achievements.

Is this possible? Yes. Is it certain? No.

While the outlook for this generation is largely positive, dangers abound, given its enormous potential power. Millennials do pose a threat to the future of this nation and the world. But if danger arrives, it won't come from the direction today's adults worry about—in the form of a selfish, alienated rabble of disaffected Ultra-Gen-X hyperslackers. Imagine, instead, an unstoppable mass hurling down the track in the opposite direction, a *cadre* of young people so cohesive and so directional that, if their aspirations are thwarted, they might overwhelm the political defenses of their elders and mobilize around a risky, even destructive agenda.

For decades, Americans have been wishing for a youth generation that would quit talking and start doing. Now that older generations are starting to produce kids like this, a new generation arises: OK, Boomers and Gen-Xers, now that you've got them, can you handle them?

Over the coming decade, the Oh-Ohs, this rising generation will introduce itself to the nation and push the nation into a new era. Once this new youth persona begins to focus on convention, community, and civic renewal, America will be on the brink of becoming someplace very new, very "millennial" in the fullest sense of the word. That's when the "end of history" stops, and the beginning of a new history, their Millennial history, starts.

Some *pundits*—marketers, especially—dub these kids "Generation Y," as though they were a mere Generation X2, *South Park* idiots beyond redemption, the ultimate price for America's post-'60s narcissism. Others, giving them names such as Generation Dot Com, depict them as an exaggerated extension of America's current mood of self-oriented commercialism.

How utterly depressing. And how utterly wrong.

Yes, there is a revolution under way among today's kids—a *good news revolution*. Their generation is going to rebel by behaving not worse, but better. Their life mission will not be to tear down old institutions that don't work, but to build up new ones that do. Look closely at youth indicators and you'll see that *Millennial attitudes and behaviors represent a sharp break from Generation X, and are running exactly counter to trends launched by the Boomers.* Across the board, Millennial kids are challenging a long list of common assumptions about what "postmodern" young people are supposed to become.

Are Millennials another "lost" generation?

No. The better word is "found." Born in an era when Americans began expressing more positive attitudes about children, the Millennials are products of a dramatic birth-rate reversal. During the Gen-X child era, planned parenting almost always meant contraceptives or abortions; during the Millennial childhood, it more often means visits to the fertility clinic.

Are they pessimists?

No. They're optimists. Surveys show that—compared to Xer teens a decade ago—today's teens are more upbeat about the world in which they're growing up. Nine in ten describe themselves as "happy," "confident," and "polite." A rapidly increasing share say that growing up is easier for them than it was for their parents. Teen suicide rates are now falling for the first time in decades.

Are they self-absorbed?

No. They're cooperative team players. From school uniforms to team learning to community service, Millennials are gravitating toward group activity. According to a recent Roper survey, more teenagers blamed "selfishness" than anything else when asked, "What is the major cause of problems in this country?" Unlike Gen Xers, they believe in their own collective power.

Are they distrustful?

No. They accept authority. Most teens say they identify with their parents' values, and over nine in ten say they "trust" and "feel close to" their parents. The proportion that report conflict with their parents is declining. Half believe that lack of parental discipline is a major social problem and large majorities favor tougher rules against misbehavior in the classroom and society at large.

Are they rule breakers?

No. They're rule followers. Today's kids are disproving the experts who once predicted a tidal wave of juvenile crime during the late 1990s. Over the last five years, the rates of homicide, violent crime, abortion, and pregnancy among teens have all plummeted at the fastest rate ever recorded. Even including the Columbine massacre, there were only half as many violent deaths at schools nationwide in the late nineties as there were in the early part of that decade.

Are they neglected?

No. They're the most watched over generation in memory. Each year, adults subject the typical kid's day to ever more structure and supervision, making it a non-stop round of parents, relatives, teachers, coaches, baby-sitters, counselors, chap-erones, minivans, surveillance cams, and curfews. Over the last decade, time spent on homework and housework is up, while time spent on weekday TV watching is down.

Are they stupid?

No. They're smarter than most people think. During the 1990s, aptitude test scores rose within every racial and ethnic group, especially in elementary schools. Eight in ten teenagers say it's "cool to be smart," while a record share of teenagers are taking AP tests and say they "look forward to school" and plan to attend college.

Have they given up on progress?

No. Today's kids believe in the future and see themselves as its cutting edge. They show a fascination for, and mastery of, new technologies—which explains why math and science scores are rising faster than verbal scores. Teens rank "scientists" and "young people" as the two groups that will cause "most changes for the bet-ter in the future."

Why is the image of this generation so off the mark? For the simple reason that the predictive assumption is wrong. Whatever the era they are living in, Americans habitually assume that the future will be a straight-line extension of the recent past. But that never occurs, either with societies or with generations.

Millennials resemble a fully charged rocket—or to use Ortega y Gasset's classic definition of a generation, "a species of biological missile hurled into space at a given instant, with a certain velocity and direction." So long as Millennials can wheel themselves onto the right launchpad and point themselves in the right direction, they can deliver excellent results. They represent an opportunity, that once fully understood and appreciated, must be acted on by people of all ages.

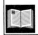 **Vocabulary**

As you think about this essay, these definitions may be helpful to you:
1. **depravities**   corrupt acts or practices
2. **seismic**   earthshaking

3. **cadre**   a nucleus or core group
4. **pundits**   those who give opinions in an authoritative manner

 Discussion Questions

1. How have the media portrayed the "Millennial Generation" in the past and how is that image changing? Why is this image so "off the mark," according to Howe and Strauss?
2. What characteristics do the authors attribute to the Millennials? If you are of the Millennial Generation, which of those characteristics describe you? Which do not?
3. What are some of the dangers the Millennials will face?
4. How are the Millennials different from Generation X, according to Howe and Strauss? Do you think the authors have created stereotypes that aren't necessarily true? Explain your thinking.
5. Do you agree that Millennials are going to change things? What kind of changes do you hope will take place? What changes do you think will take place?

 Suggestions for Your Journal

To which generation do you belong (i.e., Boomers, Xers, Millennials)? Do the characteristics attributed to your generation seem too stereotypical? How do they seem to reflect the history of our society?

If you are of the Millennial Generation, do you like the portrait that the authors have painted of your peers? How are your perceptions different from theirs? The same? If you are of another generation, what is your perception of the Millennials you know? Do you agree with the authors' description of them? Why or why not?

Do you think categorizing generations as this essay does is meaningful? If so, to what extent?

To the Graduates

Christopher Reeve

Christopher Reeve gave this commencement address to the graduates of a large mid-western university in June 2003. Reeve was an actor with many movie credits, but perhaps he is best known as "Superman." He was paralyzed after a riding accident in 1995 and spoke to that change in his life in this address. Christopher Reeve died in 2004.

I am extremely honored to address so many of you who are graduating today. I wanted to be here to pay tribute to the long-standing ideals of this university: compassion for our fellow human beings, the aspiration to be champions in all arenas of life, and the desire to make a difference.

At this university, students and faculty understand the importance of public service on both a local and global scale. Some focus on the environment, others on community outreach, education, social programs, health research, and many other programs. I salute these points of pride to congratulate you for your out-standing achievements. But I also want to sound a note of caution as you leave this sanctuary of learning, self-discovery, and ethical conduct to make your way in the outside world.

You have been taught to work hard, not to cheat, and balance your own advancement with service to others. But when you look beyond this campus, you witness seemingly endless examples of questionable conduct in government, religion, business, the media, and even sports. Our intelligence agencies are being challenged to explain their recommendation for the invasion of Iraq. The Catholic Church is embroiled in a crisis of misconduct and cover-ups. CEOs of major corporations are facing fines and imprisonment for their greed at the expense of the employees who helped create their success. The reputation of one of the most respected newspapers in the country has been severely damaged by a reporter who could not resist plagiarizing in his zeal to succeed. Even the achievements of one of our favorite baseball players will probably be eclipsed by controversy over his use of an illegal bat.

The challenge before you will be to maintain your integrity in a culture that has devalued it. You will have to bring your own personal and professional ethics with you on the journey when you leave here today, because you may not find anyone to guide you. Living a moral life in an indifferent world is likely to be more difficult than you can imagine. How will you succeed?

The answer may be found in a few simple words written by Abe Lincoln: "When I do good I feel good. When I do bad I feel bad. And that is my religion." All of us have a voice inside that will speak to us if we let it. Sometimes it is easy to hear; sometimes we have to turn down the volume of distracting noise around us so we can listen. That voice tells us if we are on the right track. It lets us know if we give as much as we take, if we welcome the opinions of others, and at least accept diversity even if we are not able to embrace it.

As you go forward, hopefully that inner voice will remind you of some of the points of pride that bring such distinction to your university. You will discover that you can go far by being conscientious, but you will go farther and find true satisfaction by being conscious. If you have already achieved self-awareness and set specific goals for yourself, that is fine. If you don't know who you are or what to do next, don't worry about it. Your life should not run on a schedule, and you may go down some dead end streets until you find the right road. Don't be afraid to question assumptions you may have lived with since child-hood. Take your time and seek true independence as you search for meaning and fulfillment.

Perhaps the greatest reward for living a conscious life is that it prepares you to cope with adversity. If you are open to change and new experiences, if you are accustomed to self-discipline, if you respect others and nurture your relation-ships, then you will have built a solid platform that will support you and help you deal with anything that comes your way. I'm not saying all of that is easy. But sitting here today I can honestly tell you that you don't need to break your neck to learn the value of living consciously. I was lucky to grow up unthreat-ened by change and eager for new experiences. Thirty years as an actor before my injury taught me self-discipline and helped me cope with rejection and failure. My marriage and my relationships with friends and family were alive and well before the accident. Since then they have grown even stronger and given me the ability to recover and go forward.

That catastrophic event also changed my perspective about other things in life. Outside of my circle of family and friends, I didn't appreciate others nearly as much as I do now. Once I trained with actual paraplegics to portray one in a film. Every evening as I drove away from the rehab center I quickly pushed those suffering patients out of my mind, relieved that I was not one of them. Less than a year later I became paralyzed myself. Did I need to learn something about compassion and humility? No doubt about it.

It was not until I was immersed in my own rehabilitation that I realized an apparent tragedy had created a unique opportunity. Spinal cord patients like the ones I once dismissed were now in the next room, traveling down the same hall-ways, and struggling right beside me in physical therapy. I came to know people of all ages and from all walks of life that I would otherwise never even have met. For all our differences, what we had in common was our disability and the desire to find a reason to hope. I was inspired by so many and gradually discov-ered that I had been given a job that would create urgency and a new direction in my life: I could do something to help.

Thanks to the education you have received and the ideals that guide this dis-tinguished university, you have already learned some of the most important principles you will ever need to know: compassion for our fellow human beings, the aspiration to be champions in all arenas of life, and the desire to make a difference. To all of you leaving today I can only say, on behalf of all those who will look to you for guidance and leadership, take those principles with you and hold them close.

Congratulations on all your achievements. I wish you the best of luck.

 Discussion Questions

1. How does Christopher Reeve define a "moral life"?
2. How does he suggest you can achieve it?
3. What is the difference between being "conscientious" and being "conscious"?
4. In what ways did Reeve's disability change his life?
5. What did he advise these graduates to consider as they enter a culture that makes it difficult to maintain integrity?

 Suggestions for Your Journal

What emotions did you feel as you read Christopher Reeve's address? How would your life change if you had to face the kind of catastrophe that he suffered? Do you live a "moral life"? If so, how? If not, do you even aspire to one? Explain.

UNIT SUMMARY

In Unit 9 you have read several authors' perceptions of how life after college might be different, along with some of their suggestions for preparing for the day after graduation. The following questions and writing assignments may help you clarify your aspirations for what you want in the future and how you might begin to prepare for it now.

Summary Questions

1. How important is having a degree to you? Do you think it is important to be educated when you graduate? How might your response affect your future career and life?
2. Levine and Cureton describe four attributes that an education must provide. Of these (hope, responsibility, appreciation of differences, and efficacy), which will be the most difficult for you to acquire? Why? The easiest? Why?
3. Briefly compare the portrait of the Millennial Generation drawn by Howe and Strauss with the description of undergraduates given by Levine and Cureton.
4. As you look forward to your years in college, have the authors of the readings in this unit given you any new insights into how you should prepare now for life after graduation? If so, what are they? What steps can you take now to prepare for your life after college (e.g., improve your communication skills or develop technological competencies)?

Suggested Writing Assignments

1. If you wrote an essay in Unit 1 about your reasons for being in college, reexamine these reasons. Are they still the same? Have they changed? Have you added any? What has influenced your thinking the most?
2. How has the prospect of finding a job after college influenced your initial choice of major? Have your experiences so far confirmed that decision? In what way? If you are considering a change, discuss some possible alternatives and why you are considering them.
3. Discuss how you intend to prepare yourself to become an effective worker in tomorrow's workplace. Describe specific ways, such as work and volunteer opportunities, campus involvement, and academic and other experiences, that will help you acquire the general competencies and skills necessary to be effective.

Suggested Readings

Carter, Carol. *Keys to Effective Learning.* Upper Saddle River, NJ: Prentice-Hall, 1999.

Mitchell, S. *American Generations: Who They Are, How They Live, What They Think.* New York: New Strategist, 1998.

Strauss, William, and Howe, Neil. *Millennials Go to College.* Great Falls, VA: LifeCourse Associates, 2003.

Author Index

Subject Index

Credits

Unit 1.

5: From William Bennett, "The Lure of Learning," Reprinted by permission of the author.

8: James Cicarelli, "A New Debate is Joined Overan Old Question: Is College an Investment or an End in Itself?" ©1987 James Cicarelli. Reprinted by permission of the author.

13: Reprinted with permission of Simon & Schuster Adult Publishing Group from *The Disciplined Mind* by Howard Gardner. Copyright © 1999 by Howard Gardner.

18: Bok Derek; *Our Underachieving Colleges.* Princeton University Press. Reprinted by permission of Princeton University Press.

23: Rudolph, Frederick. "The Rise of Football" from *American College and University: A History.* University of Georgia Press, 1990. Copyright © 1962, 1990 by Frederick Rudolph. All rights reserved.

Unit 2.

33: Gordon, Virginia. "The Developing College Student" from *Foundations: A Reader For New College Students.* Wadsworth Publishing, 2004. Used by permission of the author.

38: From Inge Bell, *This Book Not Required,* Chapter 10 "Trouble with Parents," pp. 182-203. Copyright © 1991 Sage Publications. Reprinted with permission by Sage Publications, Inc.

41: Barbara M. Newman and Philip R. Newman, "Loneliness," pp.87-90 from *When Kids go to College,* ©1992 by Ohio State University Press. Reprinted by permission of the publisher.

48: From Susan Jones Sears and Virginia N. Gordon, *Building Your Career—A Guide to Your Furture,* 3ed, (Upper Saddle River, NJ: Prentice Hall, 2002).Reprinted with permission from Pearson Education, Inc. Upper Saddle River, N.J.

52: Travis, John W. and Regina Sara Ryan. "What is Wellness?" from *Wellness Workbook: How to Achieve Enduring Health and Vitality.* Copyright © 2004, Celestial Arts. All rights reserved.

Unit 3.

63: James T. Burtchaell, "Major Decisions" reprinted by permission of the author.

66: William Raspberry, "College Major Doesn't Mean All That Much," © 1990, The Washington Post Writers Group. Reprinted with permission.

70: Howard Schein, Ned S. Laff, and Deborah Allen, "Want Good Advising? Take the Initiative!" from NACADA Monograph Series, No. 11, pp. 30-31. Copyright © 2004 by the National Academic Advising Association (NACADA). Reprinted by permission of NACADA.

75: Pauk, Walter and Ross J.W. Owens, *How to Study in College,* Eighth Edition. Copyright © 2005 by Houghton Mifflin Company. Used with permission.

82: Nancy O'Hanlon, "The Right Stuff: Research Strategies for the Internet Age," reprinted by permission of the author.

89: Thomas L. Minnick, "Fourteen Ways of Looking at Electives" from *Foundations: A Reader for New College Students.* Wadsworth Publishing, 2004. Used by permission of the author.

92: Joel J. Gold, "Please! It's Only Seven Minutes Late, Professor." Reprinted by permission of the author.

96: William R. Brown, "Why I Don't Let Students Cut My Classes." Reprinted by permission of the author.

Unit 4.

96: Howard Schein, Ned S. Laff, and Deborah Allen, "How Do I Find Out What Faculty Are Doing?" from NACADA Monograph Series, No. 11, pp. 34-35. Copyright © 2004 by the National Academic Advising Association (NACADA). Reprinted by permission of NACADA - www.nacada.ksu.edu.

106: Reprinted with the permission of Simon & Schuster Adult Publishing Group from *Thinking in the Future Tense: A Workout for the Mind* by Jennifer James. Copyright © 1996 by Jennifer James, Inc.

113: Al Siebert and Bernadine Gilpin, "Learning Styles: They Can Help or Hinder," from *The Adult Student's Guide to Survival and Success: Time For College* ©1992. Reprinted by permission of Practical Psychology Press.

118: Hellyer, Regina, Carol Robinson and Phyllis Sherwood, *Study Skills for Learning Power.* Copyright © 1998 by Houghton Mifflin Company. Used with permission.

124: Pages 12-21 from *The Unfinished Revolution* by Michael Dertouzos. Copyright © 2000 by Michael Dertouzos. Reprinted by permission of HarperCollins Publishers, Inc.

130: From *The Next Fifty Years,* edited by John Brockman, copyright © 2002 by John Brockman. Used by permission of Vintage Books, a division of Random House, Inc.

Unit 5.

137: From A.W. Bates and Gary Poole, *Effective Teaching with Technology in Higher Education* (San Francisco: Jossey-Bass, 2003). This material is used with permission of John Wiley & Sons, Inc.

145: Steven J. McDonald, "Virtual Legality," reprinted by permission of the Ohio State University Office of Legal Affairs.

149: Palloff, Rena M. and Keith Pratt. "Who is the Virtual Student?" from *The Virtual Student: A Profile and Guide to Working with Online Learners.* Copyright © 2003 by John Wiley & Sons, Inc. Reprinted with permission of John Wiley & Sons, Inc.

152: Ellen Goodman, "Technology Eliminating Conversation," from the editorial page of the *Columbus Dispatch* © 2000 the Washington Post Writers Group. Reprinted with permission.

160: Pages 120-122 from *The Unfinished Revolution* by Michael Dertouzos. Copyright © 2000 by Michael Dertouzos. Reprinted by permission of HarperCollins Publishers, Inc.

Unit 6.

168: James Carter and William Halverson, "On Academic Freedom," reprinted by permission of the author.

174: Thomas L. Minnick, "Ideas as Property" from *Foundations: A Reader For New College Students.* Wadsworth Publishing, 2004.

179: C.L. Lindsay, III. "You and the Family Educational Rights and Privacy Act" from *The College Student's Guide to the Law,* pp. 111-115. Copyright © 2005 Taylor Trade Publishing. All rights reserved. Reproduced by permission of Taylor Trade Publishing and Rowman & Littlefield Publishing Group.

182: George F. Will, "Please Stop This Talk about Values," from the FORUM section of the *Columbia Dispatch.* © 2000, The Washington Post Writers Group. Reprinted by permission of the publisher.

Unit 7.

196: Reprinted by permission of the publisher from *Making the Most of College: Students Speak their Minds* by Richard J. Light, pp. 160-168, 173-180, 185, Cambridge, Mass.: Harvard University Press, Copyright © 2001 by Richard J. Light.

200: Chana Schoenberger, "Getting to Know About You and Me," from *Newsweek,* September 20, 1993. Reprinted by permission of the author.

206: Joy E. Weeber, "What Could I Know of Racism," from the *Journal of Counseling and Development,* vol.77, no. 1. Copyright © 1999 The American Counseling Association. No further reproduction authorized without written permission of the American Counseling Association.

210: From Edward A. Delgado-Romero, "The Face of Racism," from the *Journal of Counseling & Development,* Vol.77. Copyright © 1999 The American Counseling Association. No further reproduction authorized without written permission of the American Counseling Association.

214: From Donna M. Talbot, "Personal Narrative of an Asian American's Experience with Racism," *Journal of Counseling & Development,* Vol.77. Copyright © 1999 The American Counseling Association. No further reproduction authorized without written permission of the American Counseling Association.

219: From Lisa J. Brandyberry, "Pain and Perseverance: Perspectives from an Ally," from the *Journal of Counseling & Development,* Vol.77. Copyright © 1999 The American Counseling Association. No further reproduction authorized without written permission of the American Counseling Association.

224: From "I Have a Dream", 1963, Copyright © 1963 Martin Luther King Jr., copyright renewed 1991 by Coretta Scott King. Reprinted by arrangement with the Heirs to the Estate of Martin Luther King Jr., c/o Writer's House, Inc. as agent for the proprietor.

229: "Affirmative Action and Multiculturalism," from *The Complete Idiot's Guide to Understanding Ethics* by David Bruce Ingram and Jennifer A. Parks, © 2002 by David Bruce Ingram and Jennifer A. Parks. Used by permission of Alpha Books, and imprint of Penguin Group (USA) Inc.

Unit 8.

238: Abridged from *The Pathfinder: How to Choose or Change Your Career for a Lifetime of Satisfaction and Success* by Nicholas Ayars Lore. Copyright © 1998 by Nicholas Ayars Lore. Used by permission of Simon & Schuster Adult Publishing Group.

242: "Doing the Work You Love," from *Zen and the Art of Making a Living* by Laurence G. Boldt, © 1991, 1992, 1993, 1999 by Laurence G. Boldt. Used by permission of Penguin, a division of Penguin Group (USA) Inc.

249: Mark Ballard, "Job Search: Chance or Plan?" Reprinted by permission of the author.

253: Mary Sherry, "Postgraduate Paralysis," from *Newsweek,* July 11, 1988. Reprinted by permission of the author.

260: Simonsen, Peggy. "Career Patterns for the Twenty-First Century," from *Career Compass: Navigating Your Career Strategically in the New Century,* pp. 34-47. Davies-Black Publishing, 2000. Copyright © 2000 by Peggy Simonsen. All rights reserved. Reproduced with permission of the author.

Unit 9.

268: Edmund D. Pellegrino, "Have a Degree and Being Educated." Reprinted by permission of the author.

274: Levine, Arthur and Jeanette Cureton. "A Time of Discontinuity" from *Hope and Fear Collide.* Copyright © 1998 by Jossey-Bass. Reprinted by permission of John Wiley & Sons, Inc.

278: From *Ready or Not Here Life Comes* by Mel Levine, M.D. Copyright © 2005 by Learning Ways, Inc. Abridged by permission of Simon & Schuster Adult Publishing Group.

283: From *Millenials Rising* by Neil Howe and William Strauss, copyright © 2000 by Neil Howe and William Strauss. Used by permission of Vintage Books, a division of Random House, Inc.

287: Reprinted with permission of Christopher Reeve.